Information Security and Cryptography

Series Editors

David Basin
Kenny Paterson

Advisory Board

Michael Backes
Gilles Barthe
Ronald Cramer
Ivan Damgård
Andrew D. Gordon
Joshua D. Guttman
Ueli Maurer
Tatsuaki Okamoto
Bart Preneel

For further volumes:
www.springer.com/series/4752

Cas Cremers · Sjouke Mauw

Operational Semantics and Verification of Security Protocols

Cas Cremers
Department of Computer Science
ETH Zürich
Zürich, Switzerland

Sjouke Mauw
Computer Science and
    Communications Research Unit
University of Luxembourg
Luxembourg, Luxembourg

ISSN 1619-7100   Information Security and Cryptography
ISBN 978-3-642-43053-4   ISBN 978-3-540-78636-8 (eBook)
DOI 10.1007/978-3-540-78636-8
Springer Heidelberg New York Dordrecht London

ACM Computing Classification (1998): C.2, K.6, E.3

Printed on acid-free paper

Springer is part of Springer Science+Business Media (www.springer.com)

Preface

About ten years ago, Sjouke Mauw and Erik de Vink established the computer security research group at the Eindhoven University of Technology. Given their background in formal methods, they focused on the formal modeling of security protocols and their properties. The underlying assumption was that reasoning in a relatively simple model, based on well-understood notions from the area of operational semantics, would help to understand the complexities inherent to security protocols. Soon after starting this research, Cas Cremers joined the group and took up the challenge to further develop these ideas for his PhD thesis.

Over the years, we have used the resulting model not only for theoretical research, but also for teaching the fundaments of security protocols to master students. During this time we developed the Scyther tool. The efficient tool support enabled us to quickly prove or disprove hypotheses, and enabled us to apply our approach to practical protocols.

The purpose of this book is threefold. First, it aims to present our approach in such a way that it can be used as an introduction to conducting theoretical research on security protocols. Second, it is designed to serve as a basis for teaching courses on protocol verification. Third, by providing the theoretical foundations underlying our approach, it can aid in practical protocol analysis. We hope that after reading this book, the reader has gained an understanding of the inner workings and possibilities of formal protocol analysis.

This book would have not been possible without the support of many people. First and foremost we express our great appreciation to Erik de Vink. He contributed to the conception and development of many of our technical results and we have greatly benefited from our stimulating discussions.

We are grateful to Jos Baeten and David Basin, who provided us with the opportunity to work on this research topic and the subsequent book for several years. We also express our gratitude to our editor, Ronan Nugent, who patiently provided us with support throughout the writing of this book.

The theory developed in this book and its presentation have undergone many changes over the years. We are grateful to the following people for helping to shape our ideas into their current form: David Basin, Ton van Deursen, Hugo Jonker, Barbara Kordy, Simon Meier, Matthijs Melissen, Marko Horvat, Saša Radomirović, Benedikt Schmidt, and Christoph Sprenger.

Finally, our families provided moral support throughout the writing of this book. Without them, this book would not have seen the light of day.

Zürich,   Cas Cremers
Luxembourg   Sjouke Mauw

Contents

List of Figures

List of Tables

Chapter 1
Introduction

Abstract After briefly describing the historical context of cryptography and security, we provide a motivation for studying the area of security protocols. We give an overview of the chapters of this book and their relation.

1.1 Historical Context

This book is not about cryptography.

Cryptography, or the art of "secret writing", dates back to about 600 BC, when Hebrew scholars used the so-called Atbash cipher. In order to encode the word `girl`, they would encode each character individually, by reversing the order of the alphabet: `a` is swapped with `z`, `b` is swapped with `y`, and so forth. Thus, the word `girl` would be encoded as `trio`, and vice versa. As long as nobody discovers your scheme, the fact that you are writing about a girl is secret.

Around 400 BC, the Spartans allegedly used a *Scytale* for encryption, which can be considered the first *device* used for encryption. In truth, the Scytale is just a rod with a random diameter. The idea is that both the sender and recipient know what diameter the rod should have. The sender wraps a long thin piece of paper (or, according to legend, a belt) around the rod, and writes his message from left to right on the paper, as in Fig. 1.1.

If we want to send a secret message `consoles`, and the diameter of the rod is such that two characters can be written around the rod, we write `c o n s` along the front side of the rod, as in Fig. 1.1. We turn the rod and write the remaining characters `o l e s`. Now, if we unwrap the paper from the rod, and read the characters, we find that the encrypted message is `coolness`, as can be seen in Fig. 1.2.

If the recipient wants to decode it, he wraps the paper again around a rod of the same diameter. If he uses a wrong diameter, e.g., such that three characters can be written around the rod, the message will read `clsonsoe`, and he will not receive the correct message. Here, the diameter of the rod acts as a *key*. Even when the encryption method is known to the enemy, encrypting and decrypting requires a key that is only known by the sender and the recipient.

Throughout history, the use of encoding schemes has evolved significantly. The vast majority of the schemes relied on the fact that an encoding scheme is kept se-

C. Cremers, S. Mauw, *Operational Semantics and Verification of Security Protocols*,
Information Security and Cryptography, DOI 10.1007/978-3-540-78636-8_1,

Fig. 1.1 Scytale

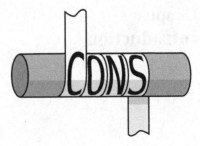

Fig. 1.2 Unfolded Scytale

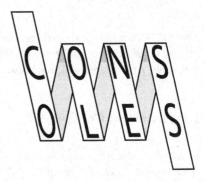

cret. This design principle is sometimes referred to as "security through obscurity", and is still often applied today.

It is possible to design stronger encryption schemes. In the 19th century, Auguste Kerckhoffs stated that an encryption scheme should be secure even if everything except the key is known to the enemy. This is often referred to as Kerckhoffs' law. In the 20th century Claude Shannon formulated a similar notion, stating that "the enemy knows the system", which is referred to as Shannon's maxim.

Just before and during the Second World War, cryptography was used extensively, also by the German forces. Although different machines were used, the most well known are the Enigma devices, based on a system with multiple rotors. Initial attempts to crack the code started as early as 1932 by Polish researchers. Based on their findings, by the end of the war a team of researchers in Bletchley Park (which included Alan Turing) was able to break coded messages on a daily basis. This result was not due to the fact that they had recovered German Enigma machines which they could analyse. Rather, it involved the development of dedicated code-breaking machines (which took several years) that were used to recover the key from the encrypted text.

From 1948 onwards, when Claude Shannon published his seminal paper on information theory [145], many scientific publications have appeared on the topic of cryptography, and for a large part these focus on finding new encryption schemes. These encryption schemes were no longer just inventions with claims, but they were developed on a more proper mathematical foundation: cryptographic schemes are derived from known hard mathematical problems. To prove the security of a scheme, one proves that if an adversary could crack the scheme, he would also be able to solve a mathematical problem that is known to be hard.

In 1976 Diffie and Hellman published their key paper in which they introduce a mechanism that later became known as asymmetric encryption [70]. We can give a somewhat imprecise metaphor to provide intuition about this scheme: the Diffie-Hellman encryption scheme allows everybody to create their own particular padlock with corresponding key. Suppose a woman called Alice wants to securely receive messages which she only can read. She creates a padlock and key. Instead of having to securely transmit the key, she keeps the key to herself, and simply hands out copies of the (open) padlock to everybody else. If her brother, Bob, wants to send a secret message to her, he puts it in a box and closes the box using Alice's padlock. Now nobody except for Alice will be able to read the message. This scheme circumvents the problem with traditional symmetric cryptography, where both the sender and the recipient must have the same key.

This breakthrough has resulted in a number of variations on these schemes, leading to international standards for encryption mechanisms. Both symmetric and asymmetric encryption schemes are used extensively today for the encryption of internet traffic, wireless communications, smart-card applications, cell phone communications, and many other applications.

From this brief historical account, one might conclude that a secure encryption scheme is the "holy grail" of communication security. Once the perfect scheme is found, all communications will be safe, and we don't ever have to worry again. Unfortunately, this is not the case. Cryptography is not enough to guarantee security in communications. And that is why this book is not about cryptography.

1.2 Black-Box Security Protocol Analysis

If you have the perfect bike lock and chain, but fix the chain around the bike in the wrong way, somebody can still steal your bike. In much the same way, the security of a computer system depends on the way the components interact. Encryption is like a bike chain. It is a useful mechanism that can be used in the construction of secure systems, but you can apply it in the wrong way. It is not a guarantee for security by itself.

Security protocols are a means to ensure some form of secure communication, and they typically use some form of encryption. Security protocols underlie most of our current communication systems, such as secure internet communications, cell phone networks, as well as the communication between credit cards, ATM machines, and banks. For these applications, it is crucial that no malicious party can disturb the intended workings of the protocol, or eavesdrop on something he was not supposed to hear. It is not sufficient to have a security protocol of which one assumes that it is secure. Instead, we want strong guarantees about its security.

In order to make a statement about the
security guarantees of a protocol, we turn
again to mathematics. We create a mathematical model of both the protocol and the
network, which is under control of an adversary. Such a model allows us to prove,
for example, that the adversary is not able
to disturb the protocol or learn any secrets.
As these models already become complex
for simple encryption schemes, it is only
feasible to reason about the security of full
protocols by abstracting away from some
(cryptographic) details. Consequently, the
need to reason about security protocols
led to the introduction of an idealised abstraction of encryption in 1983 by Dolev
and Yao [76], with two main properties.
First, cryptography is assumed to be per-

fect: a message can only be decrypted by somebody who has the right key (there
is no way to crack the scheme). Second, messages are considered to be abstract
terms: either the adversary learns the complete message (because he has the key),
or he learns nothing. We call analysis models based on these abstractions *black-box*
models, in the sense that they consider encryptions as abstract functions with some
particular properties. Instead of modelling all cryptographic details and properties,
we assume that somebody already has invented a perfect cryptographic scheme,
which we can use in building secure protocols.

Next to the two assumptions about cryptography, Dolev and Yao introduced a
third abstraction concerning computer networks. The network is assumed to be under full control of the adversary. He can remove sent messages and examine their
contents, insert his own messages, or reroute or simply transmit messages. Together,
these three properties are known as the Dolev-Yao model: cryptography is perfect,
messages are abstract terms, and the network is under full control of the adversary.

Given a security protocol, it is possible to develop mathematical techniques to derive security properties of a protocol under the Dolev-Yao assumptions. As a result,
the work of Dolev and Yao has been responsible for a branch of research which can
be roughly summarised as *black-box security protocol analysis*. However, building
the three properties sketched above into a precise mathematical model, with clear
assumptions and clearly defined security properties, has proven to be a hazardous
task.

The defining example for this area of research illustrates some of the subtleties.
It concerns the so-called Needham-Schroeder public-key protocol [124], published
in 1978, five years before the abstract model of Dolev and Yao. The basic version of
this protocol consists of three messages that are exchanged between two partners. It
is intended to provide *authentication* for both agents. It was assumed to be correct
for over 20 years; now it is considered correct or not, depending on the situation

in which it is used. The reason for this change is not to be found in more powerful analysis methods. Instead, the reason is that the assumptions about the adversary have changed.

In 1989 Burrows, Abadi and Needham published their ground-breaking paper [39] on a logic for authentication (which became known as BAN logic), which also depends on the same black-box assumptions as the Dolev-Yao model. Using this logic, they were able to prove that several protocols satisfy a form of authentication.[1] Among these protocols was the Needham-Schroeder public key protocol. Thus, it seemed that the (intuitively correct) protocol was now formally proven correct. A version of the protocol made its way into the Kerberos [27] protocol. Almost twenty years after the publication of the Needham-Schroeder protocol, in 1996, Gavin Lowe claimed to have found an attack on the protocol. It turns out that Lowe's attack required a stronger adversary than the one Dolev and Yao originally had in mind. Around 1980, networks were considered to be something that was used by honest users: attacks would come from the outside. Thus, the adversary was not one of the regular users of the system. During the 1990s, this view of networks changed: many large networks were used by users, which were not necessarily trusted. Lowe's attack requires that the adversary is, or has compromised, a regular user. As a result, the adversary model was modified, and the adversary was assumed from now on to control a number of regular users of the system.

In the same paper, Lowe introduced a mechanised procedure to find attacks on such protocols. A high-level description of the protocol is processed by a program called Casper, which models the behaviour of the protocol and the possible operations of the adversary in terms of a process algebra. Similarly, the security properties of the protocol are translated into a second set of processes that model the ideal behaviour of the system, which would occur if the security properties were satisfied. The Casper tool uses a model-checking tool that was developed for this process algebra to verify whether the actual protocol model has the same set of behaviours as the ideal behaviour model. If these behaviours are the same, the adversary has no real influence over the protocol execution. Using this procedure, Lowe was able to automatically find the attack on the Needham-Schroeder protocol, and was also able to show that no such attack exists on a repaired version of the protocol, which later became known as the Needham-Schroeder-Lowe protocol.

Since Lowe's breakthrough a large number of security protocol formalisms and tools have been developed. On the one hand, many security protocol formalisms focus solely on protocol description, and there are no tools available for them that are based on a formal semantics. On the other hand, most of the tools have only implicit links with formalisms, and lack formal definitions of the model and properties that are actually being verified. This makes it very difficult to interpret the results.

These observations lead to the central question addressed in this book, which we describe in the next paragraphs.

---

[1] In retrospect the main contribution of this paper seems to be that the logic made some of the Dolev-Yao assumptions explicit, and gave a possible mathematical definition of the notion of authentication.

1.3 Purpose and Approach

The goal of this book is to provide a methodology for the formal analysis and verification of abstract security protocols. In particular, our aim is to provide a formal semantics and intuitive formal definitions of security properties, and efficient tool support.

We start by presenting an explicit foundation in terms of an operational semantics, which allows us to formally model black-box security protocols, and define all possible behaviours of such protocols. Next, we provide formal definitions of existing and new security properties. The combination of formal definitions of protocol behaviour and security properties allows us to verify whether a property holds. We present an automatic method to verify or falsify security properties. Using a tool based on this method, we establish results about the interaction between security protocols. We further illustrate the manual application of the security protocol formalism by developing a family of multi-party protocols.

This book is based on the research on security protocols presented in [18–20, 53, 55, 56, 58–64, 113] and courses taught at ETH Zurich, Eindhoven University of Technology, and the University of Luxembourg.

1.4 Overview

We briefly sketch the organisation of this book, and summarise the chapters. This book consists of five main chapters, most of which end with a set of exercises. Chapter 2 gives a short overview of general mathematical notation used in these five chapters.

1.4.1 The Protocol Analysis Model

In Chaps. 3 and 4 the protocol analysis model is defined.

In Chap. 3, *Operational Semantics*, we present a model for defining security protocols and their behaviour. We make protocol execution in this model explicit by means of an operational semantics. The result is a role-based security protocol model that is agnostic with respect to the number of concurrent protocols. The model makes several assumptions about protocol analysis explicit, and allows, for example, for a derivation of the adversary knowledge from the protocol description. Within the protocol model, security properties are modelled as local claim events.

In Chap. 4, *Security Properties*, the model of Chap. 3 is extended with definitions of several security properties, including secrecy and existing authentication properties. We develop a strong notion of authentication, which is called injective synchronisation, and we give a hierarchy of authentication properties. We apply the formal definitions to prove properties of the Needham-Schroeder-Lowe protocol manually.

1.4.2 Applications of the Model

Chapters 5, 6 and 7 can be read independently. They build on the model defined in Chaps. 3 and 4. They each emphasise different applications of the model. Chapter 5 emphasises the algorithmic aspects of the model by providing tool support, Chap. 6 illustrates the use of the methodology to analyse existing protocols, and Chap. 7 emphasises the use of the model in protocol construction.

In Chap. 5, *Verification*, an algorithm is presented which can be used to verify security properties or find attacks, but also has the feature of being able to give a complete characterisation of a protocol. This algorithm has been implemented in a prototype tool called Scyther. The performance of this tool is state-of-the art for security protocol analysis, and we apply the tool to a large number of protocols. Further, we give a syntactic criterion for establishing injectivity of synchronisation.

The prototype tool is used in Chap. 6, *Multi-protocol Attacks*, for the automated analysis of the parallel execution of multiple protocols. This situation can occur, for example, in embedded systems, like smart-card protocols or cellular phone applications. This results in the discovery of several new attacks and results about safe practices, and illustrates that the composition of two secure protocols is not necessarily secure.

A further application of the model and tool is examined in Chap. 7, *Generalising NSL for Multi-party Authentication*, where the Needham-Schroeder-Lowe protocol is generalised to a family of multi-party authentication protocols. A proof that the generalised version of Needham-Schroeder-Lowe meets its security properties is given. The developed protocols can serve as an efficient basis for multi-party synchronising protocols.

In Chap. 8 we take a step back and look at the wider perspective. In particular, we provide references and discuss the wider context of this work, which provides pointers for further reading.

Chapter 2
Preliminaries

Abstract We describe mathematical concepts and notation used throughout the remainder of this book.

2.1 Sets and Relations

Given a set T, we write $\mathcal{P}(T)$ to denote the powerset of T, i.e., the set of all subsets of T. We write T^* to denote the set of all finite sequences of elements of T. The sequence consisting of n elements $t_0, t_1, \ldots, t_{(n-1)} \in T$ is denoted by $[t_0, t_1, \ldots, t_{(n-1)}]$, or simply by $t_0, t_1, \ldots, t_{(n-1)}$ if no confusion can occur. The empty sequence is denoted by $[\,]$. The concatenation of two sequences t and t' is denoted by $t \cdot t'$. The length of sequence $t = t_0, t_1, \ldots, t_{(n-1)}$ is n and is written as $|t|$. We write t_i to denote t's $(i+1)$th element, i.e., t_0 is the first element of t. We write $e <_t e'$ to denote $\exists i, j \colon i < j \wedge t_i = e \wedge t_j = e'$. We write $set(t)$ to denote the set of elements from t, i.e., $set(t) = \{t_i \mid 0 \le i < |t|\}$. Abusing notation, we write $e \in t$ to denote $e \in set(t)$.

Pairs are written as (x, y). The two components of a pair can be extracted by the projection operator π. More precisely, for all x and y we have that $\pi_1((x, y)) = x$ and $\pi_2((x, y)) = y$.

Let f be a function. We write $dom(f)$ to denote the domain of f and $ran(f)$ to denote the range (i.e., the codomain) of f. We write $f \colon A \to B$ to denote a total function, which maps each element of A to elements of B. We write $f \colon A \twoheadrightarrow B$ to denote a partial function, which maps some elements of A to elements of B. We say f is *injective*, notation *injective*(f), if and only if for all $x, x' \in dom(f)$ we have that $f(x) = f(x') \Rightarrow x = x'$.

A binary relation $R \colon T \times T$ is a subset of $T \times T$. It can satisfy the following properties (quantifying universally over $x, y, z \in T$):

(reflexivity)	$R(x, x)$,
(irreflexivity)	$\neg R(x, x)$,
(symmetry)	$R(x, y) \Longrightarrow R(y, x)$,
(asymmetry)	$R(x, y) \Longrightarrow \neg R(y, x)$,
(transitivity)	$R(x, y) \wedge R(y, z) \Longrightarrow R(x, z)$,
(trichotomicity)	either $R(x, y)$, $R(y, x)$, or $x = y$.

C. Cremers, S. Mauw, *Operational Semantics and Verification of Security Protocols*,   9
Information Security and Cryptography, DOI 10.1007/978-3-540-78636-8_2,
© Springer-Verlag Berlin Heidelberg 2012

Let P be one of the properties reflexivity, symmetry or transitivity. Let $R : T \times T$ be a binary relation. We define the P-closure of R as the smallest superset of R that satisfies P. We denote the transitive closure of R by R^+.

A binary relation $<: T \times T$ is a *strict partial order* if it satisfies irreflexivity, asymmetry and transitivity. A *strict total order* is a strict partial order that, in addition, satisfies trichotomicity.

Example 2.1 (Relations) Let T be the set $\{a, b, c, d\}$ and let R be the relation $\{(a, b), (b, c), (c, d)\}$. R satisfies irreflexivity and asymmetry. The reflexive closure of R is $\{(a, b), (b, c), (c, d), (a, a), (b, b), (c, c), (d, d)\}$. The transitive closure R^+ of R is $\{(a, b), (b, c), (c, d), (a, c), (a, d), (b, d)\}$. R^+ satisfies trichotomicity, irreflexivity and asymmetry; thus it is a strict total order.

2.2 BNF Grammars

Sets consisting of character strings can be defined through BNF (Backus-Naur Form) grammars [43]. A BNF grammar consists of a number of derivation rules. The left-hand side of such a derivation rule is called a *symbol*. It denotes the set that is defined through this rule. A derivation rule for the set *setname* has the form

$$setname ::= alt_1 \mid alt_2 \mid \ldots \mid alt_n.$$

The right-hand side of a derivation rule consists of a number of alternatives, which are separated by vertical bars. These alternatives represent all ways in which elements of *setname* can be generated. Every alternative itself can be a symbol, a set, a string, or a combination of these. We write $[exp]$ to denote that exp is optional and $[exp]^*$ to denote zero or more repetitions of exp.

Example 2.2 (Grammars) Let *FuncName* denote a set of function names, *FuncName* $= \{f, g, h\}$, and let *Const* denote a set of constants, *Const* $= \{c, d, e\}$. Let "(", ")", "," and "+" be strings. The following BNF grammar defines the set *Term*, which contains sums of function applications.

$$FuncApp ::= FuncName(Const\,[\,,\ Const]^*),$$

$$Term ::= FuncApp \mid Term + Term.$$

The first derivation rule defines the application of a function name to at least one constant. These constants are separated by commas. The second rule states that every function application, as defined by the first rule, is a term. Further, the recursive occurrence of the symbol *Term* on the right-hand side states that two terms separated by a $+$ also form a term.

Some elements of *Term* are $f(c)$, $f(d, d, d, c)$, $h(c) + f(d)$, and $g(c, c) + h(d, c) + h(d, c) + f(e, e, c, e)$. The following strings are *not* elements of *Term*: $c, c + c, f()$, and $f(c) + (f(d) + f(e))$.

2.3 Labelled Transition Systems

A *labelled transition system* (LTS) is a four-tuple $(S, L, \rightarrow, s_0)$, where

  (i) S is a set of states;
 (ii) L is a set of labels;
(iii) $\rightarrow: S \times L \times S$ is a ternary transition relation;
 (iv) $s_0 \in S$ is the initial state.

We abbreviate $(p, \alpha, q) \in \rightarrow$ as $p \xrightarrow{\alpha} q$. A *finite execution* of a labelled transition system $P = (S, L, \rightarrow, s_0)$ is an alternating sequence σ of states and labels, starting with s_0 and ending with a state s_n, such that if $\sigma = [s_0, \alpha_1, s_1, \alpha_2, \ldots, \alpha_n, s_n]$ then $s_i \xrightarrow{\alpha_{i+1}} s_{i+1}$ for all $0 \leq i < n$. If $[s_0, \alpha_1, s_1, \alpha_2, \ldots, \alpha_n, s_n]$ is a finite execution of LTS P, then $[\alpha_1, \alpha_2, \ldots, \alpha_n] \in L^*$ is called a *finite trace* of P. Throughout this book, the first element of a trace will have index 1.

A labelled transition system can be defined by means of a set of transition rules. A transition rule defines a number of premises $Q_1, Q_2, \ldots, Q_n (n \geq 0)$ which must all hold before a conclusion of the form $p \xrightarrow{\alpha} q$ can be drawn:

$$\frac{Q_1 \quad Q_2 \quad \cdots \quad Q_n}{p \xrightarrow{\alpha} q}.$$

Example 2.3 (LTS) We define a labelled transition system that manipulates a counter. Let $S = \mathbb{B} \times \mathbb{N}$, i.e., a state is a pair of a Boolean and a natural number. If the Boolean is *false*, an error has occurred. The initial state is $s_0 = (true, 0)$. The set of labels is defined as $L = \{inc, dec, error, reset\}$. The transition relation is defined by the following four transition rules:

$$\frac{b = true}{(b, n) \xrightarrow{inc} (b, n+1)}, \qquad \frac{b = true \quad n > 0}{(b, n) \xrightarrow{dec} (b, n-1)},$$

$$\frac{}{(b, n) \xrightarrow{error} (false, n)}, \qquad \frac{}{(b, n) \xrightarrow{reset} (true, 0)}.$$

The first two rules express that the counter can be incremented and decremented if there is no error. The counter cannot be decremented below 0. The third and fourth rules have no premises. The third rule expresses that at any time an error may occur, bringing the counter into an erroneous state. The counter can be brought back into its initial state through a reset.

An example execution of this LTS is the following:

$$(true, 0) \xrightarrow{inc} (true, 1) \xrightarrow{inc} (true, 2) \xrightarrow{dec} (true, 1)$$
$$\xrightarrow{error} (false, 1) \xrightarrow{reset} (true, 0) \xrightarrow{inc} (true, 1).$$

This gives rise to the trace $[inc, inc, dec, error, reset, inc]$.

Chapter 3
Operational Semantics

Abstract We introduce formal syntax for specifying protocols and develop an operational semantics that specifies their possible behaviours in the presence of an active adversary.

In this chapter we develop a formal operational semantics of security protocols, based on an analysis of the problem domain. The main virtue of the semantics is that it separates concerns as much as possible, clearly distinguishing protocol descriptions from their dynamic behaviour. Further characteristics of the model are a straightforward handling of parallel execution of multiple protocols, locality of security claims, the binding of fresh values to role instances, and an explicitly defined initial adversary knowledge.

We first indicate the concepts that are involved in security protocols in Sect. 3.1. In Sect. 3.2 we define how security protocols are specified in our model. We define how to model the execution of such a security protocol specification in Sect. 3.3. Then, in Sect. 3.4, we combine the previous elements into an operational semantics.

3.1 Analysis of the Problem Domain

We first conduct an analysis of the main concepts of security protocols. The purpose of this analysis is to make the design decisions explicit and to decompose the problem into smaller parts.

Figure 3.1 shows an example of a security protocol specification expressed in the graphical notation used throughout this book. This notation is based on Message Sequence Charts (MSC), which is an ITU-standardised protocol specification language [95].

In Fig. 3.1 we describe a simple example protocol, called Simple Secret Communication (SSC). The communication involves two parties, the *initiator* and the *responder*, which exchange two messages. For each party, the vertical axis denotes the order in which the indicated protocol events (like sending or receiving a message) are executed. The first message is a *request* message, sent by the initiator to the responder. Upon receipt of this request, the responder sends its reply $\{m\}_k$ to

C. Cremers, S. Mauw, *Operational Semantics and Verification of Security Protocols*,
Information Security and Cryptography, DOI 10.1007/978-3-540-78636-8_3,
© Springer-Verlag Berlin Heidelberg 2012

Fig. 3.1 A simple
communication protocol

protocol Simple Secret Communication (SSC)

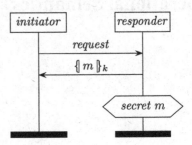

the initiator. This expression denotes the encryption of some data m with a key k.
At the end of the axis of the responder a hexagon is added to express the purpose
of the protocol. The purpose of this protocol is to ensure the secrecy of m whenever
the responder successfully finishes execution of the protocol.

Even though it might be easy to grasp the intuition behind this diagram and to
understand the protocol at an informal level, several aspects are left implicit. In
particular, because the protocol is intended to provide secret communication, we
should also know the intended threat model, or, put differently, the intended adversary model. For example, in the diagram, the capabilities of the adversary are not
made explicit, nor the fact that key k is not known to the adversary.

In order to precisely understand the meaning of this picture and to be able to
analyse whether the protocol indeed satisfies the desired secrecy property, we will
give a complete and formal definition of security protocols and their correctness.
The first step towards this goal is to identify the concepts involved.

A security protocol describes a number of behaviours, which we call *roles*. The
roles of a protocol correspond to the vertical axes in the MSC. A system running this
protocol may contain any number of communicating agents. Each agent executes
instances of one or more roles. Each such instance is called a *run*. For example, agent
Alice can perform two initiator runs and one responder run in parallel. The agents
execute their runs to achieve some security goal (e.g., the confidential exchange of
a message). While agents try to achieve their goals, an adversary may try to oppose
them. However, threats do not only come from the outside. Agents taking part in a
protocol run may be compromised by the adversary and try to invalidate the security
goals of other agents. In order to resist attacks, protocols can use *cryptographic
primitives* such as encryption or hashing.

Given this global description, we can identify the components of the security
protocol model as in Table 3.1. The relation between the components is visualised
in Fig. 3.2. Below we will discuss each of these aspects briefly, list their points of
variation and make appropriate design decisions.

Cryptographic Primitives   Cryptographic primitives are (idealised) mathematical constructs such as encryption. In our treatment of cryptographic primitives we
adopt the *black-box approach*. We focus on the properties of such primitives and

Protocol specification

Protocol execution

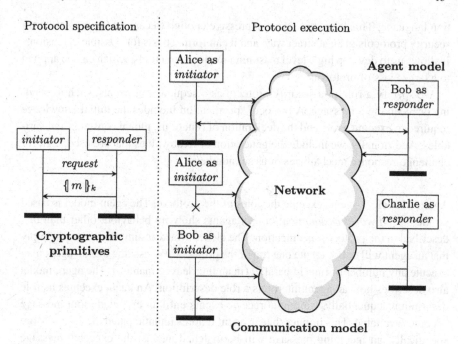

Fig. 3.2 A security protocol and its execution

Table 3.1 Components of the security protocol model

Component	Section
Protocol specification	Sect. 3.2
Cryptographic primitives	Sect. 3.2
Agent model	Sect. 3.3
Communication model	Sect. 3.3
Threat model/Adversary model	Sect. 3.3
Security requirements	Chap. 4

abstract from implementation details. We consider symmetric and asymmetric encryption, hashing and signing. The idea behind symmetric encryption is that a message encrypted with key k can be decrypted only with the same key k. Asymmetric encryption requires two keys: a secret key sk, which is only known to its owner, and a public key pk, which is made publicly available. A message encrypted with key sk can only be decrypted with key pk (and vice versa). In line with the black-box approach, we assume cryptography to be perfect, captured by the *perfect cryptography assumption*. This assumption implies that nothing can be learned of a plaintext from its encrypted version without knowing the decryption key [76].

Protocol Specification The protocol specification describes the behaviour of each of the roles in the protocol. Such a protocol specification is described in a specification language. This language is just expressive enough to capture the most relevant security protocols in an abstract way, and it can form a basis for possible extensions. It allows us to develop high-level reasoning methods and tools, which can be applied to a large class of protocols.

We specify a role in a security protocol as a sequence of events, such as sending or receiving a message. A protocol specification includes the initial knowledge required to execute a role and the declaration of functions, global constants and variables. Additionally, we include the generation of fresh values that are used, e.g., for challenge-response mechanisms or as session keys.

Agent Model   Agents execute the roles of the protocol. The agent model is based on the *closed world assumption*: honest agents show no behaviour other than that described in the protocol specification. The closed world assumption does not imply that an agent will only execute one run of the protocol. We assume that an agent may execute any number of runs in parallel (in an interleaved manner). The agent model also describes how an agent interprets a role description. An agent executes its role description sequentially, waiting at receive events until an expected input message becomes available. This implies that an agent ignores unanticipated messages. More specifically, an incoming message will be matched against the expected message format as described by the protocol specification.

Communication and Threat Model   In 1983 Dolev and Yao laid the basis for a network threat model that is currently the one most widely used [76]. In the Dolev-Yao model the adversary has complete control over the communication network, in which messages are exchanged asynchronously. The adversary can intercept any message and learn its contents. It can insert any message that it can construct from its knowledge. The adversary can additionally compromise any number of agents, thereby learning their secret keys.

Security Requirements   Security requirements state the purpose of a security protocol. Here we consider only safety properties, stating that something bad will never happen. In particular, we will study secrecy and various forms of authentication. However, the semantics is set up in such a way that a large class of security properties can be expressed easily. The details of specific security properties will be addressed in Chap. 4.

The components mentioned are not independent entities. For instance, the protocol specification makes use of the provided cryptographic primitives and the communication model is connected to the adversary model if the adversary has full control over the network.

Having introduced the relevant concepts we will now formally define each in turn.

Fig. 3.3 The
Needham-Schroeder
public-key authentication
protocol

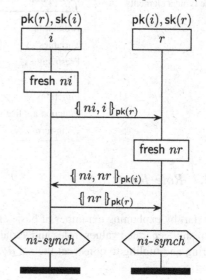

protocol Needham-Schroeder protocol (NS)

3.2 Security Protocol Specification

As a running example in this chapter, we use the short version of the Needham-Schroeder protocol from [124], referred to as *NS*. Figure 3.3 depicts this protocol. The initiator i knows its own secret key $sk(i)$ and the public key $pk(r)$ of the responder r. Symmetrically, the responder r knows its own secret key $sk(r)$ and the public key $pk(i)$ of the initiator i. We denote encryption of a message m with key k by $\{|m|\}_k$. The protocol includes a challenge-response mechanism that uses a freshly generated number. Such a fresh number is called a *nonce*, which is short for "*n*umber used *once*". The initiator first creates a fresh nonce ni, denoted by the box, and then sends its name i together with the nonce ni, encrypted with the public key $pk(r)$, to the responder. After receiving this message, the responder generates a fresh nonce nr and sends it, together with the earlier nonce ni, encrypted with the public key $pk(i)$, to i. Next, the initiator decrypts the message and returns the nonce nr of the responder, encrypted with the public key of the responder.

In the figure, hexagons denote security claims. Both the initiator and the responder claim that the property *ni-synch* holds, which stands for *non-injective synchronisation*, a form of authentication. The "*ni*" in *ni-synch* is thus not related to the name of the nonce ni. The details of security claims will be explained in Chap. 4.

A protocol specification defines the exchange of message terms between agents. The terms that occur in the protocol specification are different from those that we will define later for the execution model. We will first define role terms, which are used in the specification.

Table 3.2 Basic sets and
some typical elements

Description	Set	Typical elements
Role terms	*RoleTerm*	rt_1, rt_2
Variables	*Var*	V, W, X, Y, Z
Fresh values	*Fresh*	$ni, nr, sessionkey$
Roles	*Role*	i, r, s
Functions	*Func*	h
Function application		$h(m)$
Long-term keys		$sk(i), pk(i), k(i, r)$

3.2.1 Role Terms

We start by explaining a number of basic elements for constructing role terms, such
as freshly generated values, roles and variables. Afterwards, we add constructors for
pairing and tupling to construct the set *RoleTerm* that will be used in role descriptions.

Definition 3.1 (Basic Term Sets) We assume we are given the following sets:

- *Var*, denoting variables that are used to store received messages,
- *Fresh*, denoting values that are freshly generated for each instantiation of a role,
- *Role*, denoting roles, and
- *Func*, denoting function names of a fixed arity.

In Table 3.2 we show some typical elements of these sets, as used throughout this
book.

Definition 3.2 (Role Terms) We define the set of role terms as the basic term sets,
extended with function application, term pairing, encryption, and long-term keys.

$RoleTerm ::= \quad Var \mid Fresh \mid Role$

$\quad\mid Func([RoleTerm [, RoleTerm]^*])$

$\quad\mid (RoleTerm, RoleTerm)$

$\quad\mid \{\!|RoleTerm|\!\}_{RoleTerm}$

$\quad\mid sk(RoleTerm) \mid pk(RoleTerm) \mid k(RoleTerm, RoleTerm).$

We say a term is a basic term if it does not contain pairs or encryptions. The functions $vars : RoleTerm \to \mathcal{P}(Var)$ and $roles: RoleTerm \to \mathcal{P}(Role)$ determine the
variables and roles occurring in a term. We use the following conventions to reduce
the number of parentheses: $\{\!|a, b|\!\}_k$ denotes $\{\!|(a, b)|\!\}_k$, (a, b, c) denotes $((a, b), c)$,
and role term f (i.e., a nullary function) denotes $f()$.

We require that in every function application the number of arguments matches the arity of the function name. Functions with arity 0 are used to denote constants, such as the natural number 42. Functions with higher arity can be used to denote, e.g., hash functions.

Terms that have been encrypted with a term can only be decrypted with either the same term (for symmetric encryption) or the inverse key (for asymmetric encryption). To determine which term needs to be known to decrypt a term, we define the function $()^{-1}$ that yields the inverse of a term. Thus, for every $rt \in RoleTerm$, we write rt^{-1} to denote its inverse, where $rt^{-1} \in RoleTerm$.

Throughout this book we assume that pk and sk represent asymmetric keys, such that $\forall rt : pk(rt)^{-1} = sk(rt) \wedge sk(rt)^{-1} = pk(rt)$. For roles R, R', we write $pk(R)$ to denote the public key of R, $sk(R)$ to denote the private key of R, and $k(R, R')$ to denote the symmetric key shared between R and R'.

Example 3.3 (Encryption and Signing) Encryption of a message m with a public key $pk(R)$ is modelled as $\{\!|m|\!\}_{pk(R)}$. In order to sign a message, a role's secret key is used. This can be done in two ways, either directly, as in $\{\!|m|\!\}_{sk(R)}$, or indirectly through signing the message digest. This message digest can be constructed by applying a hash function h to the message, which results in the signed message $(m, \{\!|h(m)|\!\}_{sk(R)})$.

All role terms rt (that are not of the form $pk(X)$ or $sk(X)$ for any X), when used as an encryption key, are considered to be symmetric keys, for which we have $rt^{-1} = rt$. Thus, although we use the notation $\{\!| |\!\}$ for both types of encryption, the type of encryption that is applied can be derived from the key that is used. Note that we explicitly allow for composed keys, e.g., as in $\{\!|rt_1|\!\}_{(rt_2, rt_3)}$.

Later, we will define another type of term called run term. Together, role terms and run terms form the set of terms *Term*. On this generic set of terms we define a number of auxiliary functions.

First, we define a function *unpair* which allows us to identify the set of non-tuple terms of which a term is constructed (by tupling).

Definition 3.4 (Unpair Operator) We define the function *unpair*: $Term \rightarrow \mathcal{P}(Term)$:

$$unpair(t) = \begin{cases} unpair(t_1) \cup unpair(t_2) & \text{iff } t = (t_1, t_2) \\ \{t\} & \text{otherwise.} \end{cases}$$

We introduce a syntactic relation that allows us to identify subparts of a term.

Definition 3.5 (Subterm Relation) The syntactic subterm relation $\sqsubseteq$ is defined as the reflexive, transitive closure of the smallest relation satisfying the following for all terms $t_1, \ldots, t_n$, i such that $1 \leq i \leq n$, and function names f:

$$t_1 \sqsubseteq (t_1, t_2), \qquad t_1 \sqsubseteq \mathsf{k}(t_1, t_2),$$
$$t_2 \sqsubseteq (t_1, t_2), \qquad t_2 \sqsubseteq \mathsf{k}(t_1, t_2),$$
$$t_1 \sqsubseteq \{\!|t_1|\!\}_{t_2}, \qquad t_1 \sqsubseteq \mathsf{pk}(t_1),$$
$$t_2 \sqsubseteq \{\!|t_1|\!\}_{t_2}, \qquad t_1 \sqsubseteq \mathsf{sk}(t_1),$$
$$t_i \sqsubseteq f(t_1, \ldots, t_n).$$

Example 3.6 (Unpairing and Subterms) Let t be the term $(\{\!|p, q|\!\}_{\mathsf{sk}(R)}, (a, b), h(m))$. The unpairing of t is the set $\{\{\!|p, q|\!\}_{\mathsf{sk}(R)}, a, b, h(m)\}$. Examples of subterms of t are p, $\mathsf{sk}(R)$ and $\{\!|p, q|\!\}_{\mathsf{sk}(R)}$. Term t is a subterm of itself. The symbols h and sk are *not* subterms of t.

An agent can only construct an encrypted message if it knows the encryption key and it can only decrypt a message if it knows the corresponding decryption key.

Definition 3.7 (Term Inference Relation) Let M be a set of terms. The term inference relation $\vdash: \mathcal{P}(\textit{Term}) \times \textit{Term}$ is defined as the smallest relation satisfying for all terms t, t_i, k, and function names f,

$$t \in M \Rightarrow M \vdash t,$$
$$M \vdash t_1 \wedge M \vdash t_2 \Rightarrow M \vdash (t_1, t_2),$$
$$M \vdash t \wedge M \vdash k \Rightarrow M \vdash \{\!|t|\!\}_k,$$
$$M \vdash (t_1, t_2) \Rightarrow M \vdash t_1 \wedge M \vdash t_2,$$
$$M \vdash \{\!|t|\!\}_k \wedge M \vdash k^{-1} \Rightarrow M \vdash t,$$
$$\bigwedge_{1 \leq i \leq n} M \vdash t_i \Rightarrow M \vdash f(t_1, \ldots, t_n).$$

Example 3.8 (Inference and Encryptions) Let m and k be two terms such that $k^{-1} \neq \{\!|m|\!\}_k$. From the singleton set containing the term $\{\!|m|\!\}_k$ it is impossible to infer m or k, i.e.,

$$\{\{\!|m|\!\}_k\} \nvdash m \wedge \{\{\!|m|\!\}_k\} \nvdash k.$$

Given $\{\!|m|\!\}_k$ and k^{-1}, we can infer m:

$$\{\{\!|m|\!\}_k, k^{-1}\} \vdash m.$$

If k is an asymmetric key (and thus $k \neq k^{-1}$) and given $\{\!|m|\!\}_k$ and k^{-1}, where $k^{-1} \neq \{\!|m|\!\}_k$, it is not possible to infer k:

$$k \neq k^{-1} \wedge k^{-1} \neq \{\!|m|\!\}_k \Rightarrow \{\{\!|m|\!\}_k, k^{-1}\} \nvdash k.$$

3.2.2 Protocol Specification

We now turn to describing the protocol behaviour. We describe protocols as sets of roles. A role consists of a sequence of role events. For the definition of role events, we additionally assume being given two disjoint sets *Label* and *Claim*, which we will explain below.

Definition 3.9 (Role Events) We write $RoleEvent_R$ to denote the set of events that can be executed by the role R.

$$RoleEvent_R ::= \quad \mathsf{send}_{Label}(R, Role, RoleTerm)$$
$$| \quad \mathsf{recv}_{Label}(Role, R, RoleTerm)$$
$$| \quad \mathsf{claim}_{Label}(R, Claim\,[\,, RoleTerm]).$$

The set *RoleEvent* contains the events of all roles:

$$RoleEvent = \bigcup_{R \in Role} RoleEvent_R.$$

Event $\mathsf{send}_\ell(R, R', rt)$ denotes the sending of message rt by R, intended for R'. Likewise, $\mathsf{recv}_\ell(R, R', rt)$ denotes the receipt of message rt by R', apparently sent by R. When R executes a security claim event of the form $\mathsf{claim}_\ell(R, c, rt)$ or $\mathsf{claim}_\ell(R, c)$, security goal c is expected to hold with optional parameter rt. Security claim events are described in Chap. 4.

We leave the generation of fresh values (such as nonces) implicit, and assume that the generation of a fresh value takes place just before its first occurrence in an event.

The labels $\ell \in Label$ that tag the events serve two purposes. First, they are needed to disambiguate similar occurrences of events in a protocol specification. Second, they are used to express the relation between corresponding send and receive events. This will play a role in the communication order in Definition 3.16 and in the definition of authentication properties in the next chapter.

The behaviour of a role is specified as a sequence of role events. We require that variables first occur in so-called accessible positions.

Definition 3.10 (Accessible Subterm Relation) The accessible subterm relation $\sqsubseteq_{\mathrm{acc}}$ is defined as the reflexive, transitive closure of the smallest relation satisfying the following for all terms t_1, t_2:

$$t_1 \sqsubseteq_{\mathrm{acc}} (t_1, t_2), \qquad t_1 \sqsubseteq_{\mathrm{acc}} \{\!|t_1|\!\}_{t_2},$$
$$t_2 \sqsubseteq_{\mathrm{acc}} (t_1, t_2).$$

We consider a sequence of role events to be well-formed if all variables are initialised in an accessible position in a recv event before being used in another event. We generalise the function *vars*, which determines the variables occurring in a role term, to sequences of role events, $vars: RoleEvent^* \rightarrow \mathcal{P}(Var)$. This generalisation is straightforward. Using this function, we define well-formedness.

Definition 3.11 (Well-Formedness) The predicate $wellformed: RoleEvent^*$ is defined by:

$$wellformed(\rho) \Leftrightarrow \forall V \in vars(\rho) : \exists \rho', \ell, R, R', rt, \rho'' :$$
$$\rho = \rho' \cdot [\mathsf{recv}_\ell(R, R', rt)] \cdot \rho'' \wedge V \notin vars(\rho') \wedge V \sqsubseteq_{\mathrm{acc}} rt.$$

In addition to a list of its role events, the specification of a role also includes the initial knowledge of this role, expressed as a set of terms. The role knowledge is not needed to define the execution of the protocol, but is introduced to systematically derive the initial adversary knowledge, as explained later.

Definition 3.12 (Role Specification) Given a role R, a role specification of R consists of the initial knowledge of R and a well-formed sequence of role events. We define the set $RoleSpec$, which is the set of all role specifications, as

$$RoleSpec = \big\{(m, s) \,\big|\, m \in \mathcal{P}(RoleTerm) \wedge \forall rt \in m : vars(rt) = \emptyset \wedge$$

$$s \in (RoleEvent_R)^* \wedge wellformed(s)\big\}.$$

Thus, we require that the initial role knowledge does not contain variables.

Definition 3.13 (Protocol Specification) A protocol specification is a partial function mapping roles to role behaviours. We define the set *Protocol* of all possible protocol specifications as all partial functions from $Role \nrightarrow RoleSpec$. For every protocol $P \in Protocol$ and each role $R \in Role$, $P(R)$ is the role specification of R.

We assume a fixed protocol P in the definitions below. We write $KN_0(R)$ as a shorthand for the initial knowledge of the role R in the protocol, i.e., $P(R) = (KN_0(R), s)$, for some sequence of events s.

Without loss of generality, we assume that role events are unique within a protocol specification. This can be enforced by the labelling scheme mentioned above. Thus, we can define a function $role: RoleEvent \rightarrow Role$ that, given a role event, yields the role the event belongs to.

Example 3.14 (Role Specification) The following role specification models the initiator role of the Needham-Schroeder protocol.

$$NS(i) = \big(\ \{i, r, ni, \mathsf{sk}(i), \mathsf{pk}(i), \mathsf{pk}(r)\},$$

$$[\mathsf{send}_1(i, r, \{\!|ni, i|\!\}_{\mathsf{pk}(r)}),$$

$$\mathsf{recv}_2(r, i, \{\!|ni, V|\!\}_{\mathsf{pk}(i)}),$$

$$\mathsf{send}_3(i, r, \{\!|V|\!\}_{\mathsf{pk}(r)}),$$

$$\mathsf{claim}_4(i, ni\text{-}synch)]\ \big)$$

This role specification follows from Fig. 3.3 by selecting the left-hand axis and its associated events. Similarly, the right-hand axis leads to the definition of the responder role.

$$NS(r) = \big(\ \{i, r, nr, \mathsf{sk}(r), \mathsf{pk}(r), \mathsf{pk}(i)\},$$

$$[\mathsf{recv}_1(i, r, \{\!| W, i |\!\}_{\mathsf{pk}(r)}),$$

$$\mathsf{send}_2(r, i, \{\!| W, nr |\!\}_{\mathsf{pk}(i)}),$$

$$\mathsf{recv}_3(i, r, \{\!| nr |\!\}_{\mathsf{pk}(r)}),$$

$$\mathsf{claim}_5(r, \textit{ni-synch})]\ \big)$$

Notice that we have to clarify which constructs in the terms are variables (because they receive their values upon receiving a message) and which are constants (because they are determined by the role itself). In this example, we have that $Role = \{i, r\}$, $Fresh = \{ni, nr\}$, $Func = \emptyset$, $Label = \{1, 2, 3, 4, 5\}$, and $Var = \{V, W\}$. The two sequences are well-formed because the variables V and W occur first in receive events.

3.2.3 Event Order

Each role of the protocol corresponds to a sequence of events. For a role R, the order of the events of the sequence is denoted by $<_R$.

Definition 3.15 (Role Event Order) Let R be a role with specification $P(R) = (M, [\varepsilon_1, \ldots, \varepsilon_n])$. For R, the role event order $<_R : RoleEvent \times RoleEvent$ is defined as the strict total order defined by the sequence $[\varepsilon_1, \ldots, \varepsilon_n]$.

If the specification of R contains, e.g., the sequence of events $[\varepsilon_1, \varepsilon_2, \varepsilon_3]$, then $\varepsilon_1 <_R \varepsilon_2$, $\varepsilon_2 <_R \varepsilon_3$, and $\varepsilon_1 <_R \varepsilon_3$.

Because we specify individual roles, each communication is split into a send event in one role, and a receive event in another role. We relate two such corresponding events syntactically by using the same label, as can be observed in the role descriptions of the *NS* protocol.

The relation $\dashrightarrow$ expresses the order on events that is induced by the communications of the protocol.

Definition 3.16 (Communication Relation) The communication relation $\dashrightarrow :$ $RoleEvent \times RoleEvent$ is defined as

$$\varepsilon_1 \dashrightarrow \varepsilon_2 \ \Leftrightarrow$$

$$\exists \ell, R, R', rt_1, rt_2 : \varepsilon_1 = \mathsf{send}_\ell(R, R', rt_1) \wedge \varepsilon_2 = \mathsf{recv}_\ell(R, R', rt_2)$$

for all $\varepsilon_1, \varepsilon_2 \in RoleEvent$.

Together, the role event order and the communication relation describe a strict partial order on all events in a protocol description.

Definition 3.17 (Protocol Order) Let P be a protocol with roles $Role$. The transitive closure of the union of the role event order and the communication relation is called the protocol order $\prec_P$:

$$\prec_P = \left(\dashrightarrow \cup \bigcup_{R \in Role} <_R \right)^+ .$$

Example 3.18 (Protocol Order) For the example protocol NS, the role orderings $<_i$ and $<_r$ on the roles i and r, respectively, are defined as the strict total orders satisfying:

$$\mathsf{send}_1(i, r, \{|ni, i|\}_{\mathsf{pk}(r)}) <_i \mathsf{recv}_2(r, i, \{|ni, V|\}_{\mathsf{pk}(i)})$$

$$<_i \mathsf{send}_3(i, r, \{|V|\}_{\mathsf{pk}(r)}) <_i \mathsf{claim}_4(i, ni\text{-}synch),$$

$$\mathsf{recv}_1(i, r, \{|W, i|\}_{\mathsf{pk}(r)}) <_r \mathsf{send}_2(r, i, \{|W, nr|\}_{\mathsf{pk}(i)})$$

$$<_r \mathsf{recv}_3(i, r, \{|nr|\}_{\mathsf{pk}(r)}) <_r \mathsf{claim}_5(r, ni\text{-}synch).$$

The communication relation $\dashrightarrow$ for NS is:

$$\mathsf{send}_1(i, r, \{|ni, i|\}_{\mathsf{pk}(r)}) \dashrightarrow \mathsf{recv}_1(i, r, \{|W, i|\}_{\mathsf{pk}(r)}),$$

$$\mathsf{send}_2(r, i, \{|W, nr|\}_{\mathsf{pk}(i)}) \dashrightarrow \mathsf{recv}_2(r, i, \{|ni, V|\}_{\mathsf{pk}(i)}),$$

$$\mathsf{send}_3(i, r, \{|V|\}_{\mathsf{pk}(r)}) \dashrightarrow \mathsf{recv}_3(i, r, \{|nr|\}_{\mathsf{pk}(r)}).$$

The protocol order $\prec_{NS}$ can be depicted as follows:

$$\mathsf{send}_1(i, r, \{|ni, i|\}_{\mathsf{pk}(r)}) \quad \prec_{NS} \quad \mathsf{recv}_1(i, r, \{|W, i|\}_{\mathsf{pk}(r)})$$
$$\curlyvee_{NS} \qquad\qquad\qquad\qquad \curlyvee_{NS}$$
$$\mathsf{recv}_2(r, i, \{|ni, V|\}_{\mathsf{pk}(i)}) \quad \succ_{NS} \quad \mathsf{send}_2(r, i, \{|W, nr|\}_{\mathsf{pk}(i)})$$
$$\curlyvee_{NS} \qquad\qquad\qquad\qquad \curlyvee_{NS}$$
$$\mathsf{send}_3(i, r, \{|V|\}_{\mathsf{pk}(r)}) \quad \prec_{NS} \quad \mathsf{recv}_3(i, r, \{|nr|\}_{\mathsf{pk}(r)})$$
$$\curlyvee_{NS} \qquad\qquad\qquad\qquad \curlyvee_{NS}$$
$$\mathsf{claim}_4(i, ni\text{-}synch) \qquad\qquad \mathsf{claim}_5(r, ni\text{-}synch).$$

3.3 Describing Protocol Execution

In the previous section we have formalised the notion of a protocol description, which is a static description of how a protocol should behave. When such a protocol description is executed, dynamic aspects are introduced. These include aspects from both the agent model as well as the execution model from the domain analysis. Formalising these dynamic aspects requires the introduction of some new concepts that did not appear on the protocol description level.

3.3.1 Runs

A protocol specification describes a set of roles. These roles serve as a blueprint for the actions performed by actual agents in a system. When a protocol is executed, each agent can execute any role any number of times, possibly in parallel. We call each such a single, possibly partial, execution of a role description a *run*. From an implementation point of view, a run is conceptually similar to a *thread*. In our model, two runs executed by the same agent are independent and share no variables.

Executing a role turns a role description into a run. This process is referred to as *instantiation*. Roles can be instantiated multiple times in several runs. We assign a unique run identifier to each run. In order to instantiate a role we have to bind the role names to the names of actual agents, and we have to ensure that the freshly generated values are unique for each instantiation. We differentiate syntactically between the fresh values generated by different runs by appending the identifier of the runs to each of their names. Thus, the set of terms occurring in a run differs in several ways from the set of terms used in role descriptions.

The run terms are defined similarly to role terms. The two main differences are that fresh values, roles, and variables that are local to a run are made syntactically unique by extending them with the run identifier, and that variables and roles can be instantiated by concrete ground terms. When a run term does not contain any variables or role names, we say it is *ground*. Additionally, the run term set includes the set *AdversaryFresh* of basic run terms generated by an adversary. This set will only be used from Sect. 3.3.4 onwards, where it will be defined and explained in more detail.

We assume being given a set *RID* to denote run identifiers and a set *Agent* to denote agents.

Definition 3.19 (Run Terms) We define the set of run terms as follows:

$$
\begin{aligned}
RunTerm ::= \quad & Fresh^{\sharp RID} \\
| \ & Role^{\sharp RID} \\
| \ & Var^{\sharp RID} \\
| \ & Agent \\
| \ & Func(\ [RunTerm\ [\ ,\ RunTerm]^*]\ ) \\
| \ & (RunTerm, RunTerm) \\
| \ & \{\!|RunTerm|\!\}_{RunTerm} \\
| \ & AdversaryFresh \\
| \ & \mathsf{pk}(RunTerm)\ |\ \mathsf{sk}(RunTerm)\ |\ \mathsf{k}(RunTerm, RunTerm).
\end{aligned}
$$

We extend the inverse function $^{-1}$ to *RunTerm*. In Table 3.3 we provide some typical elements of the basic run term sets, and where appropriate, the name of the set.

Table 3.3 Basic run term
sets and some typical
elements

Description	Set	Typical elements
Run terms	*RunTerm*	$t1, t2$
Instantiated fresh values		$ni^{\#1}, nr^{\#2}, sessionkey^{\#1}$
Agents	*Agent*	A, B, C, S, E

For each run, there is a relation between the role terms and the run terms. As
explained above, this relation contains three elements: the run to which the term is
bound, the instantiation of roles by agent names and the instantiation of variables.

Definition 3.20 (Instantiations) A role term is transformed into a run term by applying an *instantiation* from the set *Inst*, defined as

$$RID \times (Role \twoheadrightarrow Agent) \times (Var \twoheadrightarrow RunTerm).$$

Often we will extract the first component, the run identifier, from an instantiation. We will use the notation *runidof*(*inst*) to denote the run identifier from an
instantiation *inst*.

Definition 3.21 (Term Instantiation)   Let *inst* $\in$ *Inst* be an instantiation, where
$inst = (\theta, \rho, \sigma)$. Let $f \in Func$ and let $rt, rt_1, \ldots, rt_n$ be role terms such that
$roles(rt) \subseteq dom(\rho)$ and $vars(rt) \subseteq dom(\sigma)$. We define instantiation, $\langle inst \rangle$:
RoleTerm $\rightarrow$ *RunTerm*, by:

$$\langle inst \rangle(rt) = \begin{cases} n^{\#\theta} & \text{if } rt = n \in Fresh, \\ \rho(R) & \text{if } rt = R \in Role \wedge R \in dom(\rho), \\ R^{\#\theta} & \text{if } rt = R \in Role \wedge R \notin dom(\rho), \\ \sigma(v) & \text{if } rt = v \in Var \wedge v \in dom(\sigma), \\ v^{\#\theta} & \text{if } rt = v \in Var \wedge v \notin dom(\sigma), \\ f(\langle inst \rangle(rt_1), \ldots, \langle inst \rangle(rt_n)) & \text{if } rt = f(rt_1, \ldots, rt_n), \\ (\langle inst \rangle(rt_1), \langle inst \rangle(rt_2)) & \text{if } rt = (rt_1, rt_2), \\ \{\!|\langle inst \rangle(rt_1)|\!\}_{\langle inst \rangle(rt_2)} & \text{if } rt = \{\!|rt_1|\!\}_{rt_2}, \\ \mathsf{sk}(\langle inst \rangle(rt_1)) & \text{if } rt = \mathsf{sk}(rt_1), \\ \mathsf{pk}(\langle inst \rangle(rt_1)) & \text{if } rt = \mathsf{pk}(rt_1), \\ \mathsf{k}(\langle inst \rangle(rt_1), \langle inst \rangle(rt_2)) & \text{if } rt = \mathsf{k}(rt_1, rt_2). \end{cases}$$

Example 3.22 (Term Instantiation) We give two examples of instantiations that may
occur in the execution of a protocol:

$$\langle 1, \{i \mapsto A, r \mapsto B\}, \emptyset \rangle (\{\!|ni, i|\!\}_{\mathsf{pk}(r)}) = \{\!|ni^{\#1}, A|\!\}_{\mathsf{pk}(B)},$$

$$\langle 2, \{i \mapsto C, r \mapsto D\}, \{W \mapsto ni^{\#1}\} \rangle (\{\!|W, nr, r|\!\}_{\mathsf{pk}(i)}) = \{\!|ni^{\#1}, nr^{\#2}, D|\!\}_{\mathsf{pk}(C)}.$$

Definition 3.23 (Run) The set of all possible runs is defined as *Run* = *Inst* $\times$
*RoleEvent**.

3.3.2 Matching

The role terms that occur in receive events in a protocol description define which run terms can be received by the agent. We formalise this relation by defining the matching predicate Match : *Inst × RoleTerm × RunTerm × Inst*. The purpose of this predicate is to match an incoming message (the third argument) to a pattern specified by a role term (the second argument), in the context of a particular instantiation. This pattern is already instantiated (the first argument), but may still contain free variables. The idea is to assign values to the free variables such that the incoming message equals the instantiated role term. The old instantiation extended with these new assignments provides the resulting instantiation (the fourth argument).

We assume we are given a function *type*: *Var* → $\mathcal{P}(RunTerm)$ that defines the set of run terms that are valid values for a variable. As we will see below, the definition of this function depends on the agent model.

Definition 3.24 (Match) For all $inst = (\theta, \rho, \sigma)$, $inst' = (\theta', \rho', \sigma') \in Inst$, $pt \in RoleTerm$ and $m \in RunTerm$, the predicate Match($inst, pt, m, inst'$) holds if and only if $\theta = \theta'$, $\rho = \rho'$ and

$$\langle inst' \rangle(pt) = m \land$$
$$\forall v \in dom(\sigma') : \sigma'(v) \in type(v) \land$$
$$\sigma \subseteq \sigma' \land$$
$$dom(\sigma') = dom(\sigma) \cup vars(pt).$$

The definition of Match ensures that (a) the instantiation of the pattern is equal to the message, (b) the instantiation is well typed, (c) the new variable assignment extends the old one, and (d) the instantiation is only extended for variables that occur in the pattern.

The definition of the *type* function depends on the agent model. For example, when expecting a fresh value, agents may accept any bit string, including agent names and encryptions. Alternatively, the implementation may add type tags to messages to ensure that agent names can be distinguished from nonces. These options are reflected in our model by using different definitions for the *type* function. We provide three possible definitions below.

The first definition of the type function corresponds to an implementation that ensures that the types of an incoming message can be established, and that variables are only instantiated with terms that are not composed by tupling or encryption.

Definition 3.25 (Type Matching) For all variables V,

$$type(V) \in \{S_1, S_2, S_3, S_4, S_5\}, \text{ where}$$
$$S_1 ::= Agent,$$
$$S_2 ::= Func([RunTerm[\, , RunTerm]^*]),$$

$$S_3 ::= \mathsf{pk}(RunTerm) \mid \mathsf{sk}(RunTerm),$$

$$S_4 ::= \mathsf{k}(RunTerm, RunTerm),$$

$$S_5 ::= Fresh^{\sharp RID} \mid AdversaryFresh.$$

We provide a second definition that focusses on term constructors.

Definition 3.26 (Constructor Matching) For all variables V,

$$type(V) \in \{T_1, T_2, RunTerm \setminus (T_1 \cup T_2)\}, \text{ where}$$

$$T_1 ::= \{\!\|RunTerm\|\!\}_{RunTerm},$$

$$T_2 ::= (RunTerm, RunTerm).$$

In this case, the match predicate cannot distinguish between an agent name and a nonce. It is thus possible that a receive event that expects a nonce term matches with a message that contains an agent name.

In the previous setting, there is still a distinction between different types. In the third definition there is only one type and this corresponds to an agent model in which no type checking is performed at all.

Definition 3.27 (No Type Matching) For all variables V,

$$type(V) = RunTerm.$$

Here, a variable can match with any term, e.g., a variable may be instantiated with a tuple.

Unless stated otherwise, we assume the type matching model from Definition 3.25.

Example 3.28 (Match) Assume $\rho = \{i \mapsto A, r \mapsto B\}$, and assume $type(X) = S_5$. Some examples for which the predicate is true are:

	inst	pt	m	inst'
Match (	$(1, \rho, \emptyset)$,	X,	$nr^{\sharp 2}$,	$(1, \rho, \{X \mapsto nr^{\sharp 2}\})$)
Match (	$(1, \rho, \emptyset)$,	$\{\!\|ni, r\|\!\}_{\mathsf{pk}(i)}$,	$\{\!\|ni^{\sharp 1}, B\|\!\}_{\mathsf{pk}(A)}$,	$(1, \rho, \emptyset)$)

In the first line, we find from the first parameter that X has not been instantiated yet. Thus, the agent expects to receive any value of type S_5, of which $nr^{\sharp 2}$ is an element. Therefore, the message fits the pattern, and receiving the message assigns $nr^{\sharp 2}$ to the variable X.

The pattern on the second line consists of a role name r and a fresh value ni, encrypted with the public key of a role i. From the instantiation with ρ we find that in this run, the r role is performed by B and the i role by A. Furthermore, the fresh value is unique to the run with run identifier 1. Thus, the message exactly matches the pattern.

Below, we give some examples where the Match predicate *does not* hold, for any instantiation $inst'$.

	$inst$	pt	m	$inst'$
$\neg$Match (	$(1, \rho, \emptyset),$	$nr,$	$nr^{\#2},$	$inst'$)
$\neg$Match (	$(1, \rho, \emptyset),$	$X,$	$(nr^{\#2}, ni^{\#1}),$	$inst'$)
$\neg$Match (	$(1, \rho, \emptyset),$	$\{\!|ni, i|\!\}_{\mathsf{pk}(i)},$	$\{\!|ni^{\#1}, B|\!\}_{\mathsf{pk}(A)},$	$inst'$)

On the first line, run 1 expects to receive its own fresh value $nr^{\#1}$. On the second line, the message does not fit the type of the variable X. On the third line the encryption key is the correct one, but the agent was expecting the name A inside, not B.

3.3.3 Run Events

To define protocol behaviour we connect the protocol descriptions (i.e., roles and their events) to their execution (i.e., instantiation of role events). We call the combination of an instantiation function with a role event a run event.

Definition 3.29 (Run Event) We define the set of run events *RunEvent* as

$$Inst \times (RoleEvent \cup \{\mathsf{create}(R) \mid R \in Role\}).$$

The additional create event is used to mark the creation of a run of a role in the operational semantics that follow.

We extend the domain of the function *role* from Sect. 3.2.2 to run events, where the role of create events is defined as the created role, and the role of other events is defined as the role of their role event.

We write *RecvRunEv* for the set of run events corresponding to receive events, *SendRunEv* for those corresponding to send events, and *ClaimRunEv* for claim events. Together with the create events, these sets combined form the set *RunEvent*.

We define a *content* extraction function for send and receive run events.

Definition 3.30 (Contents of Event) Let the function *cont*: (*RecvRunEv* $\cup$ *SendRunEv*) $\rightarrow$ *RunTerm* specify the contents of an event, i.e.,

$$cont((inst, \mathsf{send}_\ell(R, R', m))) = \langle inst \rangle(R, R', m), \quad \text{and}$$

$$cont((inst, \mathsf{recv}_\ell(R, R', m))) = \langle inst \rangle(R, R', m).$$

A protocol description allows for the creation of runs. The runs that can be created are defined by the function *runsof*.

Definition 3.31 (Possible Runs) The runs that can be created by a protocol P for a role $R \in dom(P)$ are specified by the function $runsof: Protocol \times Role \to \mathcal{P}(Run)$, defined as

$$runsof(P, R) = \big\{ ((\theta, \rho, \emptyset), s) \mid s = \pi_2(P(R)) \land$$

$$\theta \in RID \land dom(\rho) = roles(s) \land ran(\rho) = Agent \big\}.$$

Definition 3.32 (Active Run Identifiers) Given a set of runs F, we define the set of active run identifiers as

$$runIDs(F) = \big\{ \theta \mid ((\theta, \rho, \sigma), s) \in F \big\}.$$

We now have defined nearly all elements we need to model protocol execution, except for the threat model, which we discuss below.

3.3.4 Threat Model

The adversary model in our semantics is similar to the Dolev-Yao adversary model (see [76]). We assume the adversary has complete control over the network. The adversary learns any message sent over the network, can block any message, and can insert messages at will. Furthermore, we model the fact that a number of agents may be compromised by the adversary, in which case the adversary learns all the knowledge of this agent. This allows the adversary to act as if it were one of the compromised agents.

The set $Agent$ is partitioned into sets $Agent_H$ (denoting the *honest agents*) and $Agent_C$ (denoting the *compromised agents*). We often use the name E (Eve) to represent a compromised agent, i.e., $E \in Agent_C$. Agents do not know which of the agents are honest and which are not. Thus, honest agents might still start protocol sessions with compromised agents, or accept requests from compromised agents.

We infer the initial adversary knowledge from the protocol description and define it as the set of terms that compromised agents executing this protocol initially know.

Definition 3.33 (Initial Adversary Knowledge) For a protocol P, we define the initial adversary knowledge $AKN_0(P)$ as the union of the fresh terms generated by the adversary, the set of agent names, and the initial knowledge of all compromised agents in all roles:

$$AKN_0(P) = AdversaryFresh \cup Agent \cup$$

$$\bigcup_{\substack{R \in Role \\ \rho \in Role \to Agent \\ \rho(R) \in Agent_C}} \big\{ \langle \theta, \rho, \emptyset \rangle (rt) \mid \theta \in RID \land rt \in KN_0(R) \land \forall rt' \sqsubseteq rt : rt' \notin Fresh \big\}.$$

For all variables v occurring in a protocol description, we require that there exist an unbounded number of terms t that can be inferred from the initial adversary knowledge such that $t \in type(v)$. We require that the initial adversary knowledge does not contain fresh terms that may later be generated by agents, which is expressed in the above definition by the right-hand conjunct.

Example 3.34 (Initial Adversary Knowledge) For the *NS* protocol (from Example 3.14), we have that

$$AKN_0(NS) = AdversaryFresh \cup Agent$$

$$\cup \left\{ \mathsf{pk}(A) \mid A \in Agent \right\} \cup \left\{ \mathsf{sk}(A) \mid A \in Agent_C \right\}.$$

In this particular case, the initial role knowledge of both roles contributes exactly the same information to $AKN_0(NS)$. We consider role i, with $KN_0(i) = \{i, r, \mathsf{sk}(i), \mathsf{pk}(i), \mathsf{pk}(r)\}$. When such a role is executed by a compromised agent, we have that $\rho(i) \notin Agent_H$. No such restriction holds for the communication partner, and thus $\rho(r) \in Agent$. Because the role knowledge contains $\mathsf{pk}(r)$, we find that compromised agents reveal the public keys of all the agents. Finally, because $\mathsf{sk}(i) \in KN_0(i)$, we have that the secret keys of the compromised agents are known to the adversary.

3.4 Operational Semantics

We are now able to define our operational semantics for security protocols using a labelled transition system $(State, RunEvent, \rightarrow, s_0(P))$.

Definition 3.35 (State) The set of possible states of a network of agents executing roles in a security protocol is defined as

$$State = \mathcal{P}(RunTerm) \times \mathcal{P}(Run).$$

The first component of a state corresponds to the current adversary knowledge and the second component to the (remainders of the) runs that still have to be executed.

Definition 3.36 (Initial State) The initial state of a protocol is defined as

$$s_0(P) = \langle\langle AKN_0(P), \emptyset \rangle\rangle.$$

In the initial state of the system no runs have been created yet, so the initial state of the system consists of the initial adversary knowledge and the empty set of runs.

The transition relation is defined by the transition rules from Table 3.4. The four rules have a similar structure. In each rule, the left-hand side of the conclusion is the state $\langle\langle AKN, F \rangle\rangle$, where AKN is the current intruder knowledge and F is the current set of active runs. The system can transition from this state to the one on the right if

Table 3.4 Operational semantics rules

$$[create_P] \frac{R \in dom(P) \quad ((\theta, \rho, \emptyset), s) \in runsof(P, R) \quad \theta \notin runIDs(F)}{\langle\langle AKN, F \rangle\rangle \xrightarrow{((\theta,\rho,\emptyset),\text{create}(R))} \langle\langle AKN, F \cup \{((\theta, \rho, \emptyset), s)\}\rangle\rangle}$$

$$[send] \frac{e = \text{send}_\ell(R_1, R_2, m) \quad (inst, [e] \cdot s) \in F}{\langle\langle AKN, F \rangle\rangle \xrightarrow{(inst, e)} \langle\langle AKN \cup \{\langle inst \rangle(m)\}, (F \setminus \{(inst, [e] \cdot s)\}) \cup \{(inst, s)\}\rangle\rangle}$$

$$[recv] \frac{e = \text{recv}_\ell(R_1, R_2, pt) \quad (inst, [e] \cdot s) \in F \quad AKN \vdash m \quad Match(inst, pt, m, inst')}{\langle\langle AKN, F \rangle\rangle \xrightarrow{(inst', e)} \langle\langle AKN, (F \setminus \{(inst, [e] \cdot s)\}) \cup \{(inst', s)\}\rangle\rangle}$$

$$[claim] \frac{e = \text{claim}_\ell(R, c) \vee e = \text{claim}_\ell(R, c, t) \quad (inst, [e] \cdot s) \in F}{\langle\langle AKN, F \rangle\rangle \xrightarrow{(inst, e)} \langle\langle AKN, (F \setminus \{(inst, [e] \cdot s)\}) \cup \{(inst, s)\}\rangle\rangle}$$

the premises are satisfied. The new state contains an update of the set of active runs and the (possibly updated) intruder knowledge. The transitions are labelled with the executed run events.

The *create_P* rule expresses that in any state a new run from the set of possible runs $runsof(P, R)$ (see Definition 3.31) can be created. The only requirement is that its run identifier θ should not already occur in F.

The premises of the *send* rule state that there is a run in F whose next step is a send event. Upon execution of this send event the adversary learns the sent message and the run progresses to the next step.

The premises of the *recv* rule state that there is a run in F whose next step is a receive event. The difference with the send rule is that the transition is only enabled if the adversary can infer a message m that matches the pattern pt. If pt contains previously unbound variables, they are now instantiated by updating $inst$ to $inst'$. The adversary learns no new information and the run progresses.

The premises of the *claim* rule state that there is a run in F whose next step is a claim event. Except for progressing the run, they have no effect on the state. In the next chapter we explain the purpose of claim events.

A finite execution of the transition system defined above has the form $\xi = [s_0, \alpha_1, s_1, \alpha_2, \ldots, \alpha_n, s_n]$, where α_i are run events and $s_i = \langle\langle AKN_i, F_i \rangle\rangle$ are states. We define $AKN(\xi)$, the adversary knowledge after execution ξ, by $AKN(\xi) = AKN_n$.

For every finite trace $t = [\alpha_1, \alpha_2, \ldots, \alpha_n]$ of the transition system, there is a unique finite execution $[s_0, \alpha_1, s_1, \alpha_2, \ldots, \alpha_n, s_n]$. This allows us to extend the function AKN from executions to traces.

We define $traces(P)$ as the set of finite traces of the labelled transition system associated with a protocol P.

protocol Needham-Schroeder protocol (NS)

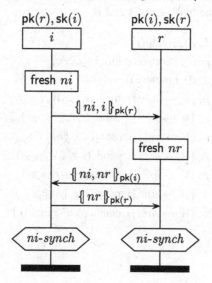

$Role = \{i, r\}$ $\quad\quad$ $Fresh = \{ni, nr\}$ $\quad\quad$ $Var = \{V, W\}$

$NS(i) = (\{i, r, ni, \mathsf{sk}(i), \mathsf{pk}(i), \mathsf{pk}(r)\},$ $\quad$ $NS(r) = (\{i, r, nr, \mathsf{sk}(r), \mathsf{pk}(r), \mathsf{pk}(i)\},$

$\quad\quad$ $[\mathsf{send}_1(i, r, \{\! | ni, i | \!\}_{\mathsf{pk}(r)}),$ $\quad\quad\quad\quad$ $[\mathsf{recv}_1(i, r, \{\! | W, i | \!\}_{\mathsf{pk}(r)}),$

$\quad\quad$ $\mathsf{recv}_2(r, i, \{\! | ni, V | \!\}_{\mathsf{pk}(i)}),$ $\quad\quad\quad\quad$ $\mathsf{send}_2(r, i, \{\! | W, nr | \!\}_{\mathsf{pk}(i)}),$

$\quad\quad$ $\mathsf{send}_3(i, r, \{\! | V | \!\}_{\mathsf{pk}(r)}),$ $\quad\quad\quad\quad$ $\mathsf{recv}_3(i, r, \{\! | nr | \!\}_{\mathsf{pk}(r)}),$

$\quad\quad$ $\mathsf{claim}_4(i, \textit{ni-synch})])$ $\quad\quad\quad\quad$ $\mathsf{claim}_5(r, \textit{ni-synch})])$

$AKN_0(NS) = AdversaryFresh \cup Agent \cup$

$\quad\quad\quad\quad\quad\quad$ $\{\mathsf{pk}(A) \mid A \in Agent\} \cup \{\mathsf{sk}(A) \mid A \in Agent_C\}$

Fig. 3.4 Overview of the specification of the *NS* protocol

3.5 Example Protocol Specification

In Fig. 3.4 we show an overview of the *NS* protocol using the notation introduced in this chapter.

Example 3.37 (Example Trace of the *NS* Protocol) Let ρ be defined by

$$\rho = \{i \mapsto A, r \mapsto B\},$$

where $\{A, B\} \subseteq Agent$. The following trace represents a single regular execution of the protocol between the two agents A and B.

$$[((1, \rho, \emptyset), \mathsf{create}(i)),$$
$$((1, \rho, \emptyset), \mathsf{send}_1(i, r, \{\!| ni, i |\!\}_{\mathsf{pk}(r)})),$$
$$((2, \rho, \emptyset), \mathsf{create}(r)),$$
$$((2, \rho, \{W \mapsto ni^{\sharp 1}\}), \mathsf{recv}_1(i, r, \{\!| W, i |\!\}_{\mathsf{pk}(r)})),$$
$$((2, \rho, \{W \mapsto ni^{\sharp 1}\}), \mathsf{send}_2(r, i, \{\!| W, nr |\!\}_{\mathsf{pk}(i)})),$$
$$((1, \rho, \{V \mapsto nr^{\sharp 2}\}), \mathsf{recv}_2(r, i, \{\!| ni, V |\!\}_{\mathsf{pk}(i)})),$$
$$((1, \rho, \{V \mapsto nr^{\sharp 2}\}), \mathsf{send}_3(i, r, \{\!| V |\!\}_{\mathsf{pk}(r)})),$$
$$((1, \rho, \{V \mapsto nr^{\sharp 2}\}), \mathsf{claim}_4(i, \textit{ni-synch})),$$
$$((2, \rho, \{W \mapsto ni^{\sharp 1}\}), \mathsf{recv}_3(i, r, \{\!| nr |\!\}_{\mathsf{pk}(r)})),$$
$$((2, \rho, \{W \mapsto ni^{\sharp 1}\}), \mathsf{claim}_5(r, \textit{ni-synch})) \,]$$

3.6 Problems

3.1 (Domain Analysis) For each of the following properties of real-world models, indicate to which element of the domain analysis they belong.

 (i) A smartcard does not support multi-threading.
 (ii) A virtual private network (VPN) is used to secure all communications.
(iii) An account is blocked after three unsuccessful login attempts.
(iv) Somebody denies having received a certain e-mail.

3.2 (Unpairing and Subterms)

 (i) What is $unpair((\{\!| p |\!\}_{\mathsf{k}(R,R')}, h(a, b)))$?
 (ii) Give all subterms of the elements of the set $unpair((\{\!| p |\!\}_{\mathsf{k}(R,R')}, h(a, b)))$.
(iii) Give a role term rt such that all subterms of rt are in $unpair(rt)$.
(iv) Prove that for every role term rt every element of $unpair(rt)$ is a subterm of rt.

3.3 (Knowledge Inference)
   Prove that the terms m and $h(k)$ can be inferred from the set

$$\left\{ \{\!| m |\!\}_{\mathsf{k}}, \ \{\!| k |\!\}_{\mathsf{pk}(b)}, \ \{\!| h(k) |\!\}_m, \ \mathsf{sk}(b) \right\}.$$

3.4 (Knowledge Inference and Subterms)

 (i) Give role terms s and t such that $\{s\} \vdash t$ but *not* $t \sqsubseteq s$.
 (ii) Give role terms s and t such that $t \sqsubseteq s$ but *not* $\{s\} \vdash t$.

3.5 (Protocol Specification) Consider the SSC protocol from Fig. 3.1.

(i) Give role specifications of the SSC protocol.
(ii) Determine $<_{initiator}$, $<_{responder}$ and $-\rightarrow$.
(iii) Determine $\prec_{SSC}$.

3.6 (Initial Intruder Knowledge) Given the SSC protocol from Problem 3.5, determine $AKN_0(SSC)$.

3.7 (Traces) Construct a trace of length 5 or more of the *NS* protocol.

3.8 (Evolution of the Adversary Knowledge) Show that the adversary knowledge is non-decreasing.

Chapter 4
Security Properties

Abstract We introduce and formalise security properties in our model. In particular, we introduce secrecy and several forms of authentication. Using these security properties, we revisit the Needham-Schroeder protocol.

In the previous chapter we presented a model for the description of security protocols and their executions in terms of traces. In this chapter we formally introduce security properties into our model.

We first define the notion of *claim events* in Sect. 4.1. We define secrecy in Sect. 4.2 and several forms of authentication in Sect. 4.3. We establish a hierarchy on authentication properties in Sect. 4.4.

4.1 Security Properties as Claim Events

We consider security properties to be an essential part of a security protocol, and a security protocol should not be considered without knowing the exact properties it is supposed to satisfy. In our model, we therefore integrate the security properties into the protocol specification by means of *claim events*.

The main idea behind claim events is locality: agents have a local view on the state of the system, based on the messages they receive. The protocol should guarantee that, based on the local view, the agent can be sure about some properties of the global state of the system, e.g., that a term is not in the adversary knowledge, or that a certain agent is active.

We provide some intuition about claim events and give formal definitions later. Intuitively, "secrecy of a term" means that if an agent communicates with non-compromised agents, the term should be secret in every trace of the protocol.

Consider the OSS protocol in Fig. 4.1. If an agent completes the initiator role i whilst communicating with an honest agent, it can be sure that the term ni it created is secret. Because the nonce is encrypted with the public key of the intended recipient, which is honest, only this agent can decrypt it. Whenever a run of the i role is completed with honest communication partners, the nonce ni generated in the run will not become known to the adversary: we say that the claim *secret ni* of the role i holds.

C. Cremers, S. Mauw, *Operational Semantics and Verification of Security Protocols*,   37
Information Security and Cryptography, DOI 10.1007/978-3-540-78636-8_4,
© Springer-Verlag Berlin Heidelberg 2012

Fig. 4.1 A protocol with a
correct and an incorrect claim

protocol One-Sided Secrecy (OSS)

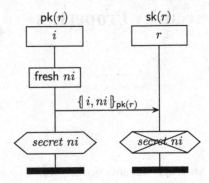

Fig. 4.2 An attack on the
secrecy claim of the
responder role

trace Attack on the OSS protocol

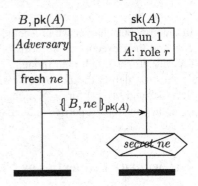

However, this does not mean that the protocol guarantees some form of global
secrecy. In particular, if an agent completes the responder role under the assumption
that its intended communication partner is honest, it cannot be sure that the received
term is secret. An invalid claim is denoted by a crossed out claim event. In Fig. 4.2
we show an attack on this protocol. Agent A executes the responder role and receives
a message that appears to come from honest agent B. However, this message was
generated by the adversary. Because the adversary knows the public key of A, it
is able to generate a message that matches the pattern that A expects, but which
contains the adversary's nonce ne. The agent A will accept the message, as there
is no authentication performed on the origin of the message. We say that the claim
secret ni of the role r does not hold. Such a falsification of a claim constitutes an
attack.

The fact that the claim of i is true, while the claim of r is false, illustrates the
difference between the local views on security by the different roles.

We define an auxiliary predicate *honest* that, given the instantiation of a role
event, specifies when the intended communication partners and the agent that executes the event are honest.

Definition 4.1 (Honest) The predicate *honest* is defined for instantiations as

$$honest((\theta, \rho, \sigma)) \iff ran(\rho) \subseteq Agent_H.$$

We define the function *actor*, which determines the agent that executes a given run event.

Definition 4.2 (Actor) The function $actor : Inst \times RoleEvent \rightarrow Agent$ is defined as

$$actor((\theta, \rho, \sigma), \varepsilon) = \rho(role(\varepsilon)).$$

4.2 Secrecy

The first security property that we define is secrecy. Secrecy expresses that certain information is not revealed to an adversary, even though this data is communicated over an untrusted network. A secrecy claim event is written as $claim_\ell(R, secret, rt)$, where ℓ is a label, R is the role executing this event and rt is the term that should be secret, i.e., not known to the adversary.

Of course, given the trust relations sketched in the previous chapter, agents communicating (secret) data with compromised agents are effectively sharing their information with the adversary. Although the communicated terms are not secret anymore in this case, this does not mean that the protocol is broken. Rather, a secrecy claim of a term holds if each time an honest agent communicates with honest agents, the term will not be known to the adversary.

Definition 4.3 (Secrecy Claim) Let P be a protocol with role R. The secrecy claim event $\gamma = claim_\ell(R, secret, rt)$ is correct if and only if

$$\forall t \in traces(P) : \forall ((\theta, \rho, \sigma), \gamma) \in t :$$

$$honest((\theta, \rho, \sigma)) \Rightarrow AKN(t) \nvdash \langle \theta, \rho, \sigma \rangle (rt).$$

The definition states that a secrecy claim γ in a protocol is true if and only if we have the following for all traces: for each run in which roles are mapped to honest agents only, and secrecy of a term is claimed, the term should not be inferable from the knowledge of the adversary.

Secrecy claims can be specified for any role term, including variables. An example of a secrecy claim for a variable can be found in the responder role of the OSS protocol (Fig. 4.1).

Example 4.4 We can now formalise our observation that the secrecy claim of the responder role of the OSS protocol does not hold. First, consider the following specification of the OSS protocol.

$$OSS(i) =$$
$$(\{i, r, ni, \mathsf{pk}(r)\},$$
$$[\mathsf{send}_1(i, r, \{\!| i, ni \,|\!\}_{\mathsf{pk}(r)}),$$
$$\mathsf{claim}_2(i, secret, ni)])$$

$$OSS(r) =$$
$$(\{i, r, \mathsf{sk}(r)\},$$
$$[\mathsf{recv}_1(i, r, \{\!| i, W \,|\!\}_{\mathsf{pk}(r)}),$$
$$\mathsf{claim}_3(r, secret, W)])$$

Let θ be any run identifier and let $\rho : Role \to Agent_H$ be defined as

$$\rho = \{i \mapsto B, r \mapsto A\}.$$

Let ne be a nonce created by the adversary, thus $ne \in AKN_0$. Then the following trace t leads to a state in which the secrecy claim is invalid:

$$[((\theta, \rho, \emptyset), \mathsf{create}(r)),$$
$$((\theta, \rho, \{W \mapsto ne\}), \mathsf{recv}_1(i, r, \{\!| i, W \,|\!\}_{\mathsf{pk}(r)})),$$
$$((\theta, \rho, \{W \mapsto ne\}), \mathsf{claim}_3(r, secret, W))].$$

Thus, we found a trace t with honest communication partners, where $\langle \theta, \rho, \{W \mapsto ne\}\rangle(W) = ne$ is claimed to be secret, while $AKN(t) \vdash ne$.

Example 4.5 Next, we prove correctness of the secrecy claim of the initiator in the OSS protocol.

We start with informally stating two properties. First, from the structure of the protocol messages we observe that the adversary knowledge will never contain secret keys of honest agents. Second, from the definition of the initial adversary knowledge, we see that fresh values created by honest agents are not in the initial adversary knowledge.

Let $t \in traces(OSS)$ be a trace of the OSS protocol containing a secrecy claim of the initiator. Thus, there is an index n such that $t_n = ((\theta, \rho, \sigma), \mathsf{claim}_2(i, secret, ni))$, for some instantiation (θ, ρ, σ) with $ran(\rho) \subseteq Agent_H$. Now we assume that the adversary learns the instantiation of ni and we will derive a contradiction.

Since $\langle \theta, \rho, \sigma \rangle(ni)$ is not in the initial adversary knowledge, there must exist a smallest k such that $AKN_k \nvdash \langle \theta, \rho, \sigma \rangle(ni)$, while $AKN_{k+1} \vdash \langle \theta, \rho, \sigma \rangle(ni)$. By inspecting the derivation rules, we see that this increase in adversary knowledge is due to an application of the send rule. Therefore, there must be a smallest index p such that $t_p = ((\theta', \rho', \sigma'), \mathsf{send}_1(i, r, \{\!| i, ni \,|\!\}_{\mathsf{pk}(r)}))$ and $\langle \theta, \rho, \sigma \rangle(ni) \sqsubseteq \langle \theta', \rho', \sigma' \rangle(\{\!| i, ni \,|\!\}_{\mathsf{pk}(r)})$. Rewriting this term inclusion gives $ni^{\sharp\theta} \sqsubseteq \{\!| \rho'(i), ni^{\sharp\theta'} \,|\!\}_{\mathsf{pk}(\rho'(r))}$. This implies that $\theta = \theta'$ and, since the operational semantics rules keep a one-to-one correspondence between θ and ρ, we also have $\rho = \rho'$. The adversary can only learn $ni^{\sharp\theta}$ from $\{\!| \rho'(i), ni^{\sharp\theta'} \,|\!\}_{\mathsf{pk}(\rho'(r))}$ if $\rho'(r)$ is a dishonest agent, which contradicts the assumption $ran(\rho) \subseteq Agent_H$.

Fig. 4.3 Protocol $HELLO_0$

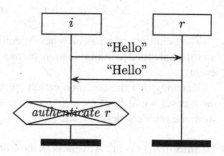

protocol Hello0

4.3 Authentication

There exist many forms of *authentication* in the literature. In its most basic form, authentication is a simple statement about the existence of a communication partner. A protocol description suggests that at least two agents are communicating. However, because the network is under the control of the adversary, not every role execution guarantees that there actually has been a communication partner. Consider the protocol in Fig. 4.3. When an agent completes the initiator role, she cannot be certain who sent the received "hello" message: it might have been sent by the adversary or any other agent.

The minimal requirement for authentication is that when A executes a protocol role she can be sure that there is at least a communication partner in the network. In most cases we want to establish something stronger, e.g., that the intended partner is aware that he is communicating with A and that the partner executes a particular role. Additionally, we may require that messages have been exchanged as specified by the protocol.

In the next sections we define several forms of authentication.

4.3.1 Aliveness

Aliveness is a form of authentication that aims to establish that an intended communication partner has executed some events, i.e., that the partner is "alive". We define four forms of aliveness, viz. *weak aliveness*, *weak aliveness in the correct role*, *recent aliveness* and *recent aliveness in the correct role*. Aliveness claim events are written as $\mathsf{claim}_\ell(R, ca, R')$, where ℓ is a label, R is the role executing this event, where $ca \in \{weak\text{-}alive, weak\text{-}alive\text{-}role, recent\text{-}alive, recent\text{-}alive\text{-}role\}$ and R' is the role that is claimed to be alive.

Definition 4.6 (Weak Aliveness) Let P be a protocol with roles R and R'. The claim event $\gamma = \mathsf{claim}_\ell(R, weak\text{-}alive, R')$ is correct if and only if

$$\forall t \in traces(P): \forall inst: (inst, \gamma) \in t \wedge honest(inst) \Rightarrow$$
$$\exists ev \in t: actor(ev) = \langle inst \rangle(R').$$

The definition of weak aliveness specifies that if an agent executes a claim event, and the intended communication partner is honest, then this partner executes an event.

Knowing that the communication partner is weakly alive is often not enough. In most cases we at least require that he is executing the role that could be expected from the protocol description.

Definition 4.7 (Weak Aliveness in the Correct Role) Let P be a protocol with roles R and R'. The claim event $\gamma = \text{claim}_\ell(R, weak\text{-}alive\text{-}role, R')$ is correct if and only if

$$\forall t \in traces(P): \forall inst: (inst, \gamma) \in t \wedge honest(inst) \Rightarrow$$
$$\exists ev \in t: actor(ev) = \langle inst \rangle(R') \wedge role(ev) = R'.$$

The notions of aliveness explained above express that the communication partner is alive, but it does not tell us whether this was before, after, or during the run in which the claim occurs. Recent aliveness expresses that the communication partner executes an event during the run in which the claim event occurs.

For the definition of recent aliveness, we extend the domain of the run identifier extraction function *runidof* from Sect. 3.3.1 to run events.

Definition 4.8 (Recent Aliveness) Let P be a protocol with roles R and R'. The claim event $\gamma = \text{claim}_\ell(R, recent\text{-}alive, R')$ is correct if and only if

$$\forall t \in traces(P) \; \forall inst: (inst, \gamma) \in t \wedge honest(inst) \Rightarrow$$
$$\exists ev \in t: actor(ev) = \langle inst \rangle(R') \wedge$$
$$\exists ev': runidof(ev') = runidof(inst) \wedge ev' <_t ev <_t (inst, \gamma).$$

Given the claim event $(inst, \gamma)$, the communication partner must have executed an event ev before this claim event, but after some other event ev' from the same run as the claim event.

Similarly to weak aliveness in the correct role, we can now also require that the communication partner is executing the correct role R'.

Definition 4.9 (Recent Aliveness in the Correct Role) Let P be a protocol with roles R and R'. The claim event $\gamma = \text{claim}_\ell(R, recent\text{-}alive\text{-}role, R')$ is correct if and only if

$$\forall t \in traces(P) \; \forall inst: (inst, \gamma) \in t \wedge honest(inst) \Rightarrow$$
$$\exists ev \in t: actor(ev) = \langle inst \rangle(R') \wedge role(ev) = R' \wedge$$
$$\exists ev': runidof(ev') = runidof(inst) \wedge ev' <_t ev <_t (inst, \gamma).$$

Fig. 4.4 Protocol $HELLO_1$ **protocol Hello1**

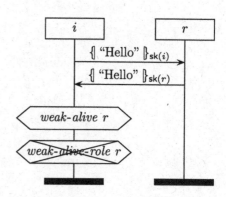

Fig. 4.5 Protocol $HELLO_2$ **protocol Hello2**

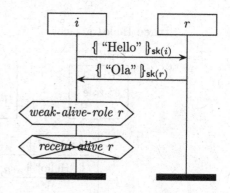

The four aliveness properties define different types of authentication. The protocols from Figs. 4.4, 4.5 and 4.6 give some distinguishing examples.

The first protocol, $HELLO_1$, satisfies *weak-alive* but not *weak-alive-role*. The second protocol, $HELLO_2$, satisfies *weak-alive* and *weak-alive-role* but not *recent-alive*. The third protocol, $HELLO_3$, satisfies *recent-alive*.

Example 4.10 An attack on the *weak-alive-role* claim of protocol $HELLO_1$ from Fig. 4.4 is shown in Fig. 4.7. Agents A and B both initiate a session of the protocol in role i. The adversary reroutes B's first message to A, who then interprets this message as the second message of her protocol execution. She then incorrectly claims that the message comes from B, executing the r role.

Correctness of the *weak-alive* claim of this protocol is proven as follows. Let $t \in traces(HELLO_1)$ be a trace of the $HELLO_1$ protocol containing a *weak-alive* claim of the initiator. Thus, there is an index n such that $t_n = ((\theta, \rho, \sigma),$ $\mathsf{claim}_3(i, weak\text{-}alive, r))$, for some instantiation (θ, ρ, σ) with $ran(\rho) \subseteq Agent_H$.

Fig. 4.6 Protocol *HELLO*₃

protocol Hello3

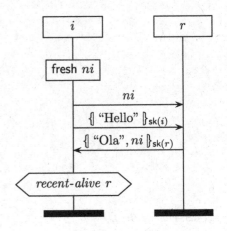

trace Hello1 attack

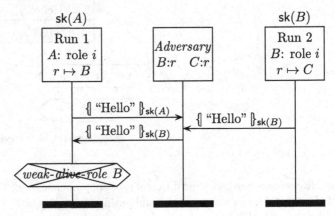

Fig. 4.7 An attack on the *HELLO*₁ protocol

Because agent $\rho(i)$ follows its role specification, it must have executed the event $((\theta, \rho, \sigma), \mathsf{recv}_2(r, i, \{\!|\, \text{"Hello"} \,|\!\}_{\mathsf{sk}(r)}))$. By inspection of the protocol specification we observe that the adversary will never learn an honest agent's secret key. In particular, $\mathsf{sk}(\rho(r))$ will remain secret. Therefore, the adversary cannot have constructed $\{\!|\, \text{"Hello"} \,|\!\}_{\mathsf{sk}(\rho(r))}$ from its components. Thus, $\{\!|\, \text{"Hello"} \,|\!\}_{\mathsf{sk}(\rho(r))}$ must have occurred as a subterm of a sent message $((\theta', \rho', \sigma'), \mathsf{send}_\ell(R_1, R_2, \{\!|\, \text{"Hello"} \,|\!\}_{\mathsf{sk}(R_1)}))$. This can only be the case if $\mathsf{sk}(\rho(r)) = \mathsf{sk}(\rho'(R_1))$, and thus $\rho(r) = \rho'(R_1)$. Thus, $\rho(r)$ has executed an event and the *weak-alive* claim is valid.

trace Hello3 attack

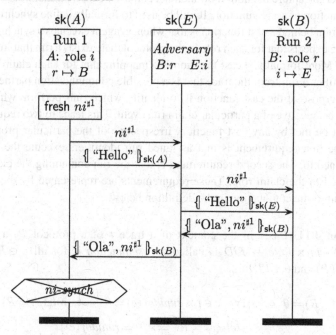

Fig. 4.8 Synchronisation does not hold for the $HELLO_3$ protocol

4.3.2 Synchronisation

The aliveness properties required that some event was executed by the communication partner, without putting restrictions on the contents of the exchanged messages.

A much stronger authentication requirement is formed by *synchronisation*. It requires that all received messages were indeed sent by the communication partner and that sent messages have indeed been received by the communication partner. This corresponds to the requirement that the actual message exchange has occurred exactly as specified by the protocol description.

We illustrate the synchronisation property by showing that it is not satisfied by the $HELLO_3$ protocol from Fig. 4.6. In Fig. 4.8 we show an attack in which A attempts to authenticate B. A sends her nonce and a signed string to B. The adversary learns the messages and modifies the second message by replacing A's signature by a signature of compromised agent E. Then the messages are forwarded (on behalf of E) to agent B, who concludes that E wants to run the protocol with him. He then answers according to the protocol specification and the adversary forwards its answer to A. At this point A rightfully assumes that there is a run executed by B. However, B responded to E instead of A. In this case, even though weak aliveness holds, synchronisation does not hold. The intended communication partners of agents A and B do not seem to correspond.

In order to capture the notion of intended communication partners, we will introduce the notion of a cast function. It will be used to formally define synchronisation. The intuition behind a cast function is that when an agent executes a synchronisation claim, she expects that for each role in the protocol there exists a run that instantiates this role. More formally, a cast function is a mapping that for each claim and each role identifies a run from the trace that is a possible communication partner.

The purpose of the cast function is to identify which runs perform which roles, from the perspective of a particular claim run event. This leads to two requirements that must be met by any cast function, irrespective of the particular protocol and trace. The first requirement is that assigned run identifiers execute the role they are assigned to. The second requirement is that the run containing the claim event is assigned to the claim role. These requirements are represented by the left- and right-hand of the conjunction in the definition below.

Definition 4.11 (*Cast*) In the context of a trace t of a protocol P, a mapping $\Gamma : RunEvent \times Role \nrightarrow RID$ is called a *cast function* if for all $c \in RunEvent$, $R \in dom(P)$ and $\theta \in RID$:

$$\Gamma(c, R) = \theta \iff \left(\forall e : e \in t \land runidof(e) = \theta \implies role(e) = R\right) \land$$
$$\left(role(c) = R \implies \theta = runidof(c)\right).$$

We write $Cast(P, t)$ to denote the collection of all cast functions for a trace t of the protocol P.

Example 4.12 (Cast Function) Let c be the *ni-synch* claim for the attack trace described in Fig. 4.8. Then the cast function for this claim event is defined by $\Gamma(c, i) = 1$ and $\Gamma(c, r) = 2$.

We use the cast function to define several synchronisation properties. Synchronisation claim events are written as $\text{claim}_\ell(R, cs)$, where ℓ is a label, R is the role executing this event and $cs \in \{ni\text{-}synch, i\text{-}synch\}$.

4.3.3 Non-injective Synchronisation

We first define *non-injective synchronisation*. Informally speaking, this property states that everything we intended to happen in the protocol description also happens in the trace.

Recall that the function $cont(e)$ extracts the instantiated contents (of the form (a, b, m)) from a send or receive run event e.

Fig. 4.9 Protocol *HELLO*₄

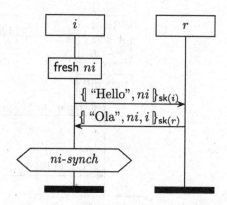

protocol Hello4

Definition 4.13 (*NI-SYNCH*) Let P be a protocol. The claim event $\gamma = \text{claim}_\ell(R, ni\text{-}synch)$ is correct if and only if

$$\forall t \in traces(P) \; \exists \Gamma \in Cast(P, t):$$

$$\forall inst : (inst, \gamma) \in t \land honest(inst) \implies$$

$$\forall \varsigma, \varrho \in RoleEvent: \varsigma \dashrightarrow \varrho \land \varrho \prec_P \gamma \implies$$

$$\exists inst'', inst' : (inst'', \varsigma) <_t (inst', \varrho) <_t (inst, \gamma) \land$$

$$runidof(inst'') = \Gamma((inst, \gamma), role(\varsigma)) \land$$

$$runidof(inst') = \Gamma((inst, \gamma), role(\varrho)) \land$$

$$cont((inst'', \varsigma)) = cont((inst', \varrho)).$$

The non-injective synchronisation property requires that there exists a cast function such that for all claim run events whose intended partners are honest, certain events occur in the trace. In particular, for all communications $\varsigma \dashrightarrow \varrho$ that occur before the claim event (according to the protocol specification) we require that the corresponding send and receive events (a) are executed by the runs indicated by the cast function, (b) occur in the right order, and (c) have the same contents.

An example of a protocol that satisfies non-injective synchronisation can be found in Fig. 4.9. In Sect. 4.5 we show how such a property can be proven correct.

It is important to notice that synchronisation only considers the contents and ordering of the messages. If the adversary just forwards the messages to the intended recipient without modifications, this is not considered an attack on synchronisation. As an example consider the trace in Fig. 4.10, which does not constitute an attack on the synchronisation of protocol *HELLO*₄.

trace Hello4 no attack

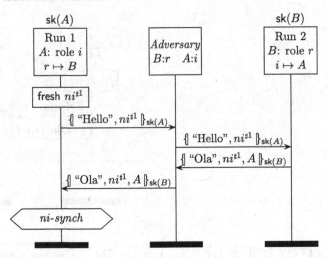

Fig. 4.10 Just forwarding the messages does not constitute an attack on synchronisation

4.3.4 Injective Synchronisation

If we look at a single protocol execution, non-injective synchronisation ensures that the protocol is executed exactly as it would be if no adversary were present. However, because agents may execute multiple runs, possibly communicating with the same agents, the adversary may still be able to induce unexpected behaviour by replaying messages from one session in another session. In particular, protocols satisfying non-injective synchronisation may still be vulnerable to so-called *replay attacks*. In a replay attack the adversary replays a message taken from a different context, thereby fooling the honest participants into thinking they have successfully completed the protocol run. Such behaviour would not be possible in the absence of an adversary.

Example 4.14 (Injectivity) The protocol in Fig. 4.11 shows an example of a protocol that satisfies synchronisation, while Fig. 4.12 shows a replay attack on this protocol. The adversary learns the message sent and can fool A in a future run to think that B has sent this message several times.

To ensure that not only single protocol executions, but also multiple executions are performed as expected, the additional property of *injectivity* is required. For a two-party protocol, consisting of a claiming initiator and a responder, this means that there must be an injective mapping from claiming initiator runs to corresponding responder runs. More precisely, two different instances of the initiator claim must correspond to two different runs of the responder.

Fig. 4.11 A protocol
vulnerable to a replay attack

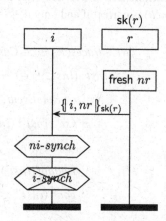

protocol Unilateral authentication

trace Replay attack

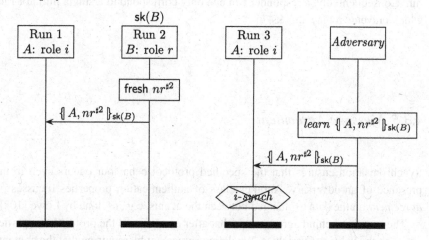

Fig. 4.12 A replay attack

To capture this requirement and to generalise it to protocols with more than two parties, we slightly modify *NI-SYNCH* and require that the cast function be injective. Recall that for each individual claim, the cast function determines the partners. By requiring that this function be injective, we ensure that each run can be a partner of at most one claim event. The resulting property is called *injective* synchronisation.

Definition 4.15 (*I-SYNCH*) Let P be a protocol. The claim event $\gamma = \mathsf{claim}_\ell(R,$ *i-synch*) is correct if and only if

$$\forall t \in traces(P)\ \exists \Gamma \in Cast(P,t)\colon injective(\Gamma)\ \wedge$$
$$\forall inst\colon (inst, \gamma) \in t \wedge honest(inst) \implies$$
$$\forall \varsigma, \varrho \in RoleEvent\colon \varsigma \dashrightarrow \varrho \wedge \varrho \prec_P \gamma \implies$$
$$\exists inst'', inst'\colon (inst'', \varsigma) <_t (inst', \varrho) <_t (inst, \gamma)\ \wedge$$
$$runidof(inst'') = \Gamma((inst, \gamma), role(\varsigma))\ \wedge$$
$$runidof(inst') = \Gamma((inst, \gamma), role(\varrho))\ \wedge$$
$$cont((inst'', \varsigma)) = cont((inst', \varrho)).$$

Example 4.16 The *HELLO*$_4$ protocol in Fig. 4.9 satisfies injective synchronisation. This can be informally motivated by observing that every initiator run has its unique nonce ni, which is used in all message exchanges with the corresponding responder run. Consequentially, a responder run can only correspond to a single initiator run, which prevents replay attacks.

4.3.5 Message Agreement

Synchronisation ensures that the specified protocol behaviour occurs even in the presence of an adversary. Another class of authentication properties focusses on *agreement* on the data exchanged between the agents, e.g., as done by Lowe [108].

The intuition behind agreement is that after execution of the protocol, the parties agree on the values of variables. We define agreement by requiring that the contents of the received messages correspond to the sent messages, as specified by the protocol. As a result, after the execution of the protocol the contents of the variables will be exactly as specified by the protocol.

The definition of agreement is very similar to the definition of synchronisation. The only difference is that synchronisation additionally requires that the communication order is respected, i.e., send events occur before corresponding receive events. We adapt Definition 4.13 and remove the requirement that send events occur before their corresponding receive event.

Agreement claim events are written as $\mathsf{claim}_\ell(R, ca)$, where ℓ is a label, R is the role executing this event and $ca \in \{ni\text{-}agree, i\text{-}agree\}$.

Definition 4.17 (*NI-AGREE*) Let P be a protocol. The claim event $\gamma = \mathsf{claim}_\ell(R, ni\text{-}agree)$ is correct if and only if

$$\forall t \in traces(P) \; \exists \Gamma \in Cast(P, t):$$

$$\forall inst: (inst, \gamma) \in t \wedge honest(inst) \implies$$

$$\forall \varsigma, \varrho \in RoleEvent: \varsigma \dashrightarrow \varrho \wedge \varrho \prec_P \gamma \implies$$

$$\exists inst'', inst': (inst'', \varsigma) <_t (inst, \gamma) \wedge (inst', \varrho) <_t (inst, \gamma) \wedge$$

$$runidof(inst'') = \Gamma((inst, \gamma), role(\varsigma)) \wedge$$

$$runidof(inst') = \Gamma((inst, \gamma), role(\varrho)) \wedge$$

$$cont((inst'', \varsigma)) = cont((inst', \varrho)).$$

The agreement predicate expresses that for all instantiated claims in any trace of a given security protocol, there exist runs for the other roles in the protocol, such that all communication events causally preceding the claim must have occurred before the claim.

Injective agreement is defined in the same way as injective synchronisation is obtained from non-injective synchronisation.

Definition 4.18 (*I-AGREE*) Let P be a protocol. The claim event $\gamma = \mathsf{claim}_\ell(R, i\text{-}agree)$ is correct if and only if

$$\forall t \in traces(P) \; \exists \Gamma \in Cast(P, t): injective(\Gamma) \wedge$$

$$\forall inst: (inst, \gamma) \in t \wedge honest(inst) \implies$$

$$\forall \varsigma, \varrho \in RoleEvent: \varsigma \dashrightarrow \varrho \wedge \varrho \prec_P \gamma \implies$$

$$\exists inst'', inst': (inst'', \varsigma) <_t (inst, \gamma) \wedge (inst', \varrho) <_t (inst, \gamma) \wedge$$

$$runidof(inst'') = \Gamma((inst, \gamma), role(\varsigma)) \wedge$$

$$runidof(inst') = \Gamma((inst, \gamma), role(\varrho)) \wedge$$

$$cont((inst'', \varsigma)) = cont((inst', \varrho)).$$

In the next section we study the relation between the various authentication properties. An example of a protocol that satisfies agreement but does not synchronise is given in Fig. 4.15.

4.4 Authentication Hierarchy

We organise the previously defined security properties according to their relative strengths. For example, every protocol that satisfies injective synchronisation also

Fig. 4.13 Hierarchy of
authentication properties

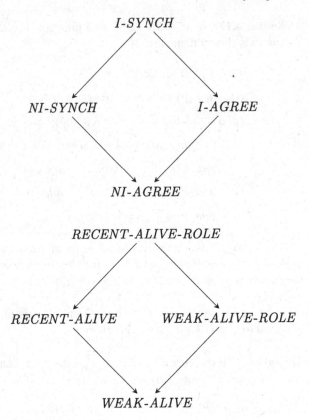

satisfies non-injective agreement. Similarly, each protocol that satisfies recent aliveness also satisfies weak aliveness.

Figure 4.13 depicts the relations between the authentication properties we have
defined previously.

The correctness of the hierarchy is captured by the following theorem.

Theorem 4.19 *Consider Fig.* 4.13. *If there is an arrow from property X to property Y, then every protocol satisfying X also satisfies Y. If there is no arrow from X
to Y, there exists a protocol satisfying property X but not Y.*

The presence of an arrow follows from the property definitions. We have already
presented a number of distinguishing examples motivating the absence of arrows
for the bottom diamond. We will give distinguishing examples for the top diamond
below.

The protocol in Fig. 4.14 satisfies *NI-SYNCH* and *NI-AGREE*, but neither
I-SYNCH nor *I-AGREE*.

The adversary will only be able to construct message $\{\!| i, r |\!\}_{\mathsf{sk}(i)}$ after having
eavesdropped this message from a previous run. Therefore, every receive event of
this message is preceded by a corresponding send event, so the protocol is both

Fig. 4.14 A protocol that is
not injective

protocol Injectivity vs. non-injectivity

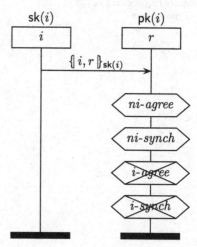

Fig. 4.15 A protocol that
satisfies agreement but does
not synchronise

protocol Synchronisation vs. agreement

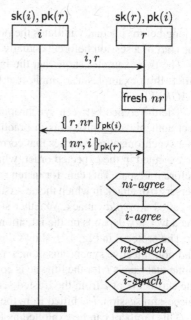

NI-SYNCH and *NI-AGREE*. However, once the adversary has learned this message,
it can replay it as often as desired, so the protocol is not injective.

A distinguishing example between synchronisation and agreement is depicted in
Fig. 4.15. This protocol satisfies injective agreement, but it does not satisfy synchronisation (both variants). This is the case, because the adversary can send message i,

Fig. 4.16 An exploitable
protocol that does not satisfy
synchronisation

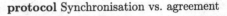

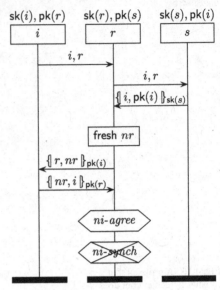

r long before *i* actually initiates the protocol, making *r* believe that *i* has requested
the start of a session before it actually did.

The two examples show that the inclusions of the top diamond in Fig. 4.13 are
strict. Both examples also imply that there are no arrows between *NI-SYNCH* and
I-AGREE.

The difference between synchronisation and agreement is subtle and most correct authentication protocols in practice satisfy both properties. The distinction is
that synchronisation requires that corresponding send and receive messages have to
be executed in the expected order, while for agreement a message may be received
before it is sent. This can, for instance, be caused by a message injection of the adversary. An attack in which the adversary injects a message before its actual creation
is called a *preplay* attack. Whether such a protocol weakness can be exploited by
the adversary depends on the intention of the protocol.

The protocol in Fig. 4.16 shows the distinction between non-injective agreement
and non-injective synchronisation. *r* is an Internet Service Provider, used by *i*. Assume that *i* pays *r* for the time he is connected. When *i* wants to connect, *r* retrieves
the certificate of *i* from the trusted server *S* and uses this to authenticate *i*. After a
successful session, *i* is billed from the moment the first message was received by *r*.

This protocol can be exploited as follows. An adversary can send the first message pre-emptively, causing *r* to initiate a session with what it believes is *i*. If at
some later time *i* decides to initiate a session with *r* and finishes it successfully, *i*
will receive a bill that is too high. In fact, although, this protocol satisfies agreement
for *r*, the first message is not authenticated at all. In contrast, this protocol does not
satisfy synchronisation. The protocol can be easily modified to satisfy *NI-SYNCH*
and thus to be resilient against the sketched type of timing attacks.

Fig. 4.17 A protocol that
does not satisfy non-injective
agreement

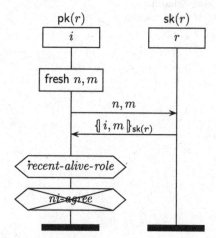

protocol Agreement vs. recent aliveness

Finally, we prove that there are no arrows between the top and bottom diamonds of Fig. 4.13. A protocol without any communication events satisfies non-injective agreement, but not recent aliveness in the correct role. The protocol from Fig. 4.17 satisfies recent aliveness in the correct role, but not non-injective agreement.

4.5 Breaking and Fixing the Needham-Schroeder Protocol

In this section we take a closer look at the Needham-Schroeder protocol which we show again in Fig. 4.18. The protocol satisfies all aliveness properties specified before, as well as synchronisation for the initiator role. We show that the Needham-Schroeder protocol does not satisfy synchronisation for the responder role by providing an attack trace. This attack was first discovered by Lowe, who also proposed a way to fix the protocol, resulting in the Needham-Schroeder-Lowe protocol [106]. We prove that the Needham-Schroeder-Lowe protocol is synchronising.

The attack is shown in a graphical form in Fig. 4.19. This attack violates the *ni-synch* claim of the r role. In the attack, an agent A executes the initiator role and communicates to a compromised agent E. This interaction can be abused by the adversary to invalidate the synchronisation claim of an agent B which intends to communicate with A.

In the first step of the attack, A sends her first message to E. The adversary learns the message, and decrypts it using the private key of E. The adversary encrypts the message again, but now using the public key of B, and fakes a message from A to B. Now B replies to A. This message is encrypted with the public key of A, so the adversary cannot decrypt this message, but he can change the original sender address to E. A thinks E has replied, and thus he decrypts the second challenge $nr^{\#2}$, and encrypts it with the public key of E. Thus, the adversary learns the value $nr^{\#2}$, and

Fig. 4.18 The
Needham-Schroeder
public-key authentication
protocol

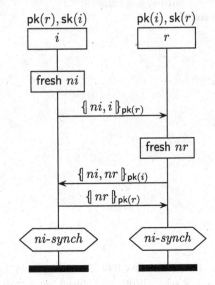

protocol Needham-Schroeder protocol (NS)

can complete the protocol with B. This constitutes an attack because the messages received by B were never sent by A. Although neither A nor B are compromised, the adversary can impersonate as A to B. Because the adversary attacks the protocol by relaying and slightly modifying messages between A and B, this type of attack is called a *man-in-the-middle* attack.

We also give a formal representation of the attack. Let $\rho_1, \rho_2 : Role \rightarrow Agent$ be defined as

$$\rho_1 = \{i \mapsto A, r \mapsto E\},$$
$$\rho_2 = \{i \mapsto A, r \mapsto B\},$$

where $\{A, B\} \subseteq Agent_H$ and $E \in Agent_C$. The following trace represents the attack:

$$
\begin{aligned}
[&((1, \rho_1, \emptyset), \mathsf{create}(i)), \\
&((1, \rho_1, \emptyset), \mathsf{send}_1(i, r, \{\!| ni, i |\!\}_{\mathsf{pk}(r)})), \\
&((2, \rho_2, \emptyset), \mathsf{create}(r)), \\
&((2, \rho_2, \{W \mapsto ni^{\#1}\}), \mathsf{recv}_1(i, r, \{\!| W, i |\!\}_{\mathsf{pk}(r)})), \\
&((2, \rho_2, \{W \mapsto ni^{\#1}\}), \mathsf{send}_2(r, i, \{\!| W, nr |\!\}_{\mathsf{pk}(i)})), \\
&((1, \rho_1, \{V \mapsto nr^{\#2}\}), \mathsf{recv}_2(r, i, \{\!| ni, V |\!\}_{\mathsf{pk}(i)})), \\
&((1, \rho_1, \{V \mapsto nr^{\#2}\}), \mathsf{send}_3(i, r, \{\!| V |\!\}_{\mathsf{pk}(r)})), \\
&((2, \rho_2, \{W \mapsto ni^{\#1}\}), \mathsf{recv}_3(i, r, \{\!| nr |\!\}_{\mathsf{pk}(r)})), \\
&((2, \rho_2, \{W \mapsto ni^{\#1}\}), \mathsf{claim}_5(r, ni\text{-}synch)) \ ].
\end{aligned}
$$

We show that non-injective synchronisation is not satisfied in this trace. We define $(inst, \gamma)$ as the claim event $((2, \rho_2, \{W \mapsto ni^{\#1}\}), \mathsf{claim}_5(r, ni\text{-}synch))$. Because $\{A, B\} \subseteq Agent_H$, we have that $honest(inst)$ holds. In this protocol, the

trace Attack on Needham-Schroeder

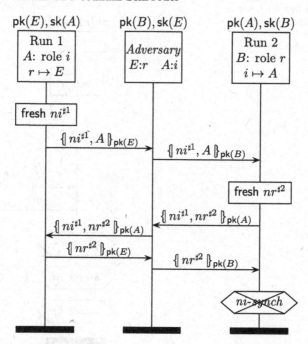

Fig. 4.19 Attack on Needham-Schroeder

claim is preceded by three communications with labels 1, 2, and 3. The definition of non-injective synchronisation requires that all three communications have occurred correctly between the claim run 2 and some other run, which is specified by $\Gamma((inst, \gamma), i)$. The definition of a cast function requires that the assigned runs perform the correct roles. Because in this trace run 1 performs the i role and run 2 performs the r role, the only candidate for the i role is run 1. Now, in order for the communications to have occurred correctly between runs 1 and 2, their contents are required to be identical. However, this is not the case, because none of the communications have matching send and receive events in the trace. In particular, the second message has different sender fields, and the payloads of the first and third messages are encrypted with different keys.

The attack is possible because when A receives the second message, she is under the assumption it was constructed by E. She therefore decrypts the message and reveals the nonce to E in the third message. However, the message was constructed by B, and therefore A should not reveal the nonce. A cannot tell who sent the second message. The fix to the protocol, as proposed by Lowe, is to include B's identity in the second message. Additionally, we add secrecy claims for the nonces and variables. The resulting Needham-Schroeder-Lowe protocol (Fig. 4.20) is specified as

Fig. 4.20 The Needham-Schroeder-Lowe public-key authentication protocol

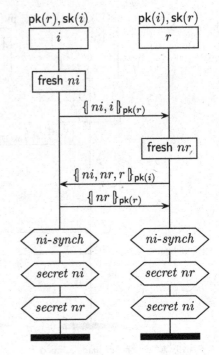

protocol NSL

follows.

$NSL(i) =$
$(\{i, r, ni, \mathsf{pk}(r), \mathsf{pk}(i), \mathsf{sk}(i)\},$
$[\mathsf{send}_1(i, r, \{\!|\, ni, i\,|\!\}_{\mathsf{pk}(r)}),$
$\mathsf{recv}_2(r, i, \{\!|\, ni, V, r\,|\!\}_{\mathsf{pk}(i)}),$
$\mathsf{send}_3(i, r, \{\!|\, V\,|\!\}_{\mathsf{pk}(r)}),$
$\mathsf{claim}_4(i, ni\text{-}synch),$
$\mathsf{claim}_6(i, secret, ni),$
$\mathsf{claim}_8(i, secret, V)]\,)$

$NSL(r) =$
$(\{i, r, nr, \mathsf{pk}(i), \mathsf{pk}(r), \mathsf{sk}(r)\},$
$[\mathsf{recv}_1(i, r, \{\!|\, W, i\,|\!\}_{\mathsf{pk}(r)}),$
$\mathsf{send}_2(r, i, \{\!|\, W, nr, r\,|\!\}_{\mathsf{pk}(i)}),$
$\mathsf{recv}_3(i, r, \{\!|\, nr\,|\!\}_{\mathsf{pk}(r)}),$
$\mathsf{claim}_5(r, ni\text{-}synch),$
$\mathsf{claim}_7(r, secret, nr),$
$\mathsf{claim}_9(r, secret, W)]\,)$

For this protocol, the initial adversary knowledge (cf. Definition 3.33) is given by

$$AKN_0 = AdversaryFresh \cup \bigcup_{a \in Agent} \{a, \mathsf{pk}(a)\} \cup \bigcup_{e \in Agent_C} \{\mathsf{sk}(e)\}.$$

We show that the Needham-Schroeder-Lowe protocol is synchronising. We introduce a number of auxiliary lemmas before stating the main result.

The first lemma expresses that roles are executed from the beginning to the end. Recall that $e <_R e'$ means that event e precedes event e' in the specification of role R.

Lemma 4.20 *Let t be a trace of a protocol and let e', e events, such that $e' <_R e$ for some role R. For all $((\theta, \rho, \sigma), e) \in t$, there exists $\sigma' \subseteq \sigma$ such that $((\theta, \rho, \sigma'), e') <_t ((\theta, \rho, \sigma), e)$.*

Proof Assume that there exists an event $((\theta, \rho, \sigma), e) \in t$ and assume that there exists an e' with $e' <_R e$. By the operational semantics rules, the role event e can only occur in a trace if there exist a reachable state $\langle\langle AKN, F \rangle\rangle$, an instantiation σ' and a sequence of events s such that $((\theta, \rho, \sigma'), [e] \cdot s) \in F$. If e is a receive event, we have $\sigma' \subseteq \sigma$, otherwise we have $\sigma' = \sigma$. In the initial state of the system, $F = \emptyset$, and therefore e must have been added to a run in F by a rule. The only rule that adds events to the runs in F is the create rule. By uniqueness of events, the created role for the run θ must be the role of e. By the role order and the inductive use of the runs in F in the operational semantics rules, the event e' must therefore occur in the created sequence before e with the same θ and ρ. The only rule that modifies σ is the receive rule (free variables are instantiated through matching) and therefore we have that the event e' must have a substitution σ' with $\sigma' \subseteq \sigma$. □

The next lemma is used to infer from an encrypted message receipt that the message must have been sent by an agent if it contains a component that is not known to the adversary.

Lemma 4.21 *Let t be a trace. For all $x, y \in Agent$, $n \in Fresh$, $m, k \in RunTerm$, $inst \in Inst$, and $\ell \in Label$, we have that if*

$$n \sqsubseteq m \wedge t \cdot [(inst, \mathsf{recv}_\ell(x, y, \{\!| m |\!\}_k))] \in traces(P) \wedge AKN(t) \nvdash \langle inst \rangle(m),$$

then there exist $inst'$, x', y', m' and ℓ', such that

$$(inst', \mathsf{send}_{\ell'}(x', y', m')) \in t \wedge \langle inst \rangle(\{\!| m |\!\}_k) \sqsubseteq \langle inst' \rangle(m').$$

Proof Because $\langle inst \rangle(\{\!| m |\!\}_k)$ is received, we have that $AKN(t) \vdash \langle inst \rangle(\{\!| m |\!\}_k)$. If the adversary learned this term by construction (encryption), it would know $\langle inst \rangle(m)$, contradicting the final conjunct of the assumption. The message could not be learned from the initial knowledge because it contains n, which is freshly generated by an agent. The adversary therefore learned the encrypted term (directly or by decryption) from a send event. □

The next lemma expresses that when two instantiations of a fresh role term (such as a nonce or session key) are equal, they were created in the same run.

Lemma 4.22 *Let (θ, ρ, σ) and $(\theta', \rho', \sigma')$ be instantiations, and let $n \in Fresh$. If $\langle \theta, \rho, \sigma \rangle(n) = \langle \theta', \rho', \sigma' \rangle(n)$ we have $\theta = \theta'$.*

Proof The lemma follows from the definition of equality as syntactic equality and Definition 3.21. □

The final lemma states that for the *NSL* protocol, the secret keys of the honest agents are not revealed to the adversary.

Lemma 4.23

$$\forall \alpha \in traces(NSL) \ \forall A \in Agent_H : AKN(\alpha) \nvdash sk(A).$$

Proof The initial adversary knowledge does not contain secret keys of honest agents as subterms. From the specification it follows that secret keys are never sent by honest agents. Therefore, the adversary has no means to obtain secret keys that it did not know initially.   □

Theorem 4.24 *The Needham-Schroeder-Lowe protocol satisfies non-injective synchronisation.*

Proof We sketch the proofs of two claims of the responder role: $claim_7$ (secrecy of nr) and $claim_5$ (non-injective synchronisation). The other claims are proven analogously.

Both proofs follow roughly the same structure. We examine the occurrence of a claim event in a trace of the system. Based on the rules of the semantics, we gradually derive more information about the trace, until we can conclude that the required property holds.

First observe that the adversary will never learn secret keys of honest agents. This follows directly from Lemma 4.23. Since the set of keys known to the adversary is constant, and all messages of the protocol are encrypted with public keys, it must be the case that if the adversary learns a basic term it learns it from decrypting an intercepted message which was encrypted with the key of a compromised agent.

Proof of $claim_7$: Secrecy of nr for the responder   Assume that there exists a trace α and an index $r7$, such that $\alpha_{r7} = ((\theta_{r7}, \rho_{r7}, \sigma_{r7}), claim_7(r, secret, nr))$ and $ran(\rho_{r7}) \subseteq Agent_H$. Now we assume that the adversary learns the instantiation of nr and we will derive a contradiction. Let k be the smallest index such that $AKN_{k+1} \vdash \langle \theta_{r7}, \rho_{r7}, \sigma_{r7} \rangle(nr)$, and thus $AKN_k \nvdash \langle \theta_{r7}, \rho_{r7}, \sigma_{r7} \rangle(nr)$. Such a smallest k exists because the initial adversary knowledge does not contain terms that are freshly generated by agents. Inspection of the derivation rules reveals that this increase in knowledge is due to an application of the send rule. Therefore, there must be a smallest index p such that $\alpha_p = ((\theta', \rho', \sigma'), send_\ell(m))$ and $\langle \theta_{r7}, \rho_{r7}, \sigma_{r7} \rangle(nr) \sqsubseteq \langle \theta', \rho', \sigma' \rangle(m)$. Since we have three possible send events in the *NSL* protocol, we have three cases: $\ell = 1, 2,$ or 3.

[$\ell = 1$] In the first case we have $\alpha_p = ((\theta', \rho', \sigma'), send_1(i, r, \{\!| ni, i |\!\}_{pk(r)}))$. Since terms ni and i both differ from nr, the adversary cannot learn the term $\langle \theta_{r7}, \rho_{r7}, \sigma_{r7} \rangle(nr)$ from $\langle \theta', \rho', \sigma' \rangle(i, r, \{\!| ni, i |\!\}_{pk(r)})$, which yields a contradiction.

[$\ell = 2$] In the second case $\alpha_p = ((\theta', \rho', \sigma'), send_2(r, i, \{\!| W, nr, r |\!\}_{pk(i)}))$. Because the adversary can learn nr we conclude that $\rho'(i)$ must be a compromised agent and either $\langle \theta_{r7}, \rho_{r7}, \sigma_{r7} \rangle(nr) = \langle \theta', \rho', \sigma' \rangle(W)$ or $\langle \theta_{r7}, \rho_{r7}, \sigma_{r7} \rangle(nr) = \langle \theta', \rho', \sigma' \rangle(nr)$. We discuss both options separately.

(i) For the former equality we derive that $AKN(\alpha) \nvdash \langle \theta', \rho', \sigma' \rangle (W)$, so we can apply Lemmas 4.20 and 4.21 to find $i1$ such that the following equation holds: $\alpha_{i1} = ((\theta_{i1}, \rho_{i1}, \sigma_{i1}), \mathsf{send}_1(i, r, \{\!|\, ni, i\, |\!\}_{\mathsf{pk}(r)}))$. This gives $\langle \theta_{i1}, \rho_{i1}, \sigma_{i1} \rangle (ni) = \langle \theta', \rho', \sigma' \rangle (W) = \langle \theta_{r7}, \rho_{r7}, \sigma_{r7} \rangle (nr)$, which cannot be the case since ni and nr are distinct terms.

(ii) That the latter equality yields a contradiction is easy to show. Using Lemma 4.22 we derive $\theta_{r7} = \theta'$ and therefore we have $\rho_{r7} = \rho'$. So $\rho_{r7}(i) = \rho'(i)$, which contradicts the assumption that $\rho_{r7}(i)$ is an honest agent.

$[\ell = 3]$ In the third case we have $\alpha_p = ((\theta', \rho', \sigma'), \mathsf{send}_3(i, r, \{\!|\, V\, |\!\}_{\mathsf{pk}(r)}))$. In order to learn $\langle \theta_{r7}, \rho_{r7}, \sigma_{r7} \rangle (nr)$ from $\langle \theta', \rho', \sigma' \rangle (i, r, \{\!|\, V\, |\!\}_{\mathsf{pk}(r)})$ we must have that $\langle \theta', \rho', \sigma' \rangle (V) = \langle \theta_{r7}, \rho_{r7}, \sigma_{r7} \rangle (nr)$ and that $\rho'(r)$ is a compromised agent. Using Lemma 4.20 we find $i2$ with $\alpha_{i2} = ((\theta', \rho', \sigma'), \mathsf{recv}_2(r, i, \{\!|\, ni, V, r\, |\!\}_{\mathsf{pk}(i)}))$. Because $AKN(\alpha) \nvdash \langle \theta', \rho', \sigma' \rangle (V)$ we can apply Lemma 4.21 to find index $r2$ with $\alpha_{r2} = ((\theta_{r2}, \rho_{r2}, \sigma_{r2}), \mathsf{send}_2(r, i, \{\!|\, W, nr, r\, |\!\}_{\mathsf{pk}(i)}))$. This gives $\rho'(r) = \rho_{r2}(r)$. (†)

Next, we derive $\langle \theta_{r2}, \rho_{r2}, \sigma_{r2} \rangle (nr) = \langle \theta', \rho', \sigma' \rangle (V) = \langle \theta_{r7}, \rho_{r7}, \sigma_{r7} \rangle (nr)$. Applying Lemma 4.22 yields $\theta_{r2} = \theta_{r7}$ and thus $\rho_{r2} = \rho_{r7}$, so $\rho'(r) = \rho_{r2}(r) = \rho_{r7}(r)$. Because $\rho'(r)$ is a compromised agent while $\rho_{r7}(r)$ is honest, we obtain a contradiction. This finishes the proof of claim_7.

Note †   Notice that the step in the proof marked with † fails for the Needham-Schroeder protocol, which gives an indication of why the hardening of the second message exchange is required.

Proof of claim_5   Let $\alpha \in traces(NSL)$. Assume that for some $r5$ and $(\theta_r, \rho_r, \sigma_{r5}) \in Inst$, with $ran(\rho_r) \subseteq Agent_H$, we have $\alpha_{r5} = ((\theta_r, \rho_r, \sigma_{r5}), \mathsf{claim}_5(r, ni\text{-}synch))$. In order to prove this synchronisation claim correct, we must find a run executing the initiator role which synchronises on the events labelled 1, 2, and 3, since all three communications precede the claim. By applying Lemma 4.20, we find $r1, r2, r3$ $(0 \le r1 < r2 < r3 < r5)$ and $\sigma_{r1} \subseteq \sigma_{r2} \subseteq \sigma_{r3} \subseteq \sigma_{r5}$, such that

$$\alpha_{r1} = ((\theta_r, \rho_r, \sigma_{r1}), \mathsf{recv}_1(i, r, \{\!|\, W, i\, |\!\}_{\mathsf{pk}(r)})),$$
$$\alpha_{r2} = ((\theta_r, \rho_r, \sigma_{r2}), \mathsf{send}_2(r, i, \{\!|\, W, nr, r\, |\!\}_{\mathsf{pk}(i)})),$$
$$\alpha_{r3} = ((\theta_r, \rho_r, \sigma_{r3}), \mathsf{recv}_3(i, r, \{\!|\, nr\, |\!\}_{\mathsf{pk}(r)})).$$

We have already proved that nr remains secret, so we can apply Lemma 4.21 to the receive event with label 3, thereby establishing index $i3$ and $(\theta_i, \rho_i, \sigma_{i3})$ such that $i3 < r3$ and the equalities $\alpha_{i3} = ((\theta_i, \rho_i, \sigma_{i3}), \mathsf{send}_3(i, r, \{\!|\, V\, |\!\}_{\mathsf{pk}(r)}))$ and $\langle \theta_r, \rho_r, \sigma_{r3} \rangle (nr) = \langle \theta_i, \rho_i, \sigma_{i3} \rangle (V)$. By applying Lemma 4.20 we obtain $i1 < i2 < i3$ such that

$$\alpha_{i1} = ((\theta_i, \rho_i, \sigma_{i1}), \mathsf{send}_1(i, r, \{\!|\, ni, i\, |\!\}_{\mathsf{pk}(r)})),$$
$$\alpha_{i2} = ((\theta_i, \rho_i, \sigma_{i2}), \mathsf{recv}_2(r, i, \{\!|\, ni, V, r\, |\!\}_{\mathsf{pk}(i)})),$$
$$\alpha_{i3} = ((\theta_i, \rho_i, \sigma_{i3}), \mathsf{send}_3(i, r, \{\!|\, V\, |\!\}_{\mathsf{pk}(r)})).$$

Now that we have found out that run θ_i is a candidate, we only have to prove that it synchronises with run θ_r. Therefore, we have to establish $r2 < i2$, $i1 < r1$ and that the corresponding send and receive events match each other.

First, we observe α_{i2}. Since variables are assigned when received first and not changed afterwards in our semantics, we have that $\langle \theta_i, \rho_i, \sigma_{i2} \rangle(V) = \langle \theta_i, \rho_i, \sigma_{i3} \rangle(V) = \langle \theta_r, \rho_r, \sigma_{r3} \rangle(nr)$, which is secret. Therefore we can again apply Lemma 4.21, thereby obtaining an index $r2' < i2$ such that $\alpha_{r2'} = ((\theta_{r'}, \rho_{r'}, \sigma_{r2'}),$ $\mathsf{send}_2(r, i, \{\!| W, nr, r |\!\}_{\mathsf{pk}(i)}))$. Because the messages of this protocol do not contain nested encryptions, we can derive the following equality: $\langle \theta_i, \rho_i, \sigma_{i2} \rangle(\{\!| ni, V, r |\!\}_{\mathsf{pk}(i)}) = \langle \theta_{r'}, \rho_{r'}, \sigma_{r2'} \rangle(\{\!| W, nr, r |\!\}_{\mathsf{pk}(i)})$. This implies that we have $\langle \theta_r, \rho_r, \sigma_{r3} \rangle(nr) = \langle \theta_i, \rho_i, \sigma_{i3} \rangle(V) = \langle \theta_{r'}, \rho_{r'}, \sigma_{r2'} \rangle(nr)$, so from Lemma 4.22 we have $\theta_r = \theta_{r'}$, and from the uniqueness of the role events we have $r2 = r2'$. This establishes synchronisation of events α_{i2} and α_{r2}.

Next, we look at α_{r1}. Because $\langle \theta_r, \rho_r, \sigma_{r1} \rangle(W)$ is secret (cf. secrecy claim 9 at the responder role), we can apply Lemma 4.21, which yields an index $i1' < r1$ such that $\alpha_{i1'} = ((\theta_{i'}, \rho_{i'}, \sigma_{i1'}), \mathsf{send}_1(i, r, \{\!| ni, i |\!\}_{\mathsf{pk}(r)}))$ and $\langle \theta_r, \rho_r, \sigma_{r1} \rangle(\{\!| W, i |\!\}_{\mathsf{pk}(r)}) = \langle \theta_{i'}, \rho_{i'}, \sigma_{i1'} \rangle(\{\!| ni, i |\!\}_{\mathsf{pk}(r)})$. Correspondence of α_{i2} and α_{r2} gives $\langle \theta_i, \rho_i, \sigma_{i2} \rangle(ni) = \langle \theta_r, \rho_r, \sigma_{r2} \rangle(W) = \langle \theta_r, \rho_r, \sigma_{r1} \rangle(W) = \langle \theta_{i'}, \rho_{i'}, \sigma_{i1'} \rangle(ni)$. By Lemma 4.22 θ_i and $\theta_{i'}$ are equal, which establishes synchronisation of events α_{r1} and α_{i1}. This finishes the synchronisation proof of claim$_5$. $\qquad\square$

4.6 Summary

In this chapter we introduced security properties to our model, defined in terms of local claim events. These local claim events denote the supposed properties of a security protocol, and are part of the protocol description. The main idea behind a claim event is locality: agents have a local view on the state of the system, based on the messages they receive. The protocol should guarantee that based on the local view the agent can be sure about some properties of the global state of the system, e.g., that something is not in the adversary's knowledge, or that a certain agent is active.

We defined secrecy and several notions of authentication, and introduced a new strong form of authentication called synchronisation. In order to compare two notions of authentication, synchronisation and agreement, we formalised two forms of agreement: injective and non-injective agreement over all variables and all roles. Due to the uniform phrasing, the two notions of authentication can be distinguished easily: agreement allows that an adversary injects a (correct and expected) message before it is sent by the originator of the message. As for agreement, we provide both an injective and a non-injective variant of synchronisation.

Our definitions of synchronisation and agreement abstract away from the protocol and the semantic model as much as possible, e.g., they do not refer to the details of the message elements. Given a trace, we only need to have an equality relation between the contents of send and receive events, and to know the ordering of the events in a protocol description, in order to be able to verify every form of authentication defined here. This contrasts with other definitions of authentication, where often much more information about the protocol and its semantics is required to verify authentication for a given trace. In fact, for our approach, the definitions do not even require a trace semantics or a full ordering on the events within a role. The definitions will also work with the partially-ordered structures of the Strand spaces model of [155], but also with the preorder on the events of a role of the AVISPA model in [94]; the only requirement on the role event order is that each event must have a finite set of preceding events. From the definitions of synchronisation and agreement, we construct a hierarchy of authentication properties depicted in Fig. 4.13. We show that with respect to the Dolev-Yao adversary model, injective synchronisation is strictly stronger than injective agreement.

In this chapter we defined notions of secrecy and authentication, but it is possible to express other security properties, such as, for example, non-repudiation, in a similar way. We have also illustrated how the security protocol model from Chap. 3 can be used to prove security properties correct. We used the model and the definitions of secrecy and synchronisation to prove two properties of the Needham-Schroeder-Lowe protocol.

The advantage of correctness proofs is that they guarantee that within the model no attacks on the security protocol exist. However, there are several disadvantages to constructing such proofs by hand. For each claim in each protocol a new proof is required. Each minor modification to the messages of a protocol can change the proof significantly. Also, if we cannot find a proof we cannot make any statement about the protocol: it may still be correct, or flawed.

Ideally, we would like to establish either correctness of a security claim of a protocol, or find a concrete attack against a claim. In Chap. 5 we address automated verification (establishing correctness) and falsification (finding attacks) of security protocol claims.

4.7 Problems

4.1 Let $\rho_1, \rho_2 : Role \rightarrow Agent$ be defined as

$$\rho_1 = \{i \mapsto A, r \mapsto E\},$$
$$\rho_2 = \{i \mapsto A, r \mapsto B\},$$

where $\{A, B\} \subseteq Agent_H$ and $E \in Agent_C$. Explain why the claim event holds in the following trace:

$$[((1, \rho_1, \emptyset), \mathsf{create}(i)),$$
$$((1, \rho_1, \emptyset), \mathsf{send}_1(i, r, \{\!| \, ni, i \, |\!\}_{\mathsf{pk}(r)})),$$
$$((2, \rho_2, \emptyset), \mathsf{create}(r)),$$
$$((2, \rho_2, \{W \mapsto ni^{\sharp 1}\}), \mathsf{recv}_1(i, r, \{\!| \, W, i \, |\!\}_{\mathsf{pk}(r)})),$$
$$((2, \rho_2, \{W \mapsto ni^{\sharp 1}\}), \mathsf{send}_2(r, i, \{\!| \, W, nr \, |\!\}_{\mathsf{pk}(i)})),$$
$$((1, \rho_1, \{V \mapsto nr^{\sharp 2}\}), \mathsf{recv}_2(r, i, \{\!| \, ni, V \, |\!\}_{\mathsf{pk}(i)})),$$
$$((1, \rho_1, \{V \mapsto nr^{\sharp 2}\}), \mathsf{send}_3(i, r, \{\!| \, V \, |\!\}_{\mathsf{pk}(r)})),$$
$$((2, \rho_2, \{W \mapsto ni^{\sharp 1}\}), \mathsf{recv}_3(i, r, \{\!| \, nr \, |\!\}_{\mathsf{pk}(r)})),$$
$$((1, \rho_1, \{V \mapsto nr^{\sharp 2}\}), \mathsf{claim}_4(i, \textit{ni-synch})) \,].$$

4.2 Consider the notion of *weak aliveness prior to the claim* (*waptc*), defined as follows:

Definition 4.25 Let P be a protocol with roles R and R'. The claim event $\gamma = \mathsf{claim}_\ell(R, waptc, R')$ is correct if and only if

$$\forall t \in traces(P): \forall inst: (inst, \gamma) \in t \wedge honest(inst) \Rightarrow$$

$$\exists ev \in t: actor(ev) = \langle inst \rangle(R') \wedge ev <_t (inst, \gamma).$$

Prove that this property is equivalent to *weak aliveness*.

4.3 (Differentiating protocols) Design authentication protocols that satisfy

(a) *recent-alive*, but not *weak-alive-role*;
(b) *weak-alive-role*, but not *recent-alive-role*;
(c) *recent-alive*, but not *recent-alive-role*.

4.4 Prove or disprove the aliveness claims of protocols $HELLO_2$ and $HELLO_3$ (Figs. 4.5 and 4.6).

4.5 (Differentiating scenarios) Give real-world scenarios that differentiate between each of the following properties. Concretely, for each of the following protocols, give a real world scenario in which it is a suitable requirement but where the other properties are not suitable.

(a) Aliveness
(b) Recent aliveness
(c) Weak aliveness

4.6 Explain why the trace in Fig. 4.8 is considered an attack, while the trace in Fig. 4.10 is not.

4.7 Give a scenario in the real world where a trace like the one in Fig. 4.10 can be considered an attack. In other words, how can an adversary take advantage of the possibility to relay messages without modifying them?

4.8 Explain why the two protocols described at the end of Sect. 4.4 are sufficient to conclude that there is no relation between any of the four classes in the top diamond and any of the four classes in the bottom diamond of Fig. 4.13.

4.9 The r role in the *NS* protocol does not satisfy non-injective synchronisation. However, it satisfies weaker authentication properties. Prove that *NS* satisfies *recent aliveness in the correct role*.

Chapter 5
Verification

Abstract We present an algorithm for the analysis of security protocols with respect to various security properties. We address design choices and efficiency considerations. Finally, we address the verification of injective synchronisation and prove that under certain conditions on their structure, synchronising protocols satisfy injectivity.

In the previous chapters we introduced a model for security protocols and various security properties, which we illustrated with manual correctness proofs. In this chapter we present an algorithm for analysing these security properties. The Scyther tool [55] contains an implementation of this algorithm. Scyther is freely available for Windows, Linux, and Mac OS X, and can be downloaded from [52].

The algorithm is based on the analysis of *trace patterns*, which represent sets of traces. Instead of analysing all individual traces, we just analyse such trace patterns. A trace pattern is defined as a partially ordered set of symbolic events. In particular, we focus on *attack patterns*, which are trace patterns that represent violations of the security property. Patterns are defined in Sect. 5.1.

Our algorithm determines whether or not a particular pattern can occur in the traces of a protocol. We present the details of the algorithm in Sect. 5.2: given a protocol and a pattern, it determines whether or not traces of the protocol exist in which the pattern occurs. We provide an example of how the algorithm traverses its search space in Sect. 5.3. In Sect. 5.4, we show how the algorithm can be used directly for all previously introduced non-injective security properties.

The performance of the algorithm depends on the used heuristics and the instantiation of parameters. We motivate our choices in Sect. 5.5 and show the resulting performance data for the Scyther tool.

Finally, we address the verification of injective synchronisation in Sect. 5.6. We prove that under certain conditions on their communication structure, synchronising protocols satisfy injectivity.

5.1 Patterns

We first introduce the main concepts underlying our algorithm. In general, any non-trivial protocol has infinitely many possible behaviours (traces). However, from the

C. Cremers, S. Mauw, *Operational Semantics and Verification of Security Protocols*,
Information Security and Cryptography, DOI 10.1007/978-3-540-78636-8_5,
© Springer-Verlag Berlin Heidelberg 2012

perspective of property verification, many of these traces are just different interleavings or renamings of similar behaviours. To capture the concept of similar traces, we introduce *trace patterns*. A trace pattern, which represents a class of traces, is defined as a *partially ordered* set of *symbolic* events.

For the properties considered until now we did not exploit all the information available in traces, e.g., the absolute position of an event in a trace was not relevant for any of the properties. We inventorise the properties of traces that were required so far to evaluate the security properties.

- Event order.
- The equivalence of events and messages.
- Positive occurrence of agent events.
- Contents of the adversary knowledge.

Some examples of elements that we did not require include the concrete position of events in a trace, the absence of agent events, or the concrete contents of a message. We therefore abstract from these elements and introduce *patterns*. A pattern represents a set of traces. This will allow us later to construct a verification algorithm for security properties that avoids considering all individual traces.

To make the different ways in which the adversary can derive a term in execution traces explicit, we introduce adversary inference events. These events correspond to term derivations based on the inference operator $\vdash$. In particular, we handle tupling implicitly, but encryption, decryption and function application are handled explicitly by introducing encr, decr and app events, respectively. We introduce two additional adversary events: init corresponds to the adversary learning its initial knowledge, and know(t) denotes that the adversary knows the term t at some point in the trace. The agent events send and recv, together with the adversary events, form the set of pattern events *PatternEvent*. To define this set, we reuse several sets defined in Chap. 3.

Definition 5.1 (Pattern Events) The set of pattern events, *PatternEvent*, is defined by the following BNF grammar:

$$
\begin{aligned}
AdvEvent ::=\ & \mathsf{decr}(\{\!|\,RunTerm\,|\!\}_{RunTerm})\ |\ \mathsf{encr}(\{\!|\,RunTerm\,|\!\}_{RunTerm})\ | \\
& \mathsf{app}(Func(RunTerm^*))\ |\ \mathsf{init}\ |\ \mathsf{know}(RunTerm), \\
SendRecv ::=\ & \mathsf{send}\ |\ \mathsf{recv}, \\
RolePos ::=\ & Role^{\#RID}\ |\ Agent, \\
CommEvent ::=\ & SendRecv_{Label}(RolePos, RolePos, RunTerm)^{\#RID}, \\
ClaimEvent ::=\ & \mathsf{claim}_{Label}(RolePos, Claim\,[\,,\,RunTerm]), \\
AgEvent ::=\ & CommEvent\ |\ ClaimEvent, \\
PatternEvent ::=\ & AdvEvent\ |\ AgEvent.
\end{aligned}
$$

To capture the interaction between events and the adversary knowledge, we define two functions from pattern events to sets of terms: *in* and *out*. The input function *in* yields the terms that are required to be in the adversary knowledge in order to enable the event, such as a message occurring in a recv event. Conversely, for events such

Table 5.1 *in* and *out* functions

e	$in(e)$	$out(e)$
$\mathrm{decr}(\{\!\|\,t'\,\|\!\}_t)$	$\{\{\!\|\,t'\,\|\!\}_t\} \cup unpair(t^{-1})$	$unpair(t')$
$\mathrm{encr}(\{\!\|\,t\,\|\!\}_{t'})$	$unpair((t,t'))$	$\{\{\!\|\,t\,\|\!\}_{t'}\}$
$\mathrm{app}(f(t_0,\ldots,t_n))$	$unpair(t_0,\ldots,t_n)$	$\{f(t_0,\ldots,t_n)\}$
init	$\emptyset$	$\bigcup_{t \in AKN_0} unpair(t)$
$\mathrm{know}(t)$	$unpair(t)$	$\emptyset$
$\mathrm{send}_\ell(t)^{\sharp\theta}$	$\emptyset$	$unpair(t)$
$\mathrm{recv}_\ell(t)^{\sharp\theta}$	$unpair(t)$	$\emptyset$
$\mathrm{claim}_\ell(t,c,t')^{\sharp\theta}$	$\emptyset$	$\emptyset$

	Trace	in	out
$t' = [$	init	$\emptyset$	$\{c,k\}$
,	$((1,\rho,\emptyset), \mathrm{create}(i))$	$\emptyset$	$\emptyset$
,	$((1,\rho,\emptyset), \mathrm{send}(i,r,\{\!\|\,m\,\|\!\}_k))$	$\emptyset$	$\{i,r,\{\!\|\,m\,\|\!\}_k\}$
,	$\mathrm{decr}(\{\!\|\,m\,\|\!\}_k)$	$\{\{\!\|\,m\,\|\!\}_k, k\}$	$\{m\}$
,	$\mathrm{app}(h((m,c)))$	$\{m,c\}$	$\{h((m,c))\}$
,	$((1,\rho,\emptyset), \mathrm{recv}(r,i,h((m,c))))$	$\{r,i,h((m,c))\}$	$\emptyset$
$]$			

Fig. 5.1 Example trace with adversary events

as send, the output function *out* yields the terms that are added to the adversary knowledge after execution of an event. The functions *in* and *out* are both of type *PatternEvent* $\to \mathcal{P}(Term)$, and are defined as in Table 5.1.

Example 5.2 (Adversary Events) Let t be the following trace for some ρ:

$$t = [((1,\rho,\emptyset), \mathrm{create}(i)),$$

$$((1,\rho,\emptyset), \mathrm{send}(i,r,\{\!\|\,m\,\|\!\}_k)), ((1,\rho,\emptyset), \mathrm{recv}(r,i,h((m,c))))].$$

Assume for this example that $AKN_0 = \{c,k\}$. The receive event is enabled, i.e., the premises of the receive rule hold, because $h((m,c))$ can be derived from the events that occurred before.

If we revisit this situation using explicit adversary events, we consider the related trace t', as defined in the left column of Fig. 5.1. It contains all the events from t in their original order, and additionally contains adversary events.

First, the adversary learns its initial knowledge $\{c,k\}$ using the init event. Then, run 1 is created before the first send occurs. The sent message occurs in its unpaired form in the *out* set of the event. To concretely derive the received term in the *in* set of the receive event, the adversary would first use $\mathrm{decr}(\{\!\|\,m\,\|\!\}_k)$, while knowing k, to obtain m. As the adversary now knows m and c, $\mathrm{app}(h((m,c)))$ can be used to obtain $h((m,c))$.

We now only need a final ingredient to define patterns. Pattern events can be regarded as partially instantiated run events. In patterns, we want to be able to specify events in which some role names or variables are already instantiated, while others are not instantiated yet. To deal with such role names and variables uniformly later, we also regard role names as pattern variables that can be local to a run, similar to variables.

Definition 5.3 (Pattern Variables *PVars*) We define the set *PVars* as the set of variables and role names that can occur in a pattern event:

$$PVars = \left\{ t^{\sharp \theta} \mid t \in Var \cup Role \wedge \theta \in RID \right\}.$$

Let $\mathcal{S}ub$ denote the set of substitutions of terms for pattern variables. We write $[t_0, \ldots, t_n / x_0, \ldots, x_n] \in \mathcal{S}ub$ to denote the substitution of t_i for x_i, for $0 \le i \le n$. We extend the functions *dom* and *ran* to substitutions: for a substitution $\phi = [t_0, \ldots, t_n / x_0, \ldots, x_n]$ we have that $dom(\phi) = \{x_0, \ldots, x_n\}$ and $ran(\phi) = \{t_0, \ldots, t_n\}$. We write $\phi(t)$ for the application of the substitution ϕ to t. We write $\phi \circ \phi'$ to denote the composition of two substitutions, i.e., for all terms t we have that $(\phi \circ \phi')(t) = \phi'(\phi(t))$.

A substitution $\phi = [t_0, \ldots, t_n / x_0, \ldots, x_n]$ is said to be *well-typed* if and only if for all $i, 0 \le i \le n$, either

$$\begin{cases} type(t_i) \cap type(x_i) \neq \emptyset, & \text{if } t_i \in PVars, \text{ or} \\ t_i \in type(x_i), & \text{otherwise.} \end{cases}$$

A variable v is called a *basic variable* if and only if $type(v)$ contains only basic terms.

We call a well-typed substitution ϕ a *unifier* of term t and term t' if and only if $\phi(t) = \phi(t')$. We call ϕ the *most general unifier* of two terms t, t', notation $\phi = MGU(t, t')$, if and only if for any other unifier ϕ' there exists a substitution ϕ'', such that $\phi' = \phi \circ \phi''$.

Informally, a pattern is a tuple $pt = (E, \rightarrow)$, where E is a set of pattern events, and $\rightarrow$ is a relation on the events from E. The relation $\rightarrow$ induces a partial order on the events, which generalises the total order on the events occurring in traces. An edge $\rightarrow$ is either said to be unlabelled, written as $e \xrightarrow{\lambda} e'$, or labelled with a run term t, e.g., $e \xrightarrow{t} e'$. Unlabelled edges represent the order of the events within a single run, whereas labelled edges capture the point at which the adversary learns a particular term. Labelled edges are also referred to as *bindings*, where the run term t in the edge $e \xrightarrow{t} e'$ is said to be *bound* to e. Labelled edges will be used by the verification algorithm in Sect. 5.2.

For any event e, we write $\phi(e)$ to denote the event resulting from substituting all terms t occurring in e by $\phi(t)$.

In the context of a pattern $(E, \rightarrow)$, we define $\rightarrow^*$ to be the reflexive, transitive closure of $\rightarrow$ (ignoring the labels).

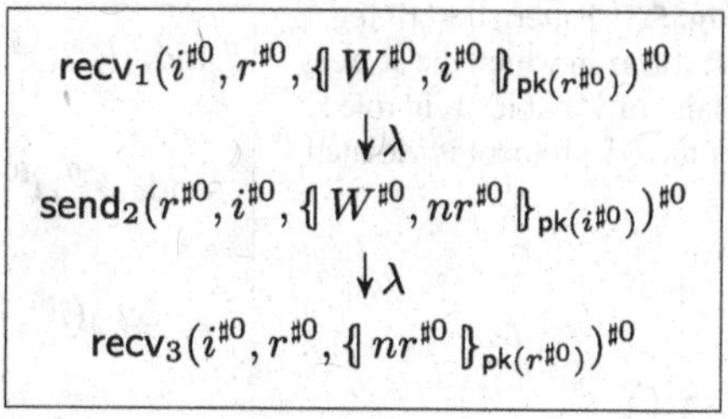

Fig. 5.2 Pattern describing
an arbitrary execution of the
send and receive events of the
r role of the NS protocol

$$\mathsf{recv}_1(i^{\#0}, r^{\#0}, \{\!\!\{\, W^{\#0}, i^{\#0} \,\}\!\!\}_{\mathsf{pk}(r^{\#0})})^{\#0}$$
$$\downarrow \lambda$$
$$\mathsf{send}_2(r^{\#0}, i^{\#0}, \{\!\!\{\, W^{\#0}, nr^{\#0} \,\}\!\!\}_{\mathsf{pk}(i^{\#0})})^{\#0}$$
$$\downarrow \lambda$$
$$\mathsf{recv}_3(i^{\#0}, r^{\#0}, \{\!\!\{\, nr^{\#0} \,\}\!\!\}_{\mathsf{pk}(r^{\#0})})^{\#0}$$

Definition 5.4 (Pattern) Let P be a protocol. Let E be a finite set of pattern events
and let $\to$ be a relation on E labelled with elements of the set $\{\lambda\} \cup RunTerm$.
We say that $(E, \to)$ is a pattern of P if and only if for all $e, e' \in E$, run terms
$t \neq \lambda$, $re, re' \in RoleEvent$, substitutions ϕ, ϕ', and run identifiers θ, the following
conditions hold:

(i) Term-labelled edges denote message causality:

$$e \xrightarrow{t} e' \Rightarrow t \in out(e) \cap in(e').$$

(ii) All agent events (cf. Definition 5.1) occurring in the pattern are from the pro-
    tocol P:

$$e \in AgEvent \Rightarrow \exists M, s, i, \phi, \theta : (M, s) \in ran(P) \wedge e = \phi(s_i)^{\#\theta},$$

where $dom(\phi) = PVars$, M is the initial knowledge of the role, and s is its
sequence of role events.

(iii) Within a run, role events are unique:

$$\left(e = \phi(re)^{\#\theta} \wedge e' = \phi'(re)^{\#\theta}\right) \Rightarrow e = e'.$$

(iv) Runs are prefix-closed with respect to the agent events in the corresponding
    role, i.e., for each role $R \in P$:

$$\left(e = \phi(re)^{\#\theta} \wedge re' <_R re\right) \Rightarrow \phi(re')^{\#\theta} \to^* e.$$

Example 5.5 (Pattern) Figure 5.2 is a graph representation of the pattern that describes an arbitrary execution of a single run of the r role of the NS protocol.
In this example, $i^{\#0}$, $r^{\#0}$, and $W^{\#0}$ are pattern variables. In particular, $type(i^{\#0}) =$
$Agent$, $type(r^{\#0}) = Agent$, and following the typed matching model, $type(W^{\#0}) =$
$AdversaryFresh \cup \{c^{\#\theta} \mid c \in Fresh \wedge \theta \in RID\}$. In this example, all agent events occur as part of a single run.

In general, when specifying patterns, the type of variables is taken from the protocol specification and the type of role names (such as $i^{\#0}$ or $r^{\#0}$) is assumed to be
$Agent$ unless stated otherwise, as we will see in the next example.

Fig. 5.3 Pattern describing
all traces in which the secrecy
claim of variable W in role r
of the *NS* protocol is violated

$$\mathsf{recv}_1(i^{\#0}, r^{\#0}, \{\!| W^{\#0}, i^{\#0} |\!\}_{\mathsf{pk}(r^{\#0})})^{\#0} \qquad \mathsf{know}(W^{\#0})$$

$$\downarrow \lambda$$

$$\mathsf{send}_2(r^{\#0}, i^{\#0}, \{\!| W^{\#0}, nr^{\#0} |\!\}_{\mathsf{pk}(i^{\#0})})^{\#0}$$

$$\downarrow \lambda$$

$$\mathsf{recv}_3(i^{\#0}, r^{\#0}, \{\!| nr^{\#0} |\!\}_{\mathsf{pk}(r^{\#0})})^{\#0}$$

$$\downarrow \lambda$$

$$\mathsf{claim}_4(r^{\#0}, secret, W^{\#0})^{\#0}$$

$$type(i^{\#0}) = Agent_H \text{ and } type(r^{\#0}) = Agent_H$$

Example 5.6 (Representing Attack Traces as Patterns) Figure 5.3 shows the pattern
that represents the set of traces in which a secrecy claim in the *NS* protocol is violated. More precisely, we consider the r role of the *NS* protocol appended with a
secrecy claim for the variable $W^{\#0}$. The additional $\mathsf{know}(W^{\#0})$ event encodes that
(the instantiation of) the term $W^{\#0}$ can be inferred from the adversary's knowledge.
Following the interpretation of the secrecy claim, an attack additionally requires that
the agents executing the claim run are honest. We capture this by restricting the type
of the pattern variables $i^{\#0}$ and $r^{\#0}$ to $Agent_H$.

We can interpret a trace as a pattern, by interpreting the trace order $\leq$ as a set of
unlabelled edges. Conversely, a pattern pt can be considered as a filter on the traces
of P, representing the set of traces of P that exhibit the pattern. In order to define
this relation, we define a function IT that projects a trace onto its non-create events
and instantiates these events.

We first extend the definition of instantiation to run events, yielding pattern
events. In particular, we define for all non-create run events e and all instantiations
$inst = (\theta, \rho, \sigma)$:

$$\langle inst \rangle(e) = \begin{cases} \mathsf{send}_\ell(\langle inst \rangle((r, r', m)))^{\#\theta} & \text{iff } e = \mathsf{send}_\ell(r, r', m), \\ \mathsf{recv}_\ell(\langle inst \rangle((r, r', m)))^{\#\theta} & \text{iff } e = \mathsf{recv}_\ell(r, r', m), \\ \mathsf{claim}_\ell(\langle inst \rangle(r), c, \langle inst \rangle(m))^{\#\theta} & \text{iff } e = \mathsf{claim}_\ell(r, c, m). \end{cases}$$

For convenience, we regard each trace tr as a set of events with an associated
total order, denoted as $tr = (E, \leq)$. Further, we often write tr_E to denote the set of
events in a trace tr, and $tr_\leq$ to denote their order.

Definition 5.7 (*IT*) We define the function $IT: RunEvent^* \to PatternEvent^*$ as follows:

$$IT([\,]) = [\,]$$

$$IT([(inst, e)] \cdot tr) = \begin{cases} [\langle inst \rangle(e)] \cdot IT(tr) & \text{if } e \text{ is not a create event, and} \\ IT(tr) & \text{otherwise.} \end{cases}$$

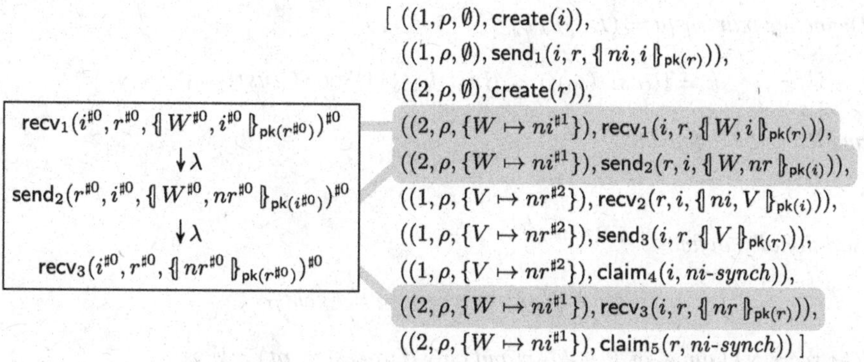

$$\begin{array}{ll}[& ((1,\rho,\emptyset),\mathsf{create}(i)),\\ & ((1,\rho,\emptyset),\mathsf{send}_1(i,r,\{\!|\,ni,i\,|\!\}_{\mathsf{pk}(r)})),\\ & ((2,\rho,\emptyset),\mathsf{create}(r)),\\ & ((2,\rho,\{W\mapsto ni^{\#1}\}),\mathsf{recv}_1(i,r,\{\!|\,W,i\,|\!\}_{\mathsf{pk}(r)})),\\ & ((2,\rho,\{W\mapsto ni^{\#1}\}),\mathsf{send}_2(r,i,\{\!|\,W,nr\,|\!\}_{\mathsf{pk}(i)})),\\ & ((1,\rho,\{V\mapsto nr^{\#2}\}),\mathsf{recv}_2(r,i,\{\!|\,ni,V\,|\!\}_{\mathsf{pk}(i)})),\\ & ((1,\rho,\{V\mapsto nr^{\#2}\}),\mathsf{send}_3(i,r,\{\!|\,V\,|\!\}_{\mathsf{pk}(r)})),\\ & ((1,\rho,\{V\mapsto nr^{\#2}\}),\mathsf{claim}_4(i,\text{ni-synch})),\\ & ((2,\rho,\{W\mapsto ni^{\#1}\}),\mathsf{recv}_3(i,r,\{\!|\,nr\,|\!\}_{\mathsf{pk}(r)})),\\ & ((2,\rho,\{W\mapsto ni^{\#1}\}),\mathsf{claim}_5(r,\text{ni-synch}))\,]\end{array}$$

Left box:
$$\mathsf{recv}_1(i^{\#0},r^{\#0},\{\!|\,W^{\#0},i^{\#0}\,|\!\}_{\mathsf{pk}(r^{\#0})})^{\#0}$$
$$\downarrow\lambda$$
$$\mathsf{send}_2(r^{\#0},i^{\#0},\{\!|\,W^{\#0},nr^{\#0}\,|\!\}_{\mathsf{pk}(i^{\#0})})^{\#0}$$
$$\downarrow\lambda$$
$$\mathsf{recv}_3(i^{\#0},r^{\#0},\{\!|\,nr^{\#0}\,|\!\}_{\mathsf{pk}(r^{\#0})})^{\#0}$$

Fig. 5.4 The correspondence between events from the pattern from Example 5.5 (*on the left*) and the events from the trace (*on the right*) representing a regular execution of the *NS* protocol

Definition 5.8 (Traces of a Protocol and a Pattern) We extend the function *traces* to capture the set of traces of a protocol that exhibit a pattern, by defining

$$traces(P,(E,\to)) = \big\{tr\in traces(P)\mid \exists\phi,\varsigma:$$
$$\big(\forall e,e'\in AgEvent: e\to^* e'\Rightarrow \phi(\varsigma(e))\leq_{IT(tr)}\phi(\varsigma(e'))\big)$$
$$\wedge\big(\forall t:\mathsf{know}(t)\in E\Rightarrow AKN(tr)\vdash\phi(\varsigma(t))\big)\big\},$$

where ϕ is a well-typed substitution from the set *PVars* to *RunTerm*, and ς is a bijective substitution from run identifiers to run identifiers.

Example 5.9 (Traces of Protocol Patterns) Example 3.37 depicts a trace of the pattern from Example 5.5. In particular, by substituting the run identifier 0 by 2, and by instantiating $i^{\#0}$ with A, $r^{\#0}$ with B, and $W^{\#0}$ with $ni^{\#1}$, the events of the pattern occur in the trace in the prescribed order. The relation between the events in the pattern and their instantiations in the trace is visualised in Fig. 5.4.

Example 5.10 (Traces of Protocol Patterns) The attack trace in Sect. 4.5 is a trace of the pattern from Example 5.6.

Many security properties can be formulated as pattern problems. We first show how the secrecy problem can be formulated as a pattern problem.

Lemma 5.11 (Secrecy as a Pattern Problem) *Let P be a protocol with a role R. Hence there exist M,s such that $P(R)=(M,s)$, where M denotes the role's knowledge and s its sequence of events. Let R contain a secrecy claim of the term rt at position i, i.e., $s_i=\mathsf{claim}_\ell(R,\text{secret},rt)$.*

Let θ be a run identifier and let ρ be the function that replaces role names by their run-bound variants, i.e., for all $r\in Role$ we define $\rho(r)=r^{\#\theta}$. Let $inst=(\theta,\rho,\emptyset)$.

Define the pattern $pt = (E, \rightarrow)$ *by*

$$E = \{\langle inst \rangle (s_0), \ldots, \langle inst \rangle (s_i)\} \cup \{\mathsf{know}(\langle inst \rangle (rt))\},$$

and let $\rightarrow$ *be defined by*

$$s_0 \xrightarrow{\lambda} s_1 \xrightarrow{\lambda} \cdots \xrightarrow{\lambda} s_i.$$

Additionally, define

$$\forall r \in dom(\rho) : type(r^{\sharp\theta}) = Agent_H.$$

The secrecy claim s_i *of* P *holds if and only if* $traces(P, pt) = \emptyset$.

Proof Recall Definition 4.3: informally, the secrecy claim is said to be correct if the adversary cannot infer the instantiation of rt in each trace in which the claim occurs in a run with honest agents.

We first show that if s_i is correct, then $traces(P, pt) = \emptyset$. We give a proof by contradiction. Assume that the statement does not hold, i.e., assume s_i is correct and that there exists a trace tr such that $tr \in traces(P, pt)$. Because tr contains the pattern pt, tr contains an instance of the secrecy claim in run θ. By the type assumption, the roles of θ are mapped to honest agents. By Definition 5.8 and the fact that $\mathsf{know}(rt)$ occurs in the pattern, the instantiation of rt from the claim event can also be inferred from the adversary knowledge after tr. This implies that s_i is not correct, contradicting the assumption.

Second, we show that if $traces(P, pt) = \emptyset$, then s_i is correct. Again we prove by contradiction, and assume that s_i is incorrect. By definition, there exists a trace in which a run occurs with the secrecy claim, whose rules are mapped to honest agents, and the adversary knows the instantiation of rt for that run. Clearly, this trace exhibits the pattern, and therefore contradicts the assumption that no such protocol traces exist.   □

Lemma 5.11 shows that analysing the secrecy property can be reduced to determining whether or not the set $traces(P, pt)$ is empty. In this case, the pattern is used to encode all possible violations (attacks) of the property. A concrete example of a pattern that corresponds to all violations of a secrecy claim is described in Example 5.6.

In Sect. 5.4 we show how to formulate other security properties as pattern problems.

5.2 Verification Algorithm

In the previous section we showed how the correctness of security claims, such as secrecy, can be restated as pattern emptiness problems. We now present an algorithm to determine a representation of the set of traces of a pattern, such that we can determine whether the set is empty, or, alternatively, construct concrete traces that exhibit the pattern. The underlying idea of the algorithm is to exploit the properties of two particular types of pattern: the *realisable* pattern and the *empty* pattern.

We first introduce realisable patterns, and show that realisable patterns always contain traces. Second, we introduce empty patterns, which contain no traces. We then present an algorithm that, given a protocol P and a pattern pt, tries to establish a set of realisable patterns $S = \{pt_1, \ldots, pt_n\}$ such that

$$traces(P, pt) = \bigcup_{0 < i \leq n} traces(P, pt_i).$$

Trivially, if $|S| = 0$, the set of traces of P and pt is empty. On the other hand, if $|S| > 0$, then there exist traces of P that exhibit the pattern. This allows us to use the algorithm to analyse security properties.

5.2.1 Well-Typed Patterns

Before we can define realisable and empty patterns, we first introduce one additional concept. In the definition of patterns, we did not require that substitutions are well-typed. This design choice simplifies the presentation of the algorithm, because some intermediate results computed during execution of the algorithm may not be well-typed. We now reintroduce this constraint by extending the well-typed predicate to protocol patterns.

Definition 5.12 (Well-Typed Pattern) Let $(E, \rightarrow)$ be a pattern of a protocol P. We say that $(E, \rightarrow)$ is a *well-typed* pattern of P if and only if

$$\forall e \in E \cap AgEvent : \exists M, s, i, \phi, \theta : (M, s) \in ran(P) \wedge e = \phi(s_i)^{\sharp\theta},$$

where ϕ is a well-typed substitution, $dom(\phi) = PVars$, M is the initial knowledge of the role, and s is its sequence of role events.

Note that the above definition is a restriction of the second clause of the pattern definition.

5.2.2 Realisable Patterns

Because we can restate the correctness of a secrecy claim as a pattern emptiness problem, and secrecy is undecidable in our setting [77], we have that checking emptiness of the set $traces(P, pt)$ is undecidable in general. However, for some patterns one can directly construct traces of the protocol that contain the pattern.

We call these patterns *realisable patterns*. Intuitively, we say that a pattern is realisable if for every event of the pattern that can only occur if the adversary knows all its "inputs", the pattern also contains preceding events that generate the corresponding "outputs". For example, if a pattern contains a receive event for a message m, the adversary must know m. If m was part of a message sent earlier in the pattern, then we can be sure that the receive event is enabled. Because we assume that the adversary can generate terms of any type, we can ignore inputs of uninstantiated variables: the adversary can always generate a suitable term.

Definition 5.13 (Realisable Patterns) Let $pt = (E, \rightarrow)$ be a pattern. We say pt is *realisable*, written as realisable(pt), if and only if $\rightarrow$ is non-cyclic, pt is well-typed, and the following holds:

$$\forall e \in E \; \forall t \in \big(in(e) \setminus PVars \big) \; \exists e' : e' \rightarrow^* e \wedge t \in out(e').$$

Example 5.14 (Patterns That Are Not Realisable) The patterns in Examples 5.5 and 5.6 are not realisable patterns, because their receive events do not have incoming edges labelled with the terms in their *in* sets. For example, let e be the first receive from Example 5.5, Fig. 5.2: we have that $in(e) = \{i^{\sharp 0}, r^{\sharp 0}, \{\!| \, W^{\sharp 0}, i^{\sharp 0} \, |\!\}_{\mathsf{pk}(r^{\sharp 0})}\}$. There is no incoming edge labelled with any of these terms. As a second example, consider the pattern in Fig. 5.3. The know event in this pattern has no incoming edge, but since $in(\mathsf{know}(W^{\sharp 0})) = \{W^{\sharp 0}\}$ and $W^{\sharp 0} \in PVars$, this is not the reason that the pattern is not realisable. Instead, the pattern is not realisable because there are no incoming edges for the encryptions in the receive events.

Example 5.15 (Realisable Patterns) Figure 5.5 shows a realisable pattern of the *NS* protocol.

From such realisable patterns, we can trivially generate traces of P that exhibit the pattern, and hence the set of traces exhibiting the pattern is non-empty. This is captured by the following lemma.

Lemma 5.16 *Let $pt = (E, \rightarrow)$ be a realisable pattern of P. Let $\leq$ be a total extension of $\rightarrow^*$, i.e., $\leq$ is a total order such that $(\rightarrow^*) \subseteq (\leq)$. Let ϕ be a well-typed substitution such that $dom(\phi) = PVars$, $ran(\phi) \subseteq \{m \mid AKN_0 \vdash m\}$. We extend the domain of ϕ to patterns in the obvious way, i.e., the substitution is applied to all terms occurring in the pattern. Then, we have that*

$$\exists tr : tr \in traces(P, pt) \wedge IT(tr) = \phi((E, \leq)),$$

where we interpret the sequence $IT(tr)$ as a set with an associated total order.

Proof Assume given a pattern $pt = (E, \rightarrow)$, a total order $\leq$, and a substitution ϕ that meet the precondition of the lemma. Then a trace $tr \in traces(P)$ can be directly constructed by applying ϕ to the events of the pattern, linearising the events by $\leq$, removing the adversary events, and reconstructing the appropriate create events. $\square$

Fig. 5.5 Realisable pattern
containing instances of the
roles of the *NS* protocol

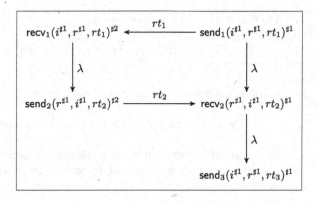

$$rt_1 = \{ ni^{\sharp 1}, i^{\sharp 1} \}_{\mathsf{pk}(r^{\sharp 1})}$$
$$rt_2 = \{ ni^{\sharp 1}, nr^{\sharp 2} \}_{\mathsf{pk}(i^{\sharp 1})}$$
$$rt_3 = \{ nr^{\sharp 2} \}_{\mathsf{pk}(r^{\sharp 1})}$$

Example 5.17 Consider the pattern from Fig. 5.5. Define $\phi = [A, B / i^{\sharp 1}, r^{\sharp 1}]$. Consider the trace from Example 3.37 in Chap. 3. The first part of this trace, up to the first claim event, is a possible trace of the pattern from Fig. 5.5.

5.2.3 Empty Patterns and Redundant Patterns

Contrary to realisable patterns, some patterns represent the empty trace set. In particular, if $\rightarrow$ is cyclic, the required order on the events cannot be established within any trace. Alternatively, if the pattern is not well-typed, no well-typed substitution exists that instantiates the variables.

Definition 5.18 (Empty Pattern) We say a pattern $(E, \rightarrow)$ is an *empty* pattern if and only if the relation $\rightarrow$ is cyclic or $(E, \rightarrow)$ is not well-typed.

Finally, we observe that patterns include additional structure which may not be visible in the corresponding trace sets. For example, in a pattern which sends a term t in two different send events, there could be a binding of t from either send to later events that receive t, even though both patterns might correspond to the same set of traces. We therefore introduce the notion of redundant patterns, which defines patterns whose trace sets can also be represented by other patterns (i.e., non-redundant patterns).

Definition 5.19 (Redundant Pattern) Let $(E, \rightarrow)$ be a pattern. We say that $(E, \rightarrow)$ is a *redundant pattern* if and only if one of the following holds:

(i) A term is not bound to a unique event,

$$\exists e, e', e'', e''', t : e \neq e'' \wedge t \neq \lambda \wedge e \xrightarrow{t} e' \wedge e'' \xrightarrow{t} e''', \text{ or}$$

(ii) A term is not bound to the earliest possible event,

$$\exists e, e', e'', t : e \neq e'' \wedge t \neq \lambda \wedge e \xrightarrow{t} e' \wedge t \in out(e'') \wedge e'' \rightarrow^* e.$$

Given a redundant pattern, it is straightforward to construct a non-redundant pattern that represents the same trace set, by re-binding all term bindings to a unique earliest event.

5.2.4 Algorithm Overview

The basic idea of the algorithm is to take a (non-redundant) pattern representing a set of traces, such as all traces violating secrecy or all traces that include an execution of a specific role. If the pattern is non-realisable, there must still be events with terms in their *in* set whose origin is not known. Then we apply a case distinction on the possible origins of such terms, resulting in a finite (possibly empty) set of patterns. Each of these new patterns additionally contains an edge identifying the source of the term, and possibly new events. We repeat this procedure, discarding any empty patterns and redundant patterns we encounter along the way, until we arrive at a set of realisable patterns that represent the same set of traces as the original pattern. For properties such as checking for secrecy of a term, where a pattern can be constructed that represents all attacks, a non-empty set of realisable patterns implies that the property is violated.

We ensure termination of the algorithm by bounding the search tree. One feature of the search is that as further case distinctions are performed, events and runs are possibly added to the pattern, but they are never removed. Because any trace of a pattern contains at least the agent events in the pattern, we know that any patterns found deeper in the search tree only contain traces with more runs. We can therefore use the number of runs as a bound for the search, ensuring termination. In practice, the algorithm often terminates before reaching the bound. We will return to the influence of the bound later.

Let $\perp$ be a special symbol to denote that the bound on the number of runs has been reached. The algorithm REFINE has signature

$$Protocol \times Pattern \times \mathbb{N} \rightarrow \mathcal{P}(Pattern) \cup \{\perp\}$$

and has the following functionality. Given a protocol P, a pattern pt of P, and an integer m denoting the bound, the algorithm returns a set S of realisable patterns and possibly the flag, i.e.,

$$\text{REFINE}(P, pt, m) = S,$$

such that the following three equations hold. First, all patterns in S are realisable.

$$\forall pt' \in S \cap Pattern : realisable(pt'). \tag{5.1}$$

Second, in case the flag $\perp$ is not in S, the set of realisable patterns represents the same set of traces as the input pattern.

$$\perp \notin S \Rightarrow traces(P, pt) = \bigcup_{pt' \in S} traces(P, pt'). \tag{5.2}$$

Third, if $\perp$ is present and the terms in the events of P contain only basic variables, any trace of the original pattern is either captured by the result, or the trace is longer than the bound m.

$$\perp \in S \Rightarrow \forall tr \in traces(P, pt) :$$
$$\left(tr \in \bigcup_{pt' \in S \setminus \{\perp\}} traces(P, pt') \vee runCount(tr) > m \right), \tag{5.3}$$

where $runCount$ is a function that returns the number of runs occurring in the trace.

Fourth, none of the patterns in S is redundant, cf. Definition 5.19.

The parameter m effectively bounds the maximum size of the considered patterns (in terms of the number of runs). However, despite this bounding of the pattern size, the algorithm is able to verify the properties of many protocols with respect to an arbitrary number of runs. The underlying reason is that for the vast majority of protocol patterns, all possible traces are captured by realisable patterns that contain only a few runs. Thus, in many practical cases, the depth of the search tree is relatively small. The bound serves to cover the rare cases in which the search tree is (too) deep. For those cases, the bound allows the algorithm to still provide useful information about the absence of "small" attacks. If the bound is reached, the outcome of the analysis is similar to the verification results provided by bounded model checking tools, such as OFMC [22], Sat-MC [13], Casper/FDR[107], or Cl-Atse [157]. We refer to this as bounded verification: if the bound is reached, we obtain the guarantee that no attacks exist whose size is smaller than the bound. In contrast, in most cases, the bound is not reached, and the algorithm proves the absence of attacks, i.e., full (unbounded) verification.

5.2.5 Pattern Refinement

Patterns can be *refined* by adding events, adding edges, or by performing well-typed substitutions. Given a protocol P, we say pt' refines pt, notation $pt' \sqsubseteq pt$, if and only if $traces(P, pt') \subseteq traces(P, pt)$.

The algorithm explores all possible ways to refine patterns into non-redundant realisable patterns. If a pattern $pt = (E, \rightarrow)$ is not realisable, and $traces(P, pt) \neq \emptyset$, there exists an event whose *in* requirements (as required for a realisable pattern) are not satisfied. Informally speaking, this corresponds to a message component for which we don't know yet how the adversary learned it. Using a heuristic *selectOpen*, we pick one of these, i.e., we select an event ge and a term gt such that $ge \in E$, $gt \in in(ge)$ and there is no e for which $e \xrightarrow{gt} ge$. We call such a tuple (ge, gt) an *open goal*. The heuristic influences the efficiency of the algorithm, and is described in Sect. 5.5.1.

We now apply a case distinction on the possible ways in which the adversary could have learned this particular message component. If $traces(P, pt)$ is not empty, then there exist patterns $pt_1, \ldots, pt_n$ that refine pt by some order $\rightarrow_{pt_i}$ and some ϕ. These patterns also contain an event e such that $e \xrightarrow{\phi(gt)}_{pt_i} \phi(ge)$, and hence $\phi(gt) \in out(e)$. Informally speaking, e is identified as the event from which the adversary learns the required message component. Note that this event may be an element of the pattern pt (under some substitution) or not.

In the case that e is a decryption event, there must exist a term $\{\!|t1|\!\}_{t2}$ such that $\phi(gt) \in unpair(t1)$. If we consider again the possible sources of the encrypted term, it may again be the result of a decryption event, and so forth. However, because events have a finite number of preceding events, we can repeatedly apply case distinction until we end up at the first non-decrypt event from which gt can be inferred by using combinations of unpairing and decryption. By the definition of patterns, which requires that messages are bound to the first event, this first event must be a protocol event. This is an essential observation for the algorithm: we collapse such (finite) sequences of repeated decryptions into a single backwards search step.

Summarising, we have that all possible sources of gt in the context of a pattern pt fall into one of the following three cases:

(i) Construction (Co):
    gt was constructed by the adversary by function application or encryption.
(ii) Decryption chain from Existing (DeEx):
    gt was extracted, possibly after repeated decryption and projection, and possibly after instantiating variables, from a message resulting from an event in pt.
(iii) Decryption chain from New (DeNew):
    gt was extracted, possibly after repeated decryption and projection, and possibly after instantiating variables, from a message resulting from a protocol event *not* in pt.

In the algorithm we perform a case distinction on the possible sources of a message according to the above cases. For the first case, a simple inspection of the message is sufficient to see whether (and how) the case applies. For the latter two cases, we need to capture all the ways in which a term $t1$ can be unified with a (sub)term of another term $t2$, possibly after repeated decryption and projection operations. To determine these, we generalise the notion of unification to so-called decryption unification.

Definition 5.20 (Most General Decryption Unifier) Let ϕ be a well-typed substitution. Let L be a sequence of pattern terms. We call (ϕ, L) a *decryption unifier* of a term $t1$ and a term $t2$, notation $(\phi, L) \in DU(t1, t2)$, if either

(i) $L = [\,] \wedge \phi(t1) \in unpair(\phi(t2))$, or
(ii) $L = L' \cdot [\{\!| t |\!\}_k], \{\!| t |\!\}_k \in unpair(\phi(t2)) \wedge (\phi, L') \in DU(t1, t)$.

We call a set of decryption unifiers S the most general decryption unifiers of $t1, t2$, notation $S = MGDU(t1, t2)$, if and only if

(i) for all $(\phi, L) \in S$ we have that $(\phi, L) \in DU(t1, t2)$, and
(ii) for any decryption unifier $(\phi, L) \in DU(t1, t2)$, there exists a decryption unifier $(\phi', L') \in MGDU$ and a substitution ϕ'', such that $\phi' = \phi \circ \phi''$.

Example 5.21 (MGDU) Let X and Y be basic variables, h a function symbol, and let $t1$, $t2$, and $t3$ be constants. Then we have that

$$MGDU(X, (t1, \{\!| Y, h(t2) |\!\}_{t3})) = \big\{ \, (\{X \mapsto t1\}, [\,]),$$
$$(\{X \mapsto Y\}, [\{\!| Y, h(t2) |\!\}_{t3}]) \big\}.$$

Example 5.22 (MGDU) Let X and Y be basic variables, h a function symbol, and let $t1$, $t2$, and $t3$ be constants. Then we have that

$$MGDU(\{\!| t2, h(X) |\!\}_{t4}, (t1, \{\!| t2, h(t3) |\!\}_Y)) = \big\{ \, (\{X \mapsto t3, Y \mapsto t4\}, [\,]) \big\}.$$

Example 5.23 (MGDU) Let X and Y be basic variables, and let $t1$, $t2$, and $t3$ be constants. Then we have that

$$MGDU(t1, \{\!| X, \{\!| Y |\!\}_{t2} |\!\}_{t3})) = \big\{ \, (\{X \mapsto t1\}, [\qquad \{\!| X, \{\!| Y |\!\}_{t2} |\!\}_{t3}])$$
$$(\{Y \mapsto t1\}, [\{\!| Y |\!\}_{t2}, \{\!| X, \{\!| Y |\!\}_{t2} |\!\}_{t3}]) \big\}.$$

We use the function *chain* to compute the set of most general decryption unifiers. Recall that *MGU* denotes the most general unifier of two terms.

$$chain(t1, t2) = \big\{ (\phi, [\,]) \mid t' \in unpair(t2) \wedge \phi = MGU(t1, t') \big\}$$
$$\cup \big\{ (\phi, L \cdot [\{\!| t |\!\}_k]) \mid \{\!| t |\!\}_k \in unpair(t2) \wedge (\phi, L) \in chain(t1, t)) \big\}.$$

The *chain* function returns a finite set of pairs.

If all variables occurring in $t2$ are basic variables, then we have that $chain(t1, t2) = MGDU(t1, t2)$. If $t2$ contains non-basic variables, we have that $chain(t1, t2) \subseteq MGDU(t1, t2)$, because cases in which the variable is instantiated with a pair might be missed.

In the algorithm, we construct chains from the *out* sets of events. For convenience, we define the function *Echain* which constructs all chains for a term from the *out* sets of a set of events.

$$Echain(t1, E) = \big\{ (e, \phi, C) \mid e \in E \wedge t2 \in out(e) \wedge (\phi, C) \in chain(t1, t2) \big\}.$$

This function also returns a finite set of pairs.

If we add protocol events to the pattern, we must ensure the pattern meets the protocol consistency requirements from the fourth clause of Definition 5.4. In particular, we must also add all events that precede the added events in the role order.[1]

The resulting algorithm REFINE is shown as Algorithm 5.1. We give an example of the way the algorithm traverses its search space in Sect. 5.3.

The algorithm is guaranteed to terminate. Each iteration either decreases the number of terms in the $in(e)$ set of an event e which have no corresponding incoming edges, or increases the number of honest agent events. From these two elements we can construct a measure that ensures termination.

The correctness of unbounded verification, corresponding to Formula (5.2), depends on the algorithm exploring all possibilities for enabling the receive events, i.e., that the case distinction on the possible sources of a message is complete.

Theorem 5.24 *Let pt be a pattern of a security protocol P, and let m be an integer. Let $S = \text{REFINE}(P, pt, m)$ such that $\perp \notin S$. Then*

$$traces(P, pt) = \bigcup_{pt' \in S} traces(P, pt').$$

Proof sketch: If the refinement algorithm returns a non-empty set S of realisable patterns, it is straightforward to see that any trace of one of these realisable patterns also exhibits the original pattern pt, based on the notion of pattern refinement. The converse, that all traces of pt are captured in S, depends on the observation that any trace that exhibits pt must be realisable. Let t be a trace of $traces(P, pt)$. The algorithm refines the pattern pt for all possible traces of P, such that one of the refinements must contain t. In particular, all receive events in t must be enabled by a (set of) preceding events. These preceding events must have non-empty out sets, and hence must be either send, decr, encr, or init events. Branching is done on the type of event, and for all possible run identifiers. These include the run identifiers occurring in the pattern as well as a fresh (i.e. not occurring in the pattern yet) run identifier. In the case that a decr event is assumed to be the enabling event, there must exist a finite chain of decrypt events, preceded by a non-decrypt event.

5.3 Example of Search Space Traversal

In this section we give an example of the search space explored by the algorithm. Consider the Yahalom-Lowe protocol with typed variables, depicted in Fig. 5.6. We

---

[1]Note that it is possible to bind a term to an event of a run, where the run identifier already occurs in the pattern, but the event does not, because the pattern contains a partial run. We handle this case implicitly under the DeEx case by considering all possible extensions of the partial runs in the pattern.

Algorithm 5.1 REFINE(P, pt, m)

Require: P is a protocol, pt is a pattern, and m is an integer.
Ensure: Returns a set of realisable patterns. The set may include the special symbol
 '$\perp$' when the complete set of realisable patterns can not be determined.
  if $runCount(pt) > m$ **then**
    return $\{\perp\}$
  else
    if $empty(P, pt) \vee redundant(P, pt)$ **then**   //   Empty or redundant? (Defs. 5.18, 5.19)
      return $\emptyset$
    else
      if $realisable(P, pt)$ **then**
        return $\{pt\}$
      else // pt is not realisable.
        $(ge, gt) \Leftarrow selectOpen(pt)$ // Apply heuristic to select an unbound term,
        // and apply case distinction on possible earliest bindings of gt.
        $Co, DeEx, DeNew \Leftarrow \emptyset, \emptyset, \emptyset$
        if $\exists t1, t2 : gt = \{\!| t1 |\!\}_{t2}$ **then**
          $pt' \Leftarrow pt \cup \{encr(gt) \xrightarrow{gt} ge\}$
          $Co \Leftarrow \text{REFINE}(P, pt', m)$
        end if
        if $\exists f, t : gt = f(t)$ **then**
          $pt' \Leftarrow pt \cup \{app(gt) \xrightarrow{gt} ge\}$
          $Co \Leftarrow Co \cup \text{REFINE}(P, pt', m)$
        end if
        for all $(e, \phi, C) \in Echain(gt, E_{pt})$ **do**
          $pt' \Leftarrow \phi(pt \cup \{e \xrightarrow{C_q} \cdots decr(C_i) \cdots \xrightarrow{gt} ge\})$
          $DeEx \Leftarrow DeEx \cup \text{REFINE}(P, pt', m)$
        end for
        for all $(e, \phi, C) \in Echain(gt, ev(P))$ **do**
          if e is not an init event **then**
            $newid \Leftarrow$ a run identifier that does not occur in pt.
            for all $x \in runIDs(pt) \cup \{newid\}$ **do**
              $\phi' \Leftarrow \phi \cup [x/\tau]$
              $pt'' \Leftarrow \phi'(pt \cup \{e \xrightarrow{C_q} \cdots decr(C_i) \cdots \xrightarrow{gt} ge\} \cup \{e' \mid e' <_{role(e)} e\})$
              $DeNew \Leftarrow DeNew \cup \text{REFINE}(P, pt'', m)$
            end for
          end if
        end for
        return $Co \cup DeEx \cup DeNew$
      end if
    end if
  end if

---

show how the pattern refinement algorithm explores the search space when provided
with an instance of the initiator role i for honest agents, typed variables, and where
the initial knowledge of the adversary is $\{kA, E\}$. In this example we assume that
the bound on the number of runs is at least 3.

We provide a high-level overview of the search space explored by the algorithm in Fig. 5.7. The details of the nodes in this tree are depicted in Figs. 5.8,
5.9, and 5.10.

Fig. 5.6 Lowe's modified
version of the Yahalom
protocol

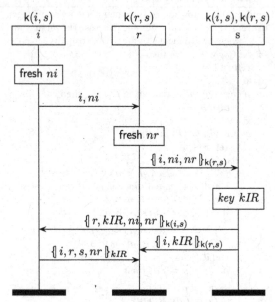

In this example, we depict the search for a pattern representing an honest instance of the i role. Initially, the role is instantiated into a pattern for an arbitrary run identifier 0, and the types of the role variables $i^{\#0}, r^{\#0}, s^{\#0}$ are restricted to $Agent_H$. The pattern that contains the ordered events of the instantiated role and the init event initialising the adversary's knowledge is depicted in Fig. 5.8 as C.0.

C.0 is not an empty pattern. Further, it is not realisable, because there is an open goal: the receive event does not have an incoming edge for the received term $\{\!|\, r^{\#0}, kIR^{\#0}, ni^{\#0}, nr^{\#0}\, |\!\}_{k(i^{\#0}, s^{\#0})}$. Since this term is not a tuple, there is only one choice for the heuristic and the case distinction will be applied to this term. We apply the case distinction on the possible origins of this encrypted term. We first consider the case of a decryption chain from events already existing in the pattern (DeEx). Because the variables are typed, $nr^{\#0}$ can not be instantiated with non-atomic terms. Therefore, there are no possible decryption chains from any of the *out* sets of the events in the pattern. Alternatively, the message might be the result of a decryption chain from an event not yet in the pattern (DeNew). This will be explored in C.2 in Fig. 5.9. The other remaining case is the construction case (Co). Because the received term is an encryption, the only option is that the term was encrypted by the adversary. This leads to C.1.

C.1 refines C.0 by adding an encryption event, which encrypts the message, and a binding from the encryption event to the receive event. Though the received message is now bound, the pattern is neither empty nor realisable, because for the encryption event we have introduced two new open goals: the message that is to be encrypted and the encryption key. Here, the heuristic determines which goal is analysed next. We assume that the heuristic selects the key $k(i, s)$.

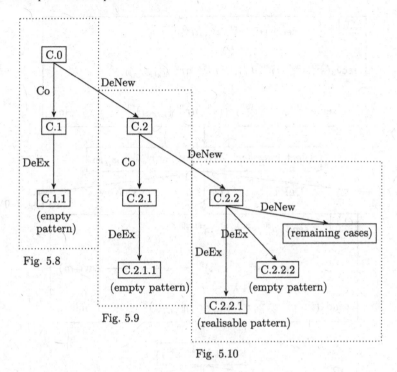

Fig. 5.7 Search tree overview

We have no construction rules for the key. We have also no decryption chains from the protocol events, as variables are typed and no protocol event sends out keys in an accessible position. The only possible source is therefore a decryption chain of length zero from initial knowledge event init, by unifying $i^{\#0}$ with A and $s^{\#0}$ with E. This leads to C.1.1.

The resulting pattern C.1.1 is empty because the instantiation of the variable $s^{\#0}$ violates the typing assumptions: $E \notin Agent_H$.

We now return to the (DeNew) case from C.0. Here, we observe that the only possible source of an encryption of the required form (a four-tuple) is the send event of the s role. Hence, we add a prefix-closed instantiation of this event with a previously unused run identifier 1. This situation is depicted in C.2. By unification we obtain that the i, r, s, and ni variables of both runs must be equal, and the corresponding variables from run 1 are substituted by those from run 0.

The resulting pattern in C.2 has only one open goal, which is the encryption $m' = \{\!| \, r^{\#0}, kI \, R^{\#0}, ni^{\#0}, nr^{\#1} \, |\!\}_{K(i^{\#0},s^{\#0})}$, which is therefore selected by the heuristic. For an encryption of this form, we observe that there can be no decryption chain from any existing event (DeEx). However, the encryption may be the result of a decryption chain (possibly of length 0) from a new event, which we will later consider in C.2.2 in Fig. 5.10.

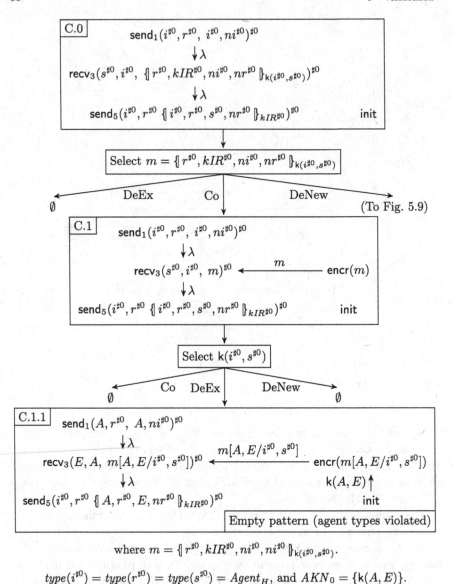

where $m = \{\!\{\, r^{\#0}, kIR^{\#0}, ni^{\#0}, ni^{\#0} \,\}\!\}_{k(i^{\#0},s^{\#0})}$.

$type(i^{\#0}) = type(r^{\#0}) = type(s^{\#0}) = Agent_H$, and $AKN_0 = \{k(A,E)\}$.

Fig. 5.8 First part of the search tree

We first consider the (Co) case of C.2. For this case, we add the appropriate encryption node, leading to C.2.1 in Fig. 5.9. C.2.1 has two open goals for the encrypt event: the message to be encrypted, and the key. Again, we assume the heuristic chooses the key $k(r^{\#0}, s^{\#0})$ to perform a case distinction on. Similar to C.1, the key can only be the result of a zero-length decryption chain from the initial knowledge event. Unification and binding leads to C.2.1.1.

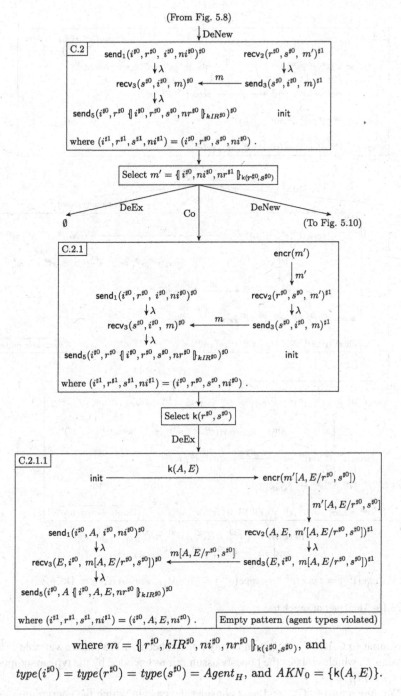

Fig. 5.9 Second part of search tree

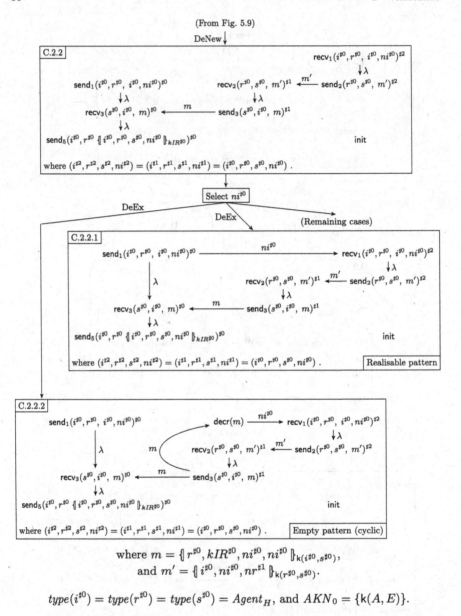

$$\text{where } m = \{\!| \, r^{\#0}, kIR^{\#0}, ni^{\#0}, ni^{\#0} \, \}\!|_{\mathsf{k}(i^{\#0}, s^{\#0})},$$
$$\text{and } m' = \{\!| \, i^{\#0}, ni^{\#0}, nr^{\#1} \, \}\!|_{\mathsf{k}(r^{\#0}, s^{\#0})}.$$

$$type(i^{\#0}) = type(r^{\#0}) = type(s^{\#0}) = Agent_H, \text{ and } AKN_0 = \{\mathsf{k}(A, E)\}.$$

Fig. 5.10 Third part of search tree

Similar to C.1.1, C.2.1.1 is an empty pattern because the pattern variable $s^{\#0}$ is equal to E, which violates the honesty assumptions encoded by the type assumption $s^{\#0} \in Agent_H$.

We now return to C.2, and next consider the case in which the encryption is the result of a decryption chain from a new event. For an encryption of this form, the only possible source is the send event of the responder role. Hence, we add this event for a previously unused run identifier 2 and the preceding events. We unify the received encryption message $\{\!| r^{\sharp 0}, kIR^{\sharp 0}, ni^{\sharp 0}, nr^{\sharp 1} |\!\}_{\mathsf{k}(i^{\sharp 0}, s^{\sharp 0})}$ with the message sent by run 2. Applying this substitution results in the variables i, r, s, and ni being equal for all three runs. This leads to C.2.2 in Fig. 5.10.

C.2.2 has only one open goal, $ni^{\sharp 0}$, because the other terms in the in set of the receive event are pattern variables. Because $ni^{\sharp 0}$ is an atomic term, it cannot be constructed. However, $ni^{\sharp 0}$ can be the result of a decryption chain from various (new or existing) events. For brevity, we do not discuss in this book all of these cases, marked in the graph as "remaining cases". We discuss two possible DeEx cases.

First, there is a decryption chain of length zero from the first send of run 0, which sends $ni^{\sharp 0}$ in plaintext. Refining the pattern with this binding leads to C.2.2.1. This pattern is realisable, as it is non-cyclic and all received messages are accounted for. Thus, it is returned as the output of the algorithm.

Another possibility is that there is a decryption chain of length 1 from the last send event of run 1. Adding the appropriate decryption event and bindings leads to C.2.2.2. However, this pattern is cyclic, and therefore empty.

The remaining cases also yield only empty patterns. The algorithm therefore returns a singleton set containing C.2.2.1.

5.4 Verifying Security Properties Using Pattern Refinement

Next we show how the algorithm is used for the analysis of security properties and characterisation.

Analysis of Secrecy   In a pre-processing step of the algorithm, security properties are automatically turned into a pattern that represents all traces that violate the property, as described in Sect. 5.1.

Then, the refinement algorithm is applied to P, pt, m for some m and returns the result set S. We distinguish three cases.

(i) $S \cap Pattern \neq \emptyset$: Following Lemma 5.16 we can directly construct traces of P that exhibit pt from each element of $S \cap Pattern$, which represent attacks. Hence secrecy is violated, and the property is falsified.

(ii) $S = \emptyset$: From Eq. (5.2) we have that there exist no traces exhibiting the pattern, hence no attacks exists. This constitutes unbounded verification.

(iii) $S = \{\bot\}$: Based on Eq. (5.3) we conclude that there are no attacks with m or fewer runs, constituting bounded verification. Observe that applying the algorithm with a larger parameter m may still yield unbounded verification or falsification.

Characterisation of Security Protocols   Characterisation, as described in [74], provides a concise finite representation of all possible protocol behaviours. The approach essentially consists of giving for all roles a finite representation of all traces that include an instance of that role. This corresponds directly to the functionality of the algorithm presented here, and can be performed by applying the algorithm to a pattern that consists of (1) the events of the role r, with the order induced by the role specification, and including only honest agent names, (2) initial adversary knowledge events init. The result of the algorithm, if it does not contain $\bot$, provides a complete characterisation. If the result contains $\bot$, it only characterises all traces which can be represented by realisable patterns that do not have more than m runs.

For example, the problem considered in Sect. 5.3 is a characterisation of the i role of the Yahalom-Lowe protocol. The result is the singleton set containing the pattern from C.2.2.1 in Fig. 5.10. Informally stated, this means that in every trace that contains an instance of the initiator role with honest agents, the pattern from C.2.2.1 must also occur.

Note that the characterisations generated by our refinement algorithm differ slightly from those in [74]. We elaborate on the differences in Chap. 8.

Analysis of Authentication Properties   To analyse authentication properties, we first apply the characterisation process and then check whether the authentication property holds for each realisable pattern. This allows for verification of, for example, aliveness or non-injective agreement. It also allows us to efficiently establish ordering related properties such as non-injective synchronisation.

Consider again the characterisation of the i role of the Yahalom-Lowe protocol, returning the single pattern from C.2.2.1 in Fig. 5.10. From this pattern, we can see that aliveness holds for the agents in the other roles, because all returned patterns (in this case only one) contain events executed by these agents. Furthermore, we can see that even non-injective synchronisation holds at the end of the i role, as all the events that precede the end of this role occur instantiated in the pattern in the correct order.

5.5 Heuristics and Parameter Choices

5.5.1 Heuristics

The heuristic *selectOpen* used in the algorithm influences both the effectiveness and efficiency of the algorithm. Recall that an open goal is a tuple (ge, gt), where $gt \in in(ge)$, that needs to be connected by an incoming edge labelled with gt in order to arrive at a realisable pattern. The heuristic selects one of possibly many such open goals, which is used for case distinction and pattern refinement. Although the algorithm will try to bind any other open goals in further iterations, any substitutions made by the case distinctions and refinement steps influence the branching factors further on. Furthermore, for some heuristics, contradictory states (corresponding to patterns with empty trace sets) may occur earlier in the iteration process. This means the heuristic is important not only for the speed of the verification, but also for improving the number of cases in which verification is complete.

As our main goal is to establish falsification or unbounded verification, we choose a heuristic that is optimal for the *effectiveness* of the algorithm: to achieve, even when choosing a small value for the parameter m, unbounded verification for as many protocols as possible. Of course, this may be less efficient for particular protocols where unbounded verification is not achieved.

Observe that the choice of heuristic influences efficiency and effectiveness of the algorithm, but it does not influence the correctness of the algorithm.

We devised over 20 candidate heuristics and investigated their effectiveness. We illustrate the five core heuristics that we considered, ordered according to their effectiveness.

- *Heuristic 1: Random.* An open goal is selected randomly for case splitting.
- *Heuristic 2: Constants.* For each open goal term t, the number of local constants that are a subterm of t is divided by the number of basic terms that are a subterm of t. The goal with the highest ratio is selected.
- *Heuristic 3:* Open goals that correspond to the keys needed for decrypt events are given higher priority, unless these keys are in the initial adversary knowledge.
- *Heuristic 4:* Give priority to goals that contain a private key as a subterm; next, give priority to goals that contain a public key; all other terms have lower priority.
- *Heuristic 5:* A combination of heuristics 2, 3 and 4, where first heuristic 4 is applied. If this yields equal priorities for a goal, heuristics 2 and 3 are applied.

The first heuristic acts as a reference point for establishing relative effectiveness of each heuristic. The second heuristic corresponds to the intuition that terms which contain more local constants of particular runs, can only be bound to very particular send events (as opposed to terms with many globals or variables), resulting in fewer case distinctions. The third heuristic captures the intuition that there should be few ways in which the adversary can gain access to a decryption key, as in general keys should not be known to the adversary. For the fourth heuristic, a strict priority is given to cases where, for example, the adversary decrypts something with a key that is never sent by the regular agents, usually corresponding to long-term keys, as these branches often lead to contradictory states. Finally, the fifth heuristic is a combination of the previous three heuristics, using a lexicographic order. For the fifth heuristic various weighting functions were also considered, of which the lexicographical order performed best in general.

Given a fairly low setting of the parameter, in particular we set $m = 4$, we investigated how each heuristic performed, when applied to a test set of 128 protocol descriptions, with 518 security claims. The test set includes the vast majority of the protocols in the SPORE library [149], various protocols from scientific papers, some variations on existing protocols, and new protocols, as modelled by users of the Scyther tool. A time limit was set for the iteration procedure, which was only used to abort tests for the first two heuristics. In Fig. 5.11 we show the impact of the heuristics on the number of states explored. From the graph it is clear that heuristic 5 explores almost 40 times fewer states than the random heuristic 1. Intuitively, this corresponds to avoiding unnecessary branching, and a tendency to arrive at contradictory trace patterns in fewer iterations.

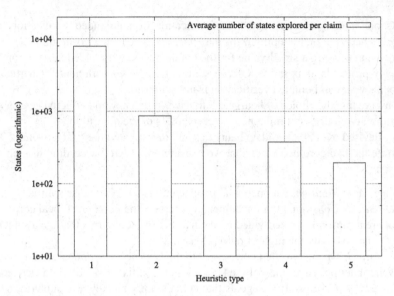

Fig. 5.11 The impact of the heuristics on the number of states traversed (for 518 claims, strict bound)

Because the effectiveness of the heuristics depends to a large degree on the particular protocol under investigation, it is difficult to give an analytical explanation of the results for the complete test set. However, it seems that the heuristics 2, 3 and 4 can be used to support each other, as is shown by the performance of heuristic 5.

The heuristic also has a direct result on the completeness of the results, which is depicted in Fig. 5.12. For heuristic 1, we get a complete result (based on complete characterisation) for less than 30 percent of the claims. This improves for each heuristic, leading to an 82 percent rating for heuristic 5. In other words, if we use heuristic 5, we have that for 82 percent of the claims in the test set, the algorithm is able to either find an attack, or verify correctness for an unbounded number of runs. In the remaining 18 percent of the cases the algorithm determines that there are no attacks involving four runs or less, but it might be possible that there are attacks involving five or more runs. We conclude that heuristic 5 is to be preferred from the set of investigated heuristics.

5.5.2 Choosing a Bound on the Number of Runs

For the protocols analysed for this book, we did not find any attacks that involved more than $x + 1$ runs, where x is the number of roles of the protocol, except for the $f^N g^N$ family of protocols from [116]. The exceptions involve a family of protocols that was specifically tailored to be correct for N runs, but incorrect for $N + 1$ runs.[2]

---

[2]This seems to suggest a correlation between the number of roles in the protocol and the runs involved in the attacks. In general, the undecidability of the problem [77] implies that there is no

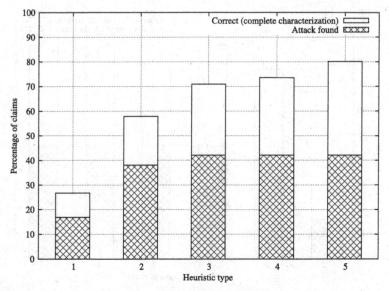

Fig. 5.12 The impact of the heuristics on the decidability (for 518 claims, strict bound)

This indicates that for practical purposes, initial verification with three or four runs would be sufficient. If verification with a low bound yields no attacks, but neither a complete characterisation, the bound can be increased.

Because a higher bound on the number of runs can improve the rate of complete characterisation, but can also increase verification time, there is an inherent trade-off between completeness and verification time. We have investigated the impact of the bound on the number of complete characterisations, within the set of protocols we used for the previous graphs. In Fig. 5.13 we show the decidability results on the test set as a function of the bound on the runs, using heuristic 5, and using no time limit for the tests. There is no difference between the decidability results of 6 and 7 run bounds, but, in general, the higher the bound, the more claims are decided. In the test case, no further attacks are found for bounds of three runs or more, but some additional claims can be proven to be correct for an unbounded number of results.

The drawback of a high bound on the number of runs is the increase in verification time. As the algorithm employs a depth-first search, memory usage is linear in the number of runs. However, for protocols and properties for which unbounded verification is not achieved and no attacks are found, the bounded verification time is exponential with respect to the number of runs. For the test set, we show verification times in Fig. 5.14 for some specific bounds on the number of runs. The figure thus corresponds to the time it took to generate the results in Fig. 5.13, on a desktop computer with an AMD 3000+ Sempron CPU running at 1.6 GHz, with 1 GB of

---

such bound for all protocols, but maybe it is possible to establish a tight lower bound for decidable subclasses [156].

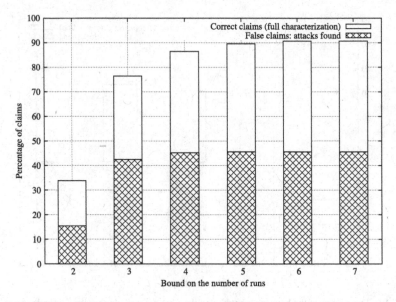

Fig. 5.13 The impact of the bound on runs on decidability for the protocols in the test set

RAM.[3] It is clear that the total verification time of a large set of protocols is exponential with respect to the maximum number of runs, even though verification time is constant for the vast majority of the protocols. This is in line with results such as those in [140].

The protocols in our test set did not include attacks involving more than a handful of runs. To evaluate the effectiveness of Scyther in finding large attacks, we analysed instances of the $f^N g^N$ family of protocols from [116], mentioned above. These protocols were specifically designed to show theoretical possibilities of the size of attacks. For each $N > 2$, the protocol $f^N g^N$ has no attacks with N or fewer runs, but there exists an attack involving $N + 1$ runs. The protocol contains only two roles and four messages, and the parameter N mainly influences the message size (by increasing the number of nonces and variables). Scyther yields the expected results: for protocols $f^N g^N$ with a bound $m \leq N$, bounded verification is performed. With a bound $m > N$, an attack is found. As an extreme example, we find the attack that involves 51 runs (on the $f^{50} g^{50}$ protocol) in 137 seconds.

5.5.3 Performance

Given the previously established choices for the heuristics and the parameter, we provide performance results for the algorithm as implemented in the Scyther tool.

---

[3]Note that, because the algorithm uses an iterative depth-first search, it uses a negligible amount of RAM.

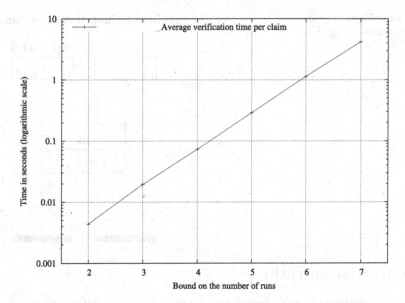

Fig. 5.14 The impact of the bound on runs on the total verification time for 518 claims

Table 5.2 Verification times in seconds (1.66 GHz Intel Centrino processor, 1 GB RAM, Linux)

Protocol	Details	Time
NSPK	attack	0.1
NSPK-FIX	verified	0.1
Otway-Rees	verified (typed variables)	0.1
Otway-Rees	attack (type flaw)	0.0
TLS (Paulson)	verified	0.2
TLS (Avispa)	attack ("Alice talks to Alice")	0.2
NSPK-FIX in parallel with NSPK-alt	attack (multi-protocol attack)	0.3
$f^{10}g^{10}$	attack using 11 runs	0.2
$f^{30}g^{30}$	attack using 31 runs	10.1
$f^{50}g^{50}$	attack using 51 runs	110.1

In Table 5.2 we show a set of modelled protocols and their analysis times. In the table, the NSPK, NSPK-FIX and Otway-Rees protocols were modelled according to SPORE [149]. The two versions of the TLS protocol are taken from a paper [132] and the AVISPA library of protocols [94]. The $f^n g^n$ protocols are instances of a family of protocols described in [116]. The protocols from this family are not intended for practical usage, but are explicitly designed to exhibit an attack involving $n + 1$ runs, but no attack with fewer runs.

Fig. 5.15 A protocol that is
not vulnerable to replay
attacks

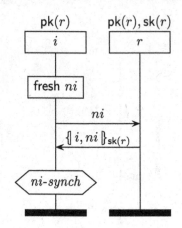

protocol Unilateral authentication

5.6 Verifying Injectivity

The algorithm introduced so far can be used to verify *non-injective* authentication properties. Because injectivity is a higher-order property, it is not possible to characterise all attacks on injectivity through a finite set of patterns. Therefore, we develop a different approach for the verification of injectivity. In particular, we focus on the verification of injectivity for protocols that satisfy non-injective synchronisation.

We propose and study a property, the LOOP property that can be syntactically verified, and we prove a theorem that shows that LOOP is sufficient to guarantee injectivity. Our result is generic in the sense that it holds for a wide range of security protocol models, and does not depend on the details of message content or nonce freshness.

5.6.1 Injective Synchronisation

As discussed in Sect. 4.3.2, protocols that satisfy *NI-SYNCH* can still be vulnerable to so-called replay attacks. Looking back at Example 4.14 in particular, we saw that the unilateral authentication protocol from Fig. 4.11 clearly does not satisfy injectivity, as is shown by the replay attack in Fig. 4.12. A simple fix would be to have the initiator determine the value of the nonce, as in Fig. 5.15. In this revised protocol, a replay attack is impossible because two different initiator runs will now require two different responder runs.

The introduction of a causal chain of messages from the initiator to the responder and back to the initiator seems sufficient to enforce injectivity. We will call such a chain a *loop*. The presence of such a loop plays a key role in the discussion on injectivity below.

We show that in our model the LOOP property guarantees that a synchronising protocol is also injective. For this result to hold, we require a specific property to hold for the adversary model. We can informally characterise this by saying that the adversary must at least be able to duplicate messages. To be more precise, the protocol model (including the adversary model) must satisfy closure of the set of execution traces under swapping of events. This class contains, for example, the model presented in Chap. 3.

We use the function *roleevent* to determine for a run event of which role event it is an instantiation. For a non-create run event $r = (inst, e)$, it is defined by $roleevent(r) = e$.

Definition 5.25 (Swap) A security protocol semantics satisfies the SWAP property if the following two conditions hold:

(i) The trace set *traces(P)* is closed with respect to non-receive swaps, i.e., for all non-create run events e' such that $roleevent(e')$ is not a receive event, it holds that

$$t \cdot [e] \cdot [e'] \cdot t' \in traces(P) \wedge runidof(e) \neq runidof(e')$$

$$\Rightarrow t \cdot [e'] \cdot [e] \cdot t' \in traces(P)$$

for all run events e and traces t, t'.

(ii) The trace set *traces(P)* is closed with respect to receive swaps, i.e., for s, r, e such that $roleevent(s)$ is a send event and $roleevent(r)$ is a receive event, we have that

$$t \cdot [s] \cdot t' \cdot [e] \cdot [r] \cdot t'' \in traces(P) \wedge runidof(e) \neq runidof(r)$$

$$\wedge\, cont(s) = cont(r) \Rightarrow t \cdot [s] \cdot t' \cdot [r] \cdot [e] \cdot t'' \in traces(P)$$

for all traces t, t', t''.

These properties state that we can shift a non-receive event to the left as long as it does not cross any other events of the same role instance. For the receive event we have an additional constraint: we can only shift it to the left if there remains an earlier send of the same message.

Lemma 5.26 (SWAP Holds for the Operational Semantics) *The operational semantics, as defined in Chap. 3, satisfies the SWAP property.*

Proof The first condition, swapping non-receives, is related to the fact that independent runs share no memory, and trivially holds based on the semantics. The second condition, swapping receives, is met because the premise of the receive rule of the semantics requires that the message is known to the adversary, and because the adversary's knowledge is non-decreasing. □

For the remainder of this section we assume the protocol P contains a claim γ. We introduce a predicate χ and a set χ' for protocols that satisfy non-injective agreement for this claim γ. Given a trace t, a claim event c, and a cast Γ that maps the roles to runs, we express the auxiliary predicate χ on the domain $traces(P) \times Cast(P, t) \times RunEvent$ by

$$\chi(t, \Gamma, c) \iff roleevent(c) = \gamma \wedge$$

$$\forall \varsigma, \varrho : \varsigma \dashrightarrow \varrho \wedge \varrho \prec_P \gamma \implies$$

$$\exists inst'', inst' : (inst'', \varsigma) <_t (inst', \varrho) <_t (inst, \gamma) \wedge$$

$$runidof(inst'') = \Gamma((inst, \gamma), role(\varsigma)) \wedge$$

$$runidof(inst') = \Gamma((inst, \gamma), role(\varrho)) \wedge$$

$$cont((inst'', \varsigma)) = cont((inst', \varrho)).$$

This predicate corresponds to part of the definition of injective synchronisation (Definition 4.15). The first conjunct of this predicate expresses the fact that the run executing the claim role is determined by the parameter c. The second conjunct expresses that in the trace t, the claim c is valid with respect to the specific cast Γ, i.e., that the partners have executed all communications as expected. In the formula this is expressed by the fact that send and receive events are executed by the expected runs, with identical contents, and in the right order.

Given a valid synchronisation claim c in a trace t, there exists a role instantiation function Γ such that $\chi(t, \Gamma, c)$ holds. The predicate χ tells us that certain events exist in the trace. Because we want to reason about these events in the following, we decide to make this set of events explicit. We define the set of events $\chi'(t, \Gamma, c)$ by

$$\chi'(t, \Gamma, c)$$

$$= \{e \in t \mid runidof(e) = \Gamma(c)(role(e)) \wedge roleevent(e) \prec_P roleevent(c)\}.$$

Assuming that χ holds, its set of events χ' has two interesting properties. If there is a receive in this set, there is also a matching send in the set. Furthermore, given an event of a role in the set, all preceding events of the same role are also in the set.

To prove our main result, the SWAP property from Definition 5.25 suffices. However, to ease the explanation of the proof, we introduce two additional lemmas. These lemmas are implied by the model and the two swap conditions.

The first lemma generalises the swapping of two events to the swapping of a set of events. In particular, the lemma holds for the events involved in a correct synchronisation claim, defined by χ. Based on the two swap properties, we can shift these events (in their original order) to the beginning of the trace. This trace transformation function $shift : \mathcal{P}(TE) \times TE^* \to TE^*$ is defined by

$$shift(E, t) = \begin{cases} t & \text{if } t \cap E = \emptyset, \\ e \cdot shift(E, u1 \cdot u2) & \text{if } t = u1 \cdot e \cdot u2 \wedge u1 \cap E = \emptyset \wedge e \in E. \end{cases}$$

Here, the intersection of a trace and a set yields the collection of elements of the set occurring in the trace. This function effectively reorders a trace. The next lemma formulates conditions assuring that the reordering of a trace in $traces(P)$ is in $traces(P)$ as well.

Lemma 5.27 *Given a protocol P and a trace t ∈ traces(P), claim event c and role instantiation function* Γ:

$$\chi(t, \Gamma, c) \wedge t' = shift(\chi'(t, \Gamma, c), t) \Rightarrow t' \in traces(P) \wedge \chi(t', \Gamma, c).$$

Proof Induction on the size of the finite set $\chi'(t, \Gamma, c)$, because $\chi(t, \Gamma, c)$ implies that the receive events can be swapped. Recall that, by convention, each event occurs at most once in a trace.   □

The lemma directly generalises to more claim instances (of the same claim). Thus, instead of a single claim run, we can consider sets of claim runs.

Lemma 5.28 *Given a trace t, a set of claim events $C \subseteq t$ and cast* $\Gamma \in Cast(P, t)$:

$$(\forall c \in C : \chi(t, \Gamma, c)) \wedge t' = shift\left(\bigcup_{c \in C} \chi'(t, \Gamma, c), t\right)$$

$$\Rightarrow t' \in traces(P) \wedge (\forall c \in C : \chi(t', \Gamma, c)).$$

Proof Similar to the proof of Lemma 5.27.   □

If we apply the *shift* function to a trace of the system, and the conditions of the lemma are met, we get a reordered trace that is also in *traces(P)*. The new trace consists of two segments: in the first segment there are only the preceding events of the claim events in C, and all other events are in the second segment.

Intuitively, these lemmas express that the events involved in a valid synchronisation claim are independent of the other events in the trace. A valid synchronisation can occur at any point in the trace, because it does not require the involvement of other runs, or of the adversary. However, other events in the trace might depend on events involved in the synchronisation. Although we cannot shift the synchronising events to the right, we can shift them to the left, which ensures that any dependencies will not be broken.

We use Lemma 5.27 and Lemma 5.28 in the injectivity proof in the next section.

5.6.2 The LOOP Property

We define a property of protocols, which we call the LOOP property. For protocols with only two roles, it resembles a ping-pong property. First the claim role executes an event, then the other role, and then the claim role again. For example, the LOOP property does not hold for the protocol in Fig. 4.12, but it does hold for the protocols in Figs. 5.15 and 3.3.

We generalise this for multi-party protocols with any number of roles. We require that the partner roles have an event that must occur after the start of the claim run, but before the claim event itself.

Definition 5.29 (LOOP)   A security protocol P has the LOOP property with respect to a claim γ if

$$\forall \varepsilon \prec_P \gamma, role(\varepsilon) \neq role(\gamma):$$

$$\exists \varepsilon', \varepsilon'' : \varepsilon' \prec_P \varepsilon'' \prec_P \gamma \wedge role(\varepsilon') = role(\gamma) \wedge role(\varepsilon'') = role(\varepsilon). \qquad (5.4)$$

The property tells us that for each role that has an event ε that precedes the claim γ, there exists a loop from the claim role to the role and back. This structure is identified in the formula by $\varepsilon' \prec_P \varepsilon'' \prec_P \gamma$. We use LOOP$(P, \gamma)$ to denote that security protocol P has the LOOP property with respect to claim γ.

Lemma 5.30 *Given a security protocol P with a claim γ. If all roles $R \neq role(\gamma)$ that have events preceding γ start with a receive event, then we have that* LOOP(P, γ).

Proof The proof of this lemma follows from the definition of the protocol order $\prec_P$. Let P be a protocol with a claim γ. Let $R \neq role(\gamma)$ be a role with an event ε that precedes the claim. Based on the precondition of the lemma, it starts with a receive, and thus there must be a preceding event with the same label on a different role R'. If $R' = role(\gamma)$ then we clearly have established a loop. On the other hand, if we have $R' \neq role(\gamma)$, we again have that this role must have a preceding event on another role. As the set of role events is finite, we ultimately end up at an event of the claim role. Thus we can conclude that LOOP(P, γ) holds. $\square$

This lemma tells us that the LOOP property always holds for the initiating role of a protocol. Thus, we only have to check whether the LOOP property holds for responder roles.

We proceed with the main theorem of this section, which provides a syntactic condition for the injectivity of a synchronising protocol.

Theorem 5.31 (LOOP)   *Let P be a protocol with claim event γ. Then we have that*

$$NI\text{-}SYNCH(P, \gamma) \wedge LOOP(P, \gamma) \Rightarrow I\text{-}SYNCH(P, \gamma).$$

Proof By contradiction. Assume that the implication does not hold. Thus we have

$$NI\text{-}SYNCH(P, \gamma) \wedge LOOP(P, \gamma) \wedge \neg I\text{-}SYNCH(P, \gamma). \qquad (5.5)$$

The remainder of the proof is done in two steps. The first step of the proof establishes a trace t of the protocol in which there are two runs that synchronise with the same run. In the second step we use the shifting lemmas to transform t into another trace of the protocol. For this new trace, we will show that *NI-SYNCH* cannot hold, which contradicts the assumptions.

From now on, we will omit the type information for t and Γ in the quantifiers and assume that $t \in traces(P)$.

Given that the protocol synchronises, but is not injective, we derive from Definitions 4.13 and 4.15 and formula (5.5) that

$$\forall t \ \exists \Gamma \ \forall c \in t : roleevent(c) = \gamma \Rightarrow \chi(t, \Gamma, c) \wedge$$

$$\neg \ \forall t \exists \Gamma \ injective \forall c \in t : roleevent(c) = \gamma \Rightarrow \chi(t, \Gamma, c). \qquad (5.6)$$

We push the negation through the quantifiers, yielding

$$\forall t \ \exists \Gamma \ \forall c \in t : roleevent(c) = \gamma \Rightarrow \chi(t, \Gamma, c) \wedge$$

$$\exists t \ \forall \Gamma \neg (\Gamma \ injective \wedge \forall c \in t : roleevent(c) = \gamma \Rightarrow \chi(t, \Gamma, c)). \qquad (5.7)$$

Based on the existential quantifiers in (5.7), we choose a trace t and instantiation function Γ such that

$$\forall c \in t : roleevent(c) = \gamma \Rightarrow \chi(t, \Gamma, c) \wedge$$

$$\neg (\Gamma \ injective \wedge \forall c \in t : roleevent(c) = \gamma \Rightarrow \chi(t, \Gamma, c)). \qquad (5.8)$$

Note that in (5.8) the left conjunct also occurs as a sub-formula in the right conjunct. Rewriting yields

$$\forall c \in t : roleevent(c) = \gamma \Rightarrow \chi(t, \Gamma, c) \wedge \neg (\Gamma \ injective). \qquad (5.9)$$

Making the non-injectivity for the function Γ explicit as explained in Definition 4.11, there must exist two claim events, for which χ holds:

$$\exists c1, c2, R1, R2 : \chi(t, \Gamma, c1) \wedge \chi(t, \Gamma, c2)$$

$$\wedge \ \Gamma(c1)(R1) = \Gamma(c2)(R2) \wedge (c1 \neq c2 \vee R1 \neq R2). \qquad (5.10)$$

From the predicate χ and Eq. (5.10), we have that the run $\Gamma(c1)(R1)$ must be executing the role $R1$. Because $\Gamma(c1)(R1) = \Gamma(c2)(R2)$ it is also executing role $R2$. Runs only execute a single role, and thus we derive that $R1 = R2$. The fourth conjunct now reduces to $c1 \neq c2$.

Put $R = R1 = R2$. We choose two claim events $c1, c2$ such that Formula (5.10) holds for R. Now there exists a run identifier θ such that

$$\Gamma(c1)(R) = \Gamma(c2)(R) = \theta.$$

From the definition of χ, we obtain that if R would be equal to $role(\gamma)$, we would have $\theta = c1$ and $\theta = c2$, implying $c1 = c2$ and contradicting Equation (5.10). Thus, we have $R \neq role(\gamma)$.

We have now established that the trace t contains events from at least three role instances. Two of these, $[c1]_\pi$ and $[c2]_\pi$, are executing the claim role, while the third, θ is executing a different role R. Furthermore, we have that the claims $c1$ and $c2$ synchronise with θ.

This completes the first step of the proof. We will now proceed by transforming t into a trace for which NI-SYNCH cannot hold, for the second part of the proof.

Because we have $\chi(t, \Gamma, c1)$ and $\chi(t, \Gamma, c2)$, on the basis of Lemma 5.28 we can apply *shift* using $c1$ and $c2$ to get a trace $t' \in traces(P)$

$$t' = shift(\chi'(t, \Gamma, c1) \cup \chi'(t, \Gamma, c2), t).$$

In the trace t' we now have two distinct segments. All events involved with the synchronisation of $c1$ and $c2$ are now in the initial segment of t'. This includes the events of θ that precede the claim. The second segment of t' contains all other events that are not involved in the preceding events of $c1$ and $c2$.

We will now reorder the initial segment of t'. To this end, we apply the *shift* function a second time, now only for $c1$. This will also yield a trace of the protocol, because the conditions of Lemma 5.28 hold for t', as the application of *shift* to t maintained the order of the events in the shifted set, which implies that $\chi(t', \Gamma, c1)$ holds. Thus, we also know that the trace t'' is an element of $traces(P)$, where

$$t'' = shift(\chi'(t', \Gamma, c1), t').$$

Because the *shift* function maintains the order of the involved events, we have that $t'' = u1 \cdot u2 \cdot u3$, where

$$set(u1) = \chi'(t', \Gamma, c1),$$

$$set(u2) = \chi'(t, \Gamma, c2) \setminus \chi'(t', \Gamma, c1).$$

All events that are not involved with the synchronisation claims $c1$ and $c2$, are in $u3$.

Observe that $u1$ includes all events of θ that are involved with the claim of the run $c1$. As all events are unique, these are not part of $u2$. From the construction of the involved events set, we know that all involved events of role R are also in θ, because all other role instances are executing other roles (as indicated by Γ). This implies that there are no events of role R in the $u2$ segment at all: these are all in $u1$.

Now we have arrived at a contradiction. t'' is in the set $traces(P)$. The loop property combined with *NI-SYNCH* requires that for each role, there is an event after the first event of the claim role that occurs before the claim. For the run $c2$ all events are in $u2$ (including the start and the claim), but in this segment there is no event of role R. Thus, there can be no Γ for t'' such that $\chi(t'', \Gamma, c2)$ holds. This implies that *NI-SYNCH* does not hold for the protocol, which contradicts the assumptions.   □

Thus, we have established that LOOP is a sufficient condition to guarantee injectivity for protocols that satisfy *NI-SYNCH*.

Example 5.32 The *NSL* protocol satisfies non-injective synchronisation (Theorem 4.24) and it contains loops for both roles. Therefore, we can apply Theorem 5.31 and establish injective synchronisation for both roles.

5.6.3 Model Assumptions

Theorem 5.31 states that, for a large class of security protocol models including the model defined in Chap. 3, injectivity of authentication protocols is easy to verify, once synchronisation has been established. Until now, injectivity and authentication have been strongly connected. Our new results establish that it suffices to verify the non-injective variant of synchronisation. Verifying injectivity is a simple and separate task, which does not depend on any specific (data) model. Our result does not depend on all the details of our protocol model. Instead, as already mentioned, we have characterised a class of models in which Theorem 5.31 holds. This class contains nearly all models found in the literature, such as the Strand spaces model, Casper/FDR without time, and term rewrite systems [84, 107, 155], as well as many models that allow for non-linear (branching) protocol specifications. These models share the following properties:

(i) Multiple instances of the protocol are truly independent. They do not share variables, memory, or time.
(ii) The adversary has the ability to duplicate messages, as holds, for example, in the standard Dolev-Yao adversary model.

The question arises whether the theorem also holds in an adversary-less model. This is in fact the case, but of less interest, because injectivity always holds for synchronising or agreeing protocols when there is no adversary.

Automated verification of the LOOP property can be implemented easily. The algorithm is an instance of the reachability problem in a finite acyclic graph, and therefore has linear complexity.

Almost all correct authentication protocols in the literature satisfy the *NI-SYNCH* property as well as LOOP. It seems that LOOP is a necessary condition for injectivity, in particular for the Dolev-Yao adversary model. However, for peculiar adversary models, LOOP is not a necessary condition for injectivity. In the models where LOOP is also a necessary condition for injectivity, our results imply a minimum number of messages in a multi-party authentication protocol. The LOOP property guarantees injectivity for synchronising protocols. However, the example in Fig. 5.16 shows that LOOP does not suffice to guarantee injectivity. The protocol satisfies the loop property for the claim role, and the protocol satisfies non-injective agreement, but not injective agreement.

5.7 Further Features of the Scyther Tool

Data Agreement Besides the properties mentioned here, the Scyther tool [52, 55] supports non-injective agreement on data items, as defined by Lowe [108, 141]. This feature was used for the analysis, and subsequent repair, of the ISO/IEC 9798 standard for entity authentication [20].

Fig. 5.16 A unilateral agreement protocol, with LOOP, but not injective

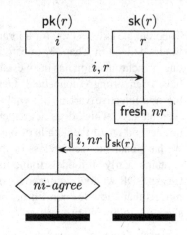

protocol LOOP **and agreement**

Adversary Models   Scyther has been extended with a large set of different adversary types, which have additional capabilities when compared to the Dolev-Yao adversary model [19]. These additional capabilities include learning the long-term keys of an agent and learning (parts of) the internal state of an agent, such as random values. Furthermore, for protocols that compute session keys, the adversary may be able to learn them. These capabilities enable the analysis of advanced security properties, such as *(weak) perfect forward secrecy*, resilience against *key compromise impersonation*, and many other properties. Supporting such properties makes Scyther directly applicable to the domain of *authenticated key exchange* protocols and their intended security properties [57]. Further details are described in [19].

Because of its support for several adversary models, Scyther is also able to compute so-called protocol security hierarchies. The underlying idea is that given a finite set of adversary models S and a set of protocols T, the Scyther tool can be used to determine which protocols are correct with respect to which adversary models. We write correct(P, s) to denote that all the claims of P hold with respect to adversary model s. Let $\leq_A$ denote a partial order on the adversary models in S. For example, one can define such a partial order on the basis of trace inclusion: for $s, s' \in S$,

$$ s \leq_A s' \iff \forall P \in Protocol : traces_s(P) \subseteq traces_{s'}(P), $$

where $traces_s(P)$ denotes the traces of the protocol P in the context of adversary model s.

Using the results of the analysis and the order on the adversary models, we can determine an order $\leq_{PSH}$ on the protocols in T. In particular, for $P, P' \in T$,

$$ P \leq_{PSH} P' \iff \forall s \in S : \big(\text{correct}(P, s) \Rightarrow \text{correct}(P', s)\big). $$

If $P \leq_{PSH} P'$, we say that P' is at least as strong as P, and we refer to this partial order as the security protocol hierarchy [18].

Applications   Besides the applications mentioned in this book, Scyther has also been used for the analysis of the Internet Key Exchange protocol IKE [58] and the analysis of many authenticated key exchange protocols [18, 19, 57].

5.8 Problems

5.1 Let P be a protocol and let $(E, \rightarrow)$ be a pattern of P. Prove that for all $tr \in traces(P, (E, \rightarrow))$ the following holds: $|tr| \geq |E \cap RunEvent|$.

5.2 Show that the pattern from Fig. 5.5 meets the pattern criteria of Definition 5.4 with respect to the NS protocol.

5.3 Give a formal definition of injective aliveness.

5.4 Prove that the i role of the protocol in Fig. 5.16 does not satisfy injective agreement.

5.5 Prove that the i role of the protocol in Fig. 5.16 does not satisfy non-injective synchronisation.

5.6 Reformulate Theorem 5.31 for a notion of injective aliveness and either prove it correct or find a counter example.

Chapter 6
Multi-protocol Attacks

Abstract We introduce the notion of multi-protocol attacks. Using the tool presented in the previous chapter, we analyse a large number of protocols. From the results we obtain two common patterns that occur in multi-protocol attacks.

In this chapter we apply some of the methodologies and tools developed in the previous chapters. We turn our attention to one of the assumptions underlying modern security protocol analysis, namely that the protocol under scrutiny is the only protocol that is executed in the system.

As indicated in the previous chapters, a number of successful formal methods and corresponding tools exist for the analysis of security protocols. These methods are generally limited to the verification of protocols that run in isolation. In other words, the formal models generally assume that there is only one protocol being executed over the network.

However, the assumption that a protocol is the only one that is executed over the untrusted network is often not realistic. In the case where multiple protocols are used over a shared untrusted network, the problem of verifying security properties becomes significantly harder. The reason for this is the fact that security properties are not compositional. It may happen that two protocols that are correct when run in isolation are vulnerable to new attacks when used over the same network.

An attack that necessarily involves more than one protocol is called a *multi-protocol attack*. The existence of such attacks was established first by Kelsey, Schneier and Wagner (see [97]). They showed that, for any given correct protocol, another correct protocol can be constructed, such that when these two protocols are executed over the same network, the adversary can use messages from the second protocol to mount an attack against the first protocol. The examples found in the literature involve protocols that were constructed especially for the purpose of breaking some particular protocol. Kelsey et al. coined this type of attack the "chosen protocol attack".

An interesting question is whether the same phenomenon occurs for combinations of existing protocols. The fact that it is possible to construct a protocol that induces a multi-protocol attack does not imply that all combinations of correct protocols are incorrect. It can be shown that if *all* protocols that use the same network and key infrastructure satisfy certain requirements, e.g., parts of messages of

C. Cremers, S. Mauw, *Operational Semantics and Verification of Security Protocols*, 107
Information Security and Cryptography, DOI 10.1007/978-3-540-78636-8_6,
© Springer-Verlag Berlin Heidelberg 2012

one protocol can never be mistaken for parts of messages of the other protocols, compositionality of the individual security properties is guaranteed. In that case, in order to prove correctness of the system it suffices to prove correctness of the protocols in isolation. Different formulations of sufficient conditions for compositionality have been established in the literature, e.g., [8, 90]. However, the standard protocols found in the literature do not meet these requirements, as many of these protocols have very similar messages. Thus the theoretical possibility of multi-protocol attacks remains.

Our modelling of security properties as claim events simplifies the analysis of multi-protocol attacks, as we can simply add roles to the protocol in order to analyse the claims in the context of multiple protocols. In line with the semantics, the tool can handle multi-protocol analysis in a straightforward manner by concatenating multiple protocol descriptions. Providing the tool with the concatenation of two protocol descriptions amounts to verification of their security properties when both protocols are executed over the same network. Using the tool, we verified the composition of all pairs from 38 protocols from the literature. The tests reveal a significant number of multi-protocol attacks.

We proceed by defining in Sect. 6.1 the notion of multi-protocol attacks, and we describe the experiments in Sect. 6.2. The results of the experiments are analysed in Sect. 6.3, and two practical attack scenarios are treated in Sect. 6.4. We briefly discuss some preventive measures in Sect. 6.5 and draw conclusions in Sect. 6.6.

6.1 Multi-protocol Attacks

In our semantics, there is no explicit notion of "a single protocol". A protocol is simply a collection of roles. If we take the union of two disjoint protocols, the result is still a protocol. Intuitively, we take "a single protocol" to mean a set of roles that are connected by means of the communication relation $-\!\!\!-\!\!\!\rightarrow$ from Definition 3.16. If we join two such protocols, not all roles will be connected. We say that such a set of role descriptions contains multiple protocols.

Definition 6.1 (Connected Roles) Let P be a protocol. We denote by $=\!\!-\!\!\!\rightarrow$ the symmetric, reflexive, and transitive closure of the communication relation $-\!\!\!-\!\!\!\rightarrow$. We say that two roles R and R' are *connected* if and only if

$$\exists e, e' : e \in P(R) \wedge e' \in P(R') \wedge e =\!\!-\!\!\!\rightarrow e'.$$

Definition 6.2 (Single/Multiple Protocols) Given a protocol specification P, the multiplicity of P is defined as the number of equivalence classes defined by the connected roles relation. If the multiplicity is equal to 1 we say that P contains a single protocol. If the multiplicity is more than 1, we say that P contains multiple protocols.

Table 6.1   List of protocols tested in a multi-protocol environment

Protocols	
Andrew Secure RPC-concrete	Otway-Rees
Andrew Secure RPC-BAN	SOPH
Andrew Secure RPC-LoweBAN	spliceAS-CJ
Bilateral Key Exchange (BKE)	spliceAS-HC
Boyd	spliceAS
CCITT 509 BAN 3	TMN
DenningSacco-Lowe	Wide Mouthed Frog Brutus
DenningSacco	Wide Mouthed Frog Lowe
Gong nonce	Wide Mouthed Frog
Gong nonce (b)	Woo Lam Pi-1
ISO/IEC 117702 13	Woo Lam Pi-2
Kao Chow	Woo Lam Pi-3
Kao Chow-2	Woo Lam Pi-f
Kao Chow-3	Woo Lam
KSL	Yahalom-BAN-Paulson-modified
NeedhamSchroeder-SK-amended	Yahalom-BAN-Paulson
NeedhamSchroeder-SK	Yahalom-BAN
NS3	Yahalom-Lowe
NSL3	Yahalom

All protocols shown up to this point are single protocols. There is only one equivalence class of connected roles. If we join the role specifications of two or more protocols with disjoint role sets, the result contains multiple protocols.

Definition 6.3 (Multi-protocol Attack)   Let P be a protocol description that contains a single protocol that contains a security claim γ. We say that there exists a multi-protocol attack on γ if and only if (1) there is no attack on γ in the context of P, and (2) there exists a protocol description MP that contains multiple protocols, among which is P, i.e.,

$$\forall R \in dom(P): \quad MP(R) = P(R),$$

such that there exists an attack on γ in the context of MP.

6.2   Experiments

In this section we describe a number of experiments to determine whether multi-protocol attacks can occur on existing protocols from the literature.

The set of protocols included in the test is shown in Table 6.1. The protocols were selected from the literature: the Clark and Jacob library in [44], the related SPORE library in [149], and the work on protocols for authentication and key establishment in [37] by Boyd and Mathuria. This resulted in a set of 38 protocols. For these experiments, three security properties were considered: secrecy and two forms of authentication, viz. non-injective agreement and non-injective synchronisation, as defined in Chap. 4.

In general, the computational costs of verifying properties in multi-protocol environments are exponential with respect to the number of protocols; see e.g., [77, 156]. Currently it is therefore infeasible to verify an environment with all these protocols in parallel. Instead, we choose to test all possible combinations of two protocols from this set. This method allows us to find multi-protocol attacks that involve two protocols. When such a test yields an attack, we verify automatically whether the attack requires multiple protocols, or can be mounted against a single protocol, in which case the attack is not a multi-protocol attack and is discarded.

The verification results also depend on the type of *matching* used, in particular, on whether or not so-called *type-flaw* attacks are possible. We explain this in more detail in the next section. All tests were conducted in three variants, once for a fully typed definition of match, once allowing for basic type flaws, and once untyped. This was achieved by varying the definition of the Match predicate as described in Sect. 3.3.2. In total, over 14,000 tests were performed to obtain these results.

6.3 Results

The tests reveal that there is a large number of multi-protocol attacks possible on the selected set of protocols. Out of the 38 protocols from the literature, 29 had security claims that are correct in isolation, but had attacks when put in parallel with another protocol from the set.

We provide a full overview of the discovered multi-protocol attacks in Table 6.2. In this table, the left-hand column lists all protocol claims for which we found multi-protocol attacks. The top row lists the protocol that was used to break the claim. For each combination of a claim of the left column and a protocol from the top row, there are three possibilities.

The first possibility is an empty cell, which denotes that no multi-protocol attack exists, i.e., we found no attack on the claim even in the presence of the protocol from the top row.

The other two possibilities are an open or closed dot (o or ●). These denote that a multi-protocol attack was found where the adversary uses the top row protocol to attack the claim. In particular, an open dot (o) denotes that the attack either involves a type flaw (basic type flaw or full type flaw) or requires a self-initiation scenario, i.e., Alice is able to start a session with herself as the intended partner. In contrast, a closed dot (●) denotes that there is a multi-protocol attack that does not require type flaws or self-initiation.

The table shows that the interaction between the various protocols is significant and not isolated to a few cases. However, many attacks found belong to the "re-

Table 6.2 Overview of protocol claims with multi-protocol attacks

Protocol	Claim	andrew-Concrete	andrew-LoweBan	boyd	denningSacco	denningSacco-Lowe	gongnonce	gongnonceb	isoiec11770213	kaochow	kaochow-2	kaochow-3	ksl	needhamschroedersk	needhamschroedersk-amend	otwayrees	soph	tmn	wmf	wmf-Lowe	woolam	woolamPi-1	woolamPi-2	woolamPi-3	woolamPi-f	yahalom	yahalom-BAN	yahalom-BAN-Paulson	yahalom-BAN-Paulson-mod	yahalom-Lowe
andrew-Ban	I Niagree																						o							
andrew-Ban	I Nisynch																						o							
andrew-Ban	I Secret(kir)																						o							
andrew-Concrete	R Secret(kir)																					o								
andrew-LoweBan	I Nisynch								o																					
andrew-LoweBan	R Nisynch																											o	o	o
andrew-LoweBan	R Secret(kir)																											o	o	o
boyd	I Secret(m(·))								o													o	o	o	o					
boyd	R Secret(m(·))								o													o	o	o	o					
denningSacco	I Niagree	●			●	o	o			o	o	o		o	o			o			o	o	o	●	o		o	o	o	o
denningSacco	I Secret(Kir)					o	o			o	o	o		o	o						o	o	o	●	o		o	o		o
denningSacco	R Niagree	●	o		●			o				o						o			o	o	o	o	o		o	o		o
denningSacco	R Secret(Kir)		o					o				o									o	o	o	o	o		o	o		o
denningSacco-Lowe	I Niagree	●			●		o	o		o	o	o		o	o						o	o	●	●	o		o	o		o
denningSacco-Lowe	I Secret(Kir)						o	o		o	o	o		o	o						o	o	●	●	o		o			o
denningSacco-Lowe	R Niagree	●	o		●			o				o									o	o	o	o	o		o	o		o
denningSacco-Lowe	R Secret(Kir)		o					o				o									o	o	o	o	o		o	o		o
gongnonce	I Secret(kr)																					o	o	o						
gongnonce	R Secret(ki)																					o	o	o						
gongnonceb	I Secret(ki)									o	o																			
gongnonceb	I Secret(kr)									o	o																			
gongnonceb	R Secret(ki)									o	o																			
gongnonceb	R Secret(kr)									o	o																			
isoiec11770213	I Secret(kir)															o						o	o							
isoiec11770213	R Secret(kir)																										o	o		o
kaochow	I Secret(kir)			o	o																o	o	o	o						
kaochow	R Secret(kir)			o	o				o											o	o	●	●	●	●	o		o	o	o
kaochow-2	I Secret(kir)																					o	●	●	●					
kaochow-2	R Secret(kir)						o															●	●	●	●					
kaochow-3	I Secret(kir)			o	o																	o	o	o						
kaochow-3	R Secret(kir)			o	o		o															●	●	●	●					
ksl	I Secret(Kir)																									o				
ksl	R Secret(Kir)																									o				
needhamschroedersk	I Nisynch	●											●																	
needhamschroedersk	R Nisynch	●											●									o	o				o		o	
needhamschroedersk	R Secret(Kir)																					o	o				o		o	
needhamschroedersk-amend	R Secret(Nr)																					o								
nsl3	I Secret(nr)																o													
nsl3	R Secret(nr)																o													
otwayrees	I Secret(Kir)								o													o	o							
otwayrees	R Secret(Kir)								o													o								
spliceAS	I Secret(N2)																	o												
spliceAS	R Secret(N2)																	o												
spliceAS-CJ	I Secret(N2)																●													
spliceAS-CJ	R Secret(N2)																●													
spliceAS-HC	I Secret(N2)																	o												
spliceAS-HC	R Secret(N2)																	o												
wmf	I Secret(Kir)				o	o																								
wmf	R Secret(Kir)				o	o			o												o	o	o	o						
wmf-Lowe	R Secret(Kir)			o					o												o	o	o	o	o	o		o		o
wmfbrutus	B Secret(kab)																						●	●				o	o	o
woolam	I Secret(Kir)				o	o			o											o		o	●	●				o		o
yahalom	I Secret(Kir)									o												o	o	o	●					
yahalom	R Secret(Kir)									o												o	o	o						
yahalom	S Secret(Nr)	o	o	o	o				o					o							o	o	o	●	●	o				
yahalom-BAN	I Secret(Kir)									o												o	o	●	●	o				
yahalom-BAN	R Secret(Kir)									o												o	o	●	●	o				
yahalom-BAN-Paulson	A Secret(kab)										o											o	o	●	●					
yahalom-BAN-Paulson	B Secret(kab)										o													o						
yahalom-BAN-Paulson-mod	A Secret(kab)										o											o	●	●	o					
yahalom-BAN-Paulson-mod	B Secret(kab)										o											o	●	●	o					
yahalom-Lowe	I Nisynch	●							o	o												o	o	●	●	o		●		●
yahalom-Lowe	I Secret(Kir)								o	o												o	o	●	●	o				
yahalom-Lowe	R Nisynch								o																			●		●
yahalom-Lowe	R Secret(Kir)								o																	o				

stricted" category denoted by the open dot (○), which makes them more unlikely to be exploited in practice.

The table shows that the simpler multi-protocol attacks (●) mainly occur due to two potential problems: the problem of protocol variants (or protocol updates) and the problem of protocols that can be used as encryption/decryption oracles with few restrictions.

With respect to the first potential problem, we observe that many attacks occur close to the diagonal of the table. These attacks exploit closely related versions of the target protocol. For example, the Denning-Sacco protocol can be attacked using Lowe's modified version of that protocol. Similarly, Lowe's variant of the Yahalom protocol can be attacked using either the original Yahalom protocol or the BAN/Paulson variant. The underlying reason is that the variants contain many similar messages, which gives rise to protocol update attacks, which we will discuss in Sect. 6.4.1.

With respect to the second potential problem, which encompasses protocols that can be used in an oracle-like fashion, we observe many attacks occurring in the columns labelled with Andrew-Concrete, SOPH, or Woo-Lam-Pi variants. These protocols contain simple challenge-response mechanisms which allow the adversary to either encrypt or decrypt a nonce of its choosing, without producing or requiring much structure in the encrypted message.

We further elaborate on the effect of the matching type on the presence of multi-protocol attacks. Observe that the three types of matching that were used in the test have a clear hierarchy. Any attack that occurs in the strict type model will also occur in the other two models. Similarly, any attack occurring in the model that allows for basic type flaws will also be an attack in the untyped model.

For multi-protocol attacks, however, there is no such inherent monotonicity. This is caused by the fact that the multi-protocol definition states that the property should be correct in the context of the single protocol. Consider for example the Otway-Rees protocol. For this protocol, the secrecy claims are true in the strict type model, so it may be the case that there exist multi-protocol attacks on these claims in the strict type model. For the untyped model, however, there exist type-flaw attacks on both these claims.

We discuss each of these three typing categories separately.

6.3.1 Strict Type Matching: No Type Flaws

We start off with the most restricted model, in which it is assumed that the agents can somehow check the type of the data they receive, and thus only accept terms of the correct type. For the protocols from the literature we found 27 two-protocol attacks. We found attacks violating authentication as well as secrecy requirements.

The vast majority of these attacks involve variants of the Woo-Lam Pi protocol described in [159]. These protocols contain a read/send pattern which can be used as a so-called encryption oracle, a protocol mechanism that allows an adversary to encrypt arbitrary values with some key. In this case arbitrary nonces can be encrypted

Table 6.3 Influence of matching predicate

Matching predicate	Number of attacks
No type flaws possible	27
Basic type flaws possible	69
All type flaws possible	307

with the symmetric key shared by an agent and the server. This enables many attacks on other protocols that involve this shared key.

The remainder of the attacks share a common pattern that we call *ambiguous authentication*, which will be explained in detail in Sect. 6.4.2.

6.3.2 Simple Type Matching: Basic Type Flaws Only

If we relax the typing constraints on messages, such that variables can contain any term that is not a tuple or an encryption, the number of attack possibilities increases dramatically. Attacks in this category are called basic type-flaw attacks. Specifically, many attacks become possible because (session) keys can be mistaken for nonces, which might enable the adversary to learn the session keys. This can also cause new authentication attacks. In these tests, 69 attacks were found using basic type-flaw mistakes.

6.3.3 Untyped Matching: All Type Flaws

With untyped matching, in which random values can now be mistaken for any tuple term or encrypted term, the number of possible message interferences is further increased. This opens up many new possibilities for protocol interference. We found 307 multi-protocol attacks based on all type flaws.

To conclude, we have summarised the influence of the strictness of the matching predicate (and thus the susceptibility to type-flaw attacks) in Table 6.3.

Although this was outside of the scope of the main tests, we also searched for and found examples of three-protocol attacks. For example, the Yahalom-Lowe claim of the secrecy of the received session key is correct in isolation, and is also correct in combination with any other protocol from the test, but can be violated in the presence of the Denning-Sacco shared key and Yahalom-BAN protocols if all type flaws are possible.

6.3.4 Attack Example

As an example of a basic type-flaw multi-protocol attack, we show an attack on the Woo-Lam mutual authentication protocol from [159], together with the Yahalom-

protocol Woo-Lam mutual authentication

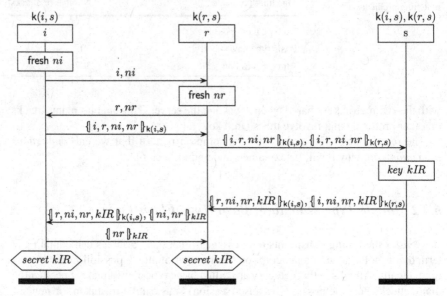

Fig. 6.1 The Woo and Lam mutual authentication protocol

Lowe protocol from [109]. The Woo-Lam mutual authentication protocol is shown in Fig. 6.1, and the Yahalom-Lowe protocol is shown in Fig. 6.2.

Both protocols have similar goals and preconditions. They use symmetric encryption and a trusted server to generate a fresh session key for authentication communication between two agents. They even operate in a similar way: the initiator i and responder r both create a nonce, which they send to the server. The server creates a new session key kIR, and distributes the key, combined with the nonces, back to i and r. They check the nonces, to confirm that the key is indeed fresh.

In Fig. 6.3 we show a multi-protocol attack on these protocols, exploiting a basic type flaw. This attack is possible if the agent cannot distinguish between a session key and a nonce, assuming that it has not encountered either before.

The attack proceeds as follows. An agent A starts the Woo-Lam protocol in the i role, wants to communicate with another instance of A, and sends a fresh nonce $ni^{\sharp 1}$. The adversary intercepts the nonce. The agent A starts a Yahalom-Lowe session in parallel, in the i role. A creates and sends a second nonce $ni^{\sharp 2}$. This is also intercepted by the adversary.

The adversary now sends the nonce $ni^{\sharp 2}$ to A in the Woo-Lam protocol, as if it were sent by a Woo-Lam responder role. The agent responds with a server request with the names of both agents and the nonces $\{\!|A, A, ni^{\sharp 1}, ni^{\sharp 2}|\!\}_{k(A,S)}$. This message is intercepted, concatenated with itself, and sent to the Woo-Lam server S. The server generates a fresh session key and sends back two (identical) messages, $\{\!|A, ni^{\sharp 1}, ni^{\sharp 2}, kIR^{\sharp 3}|\!\}_{k(A,S)}$. One of these is redirected to the Yahalom-Lowe i role. This role is expecting a message of the form $\{\!|A, \mathrm{Key}, ni^{\sharp 2}, \mathrm{Nonce}|\!\}_{k(A,S)}$, where

Fig. 6.2 Lowe's modified version of the Yahalom protocol

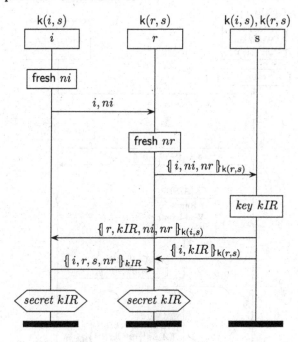

protocol Yahalom-Lowe

Key is a new key and Nonce is a nonce that it he has not encountered before. Thus, it cannot tell the difference between these terms. Because of type confusion, it accepts the message, under the assumption that $ni^{\#1}$ is the fresh session key, and that $kIR^{\#3}$ is the responder nonce. Thus, it encrypts the key using the nonce, sends $\{\!|A, A, ni^{\#2}, kIR^{\#3}|\!\}_{ni^{\#1}}$ and claims that $ni^{\#1}$ is secret. Because the adversary knows $ni^{\#1}$, this is clearly not the case. This is an attack on the Yahalom-Lowe i role. However, we can continue the attack. The adversary intercepts this last message. Because it knows $ni^{\#1}$, it can decrypt the message, and learns the key $kIR^{\#3}$. This enables him to create the last message that is expected by the Woo-Lam i role. This role then claims secrecy of $kIR^{\#3}$, which is also known to the adversary.

This basic type-flaw attack enables an adversary to break two protocols at the same time.

6.4 Attack Scenarios

The experiments have revealed that although many multi-protocol attacks can occur, their scope is limited if type-flaw attacks are prevented. But even if such attacks are excluded, two main scenarios remain in which multi-protocol attacks are likely to occur. We discuss the scenarios in this section, and we discuss some preventive measures in the next section.

trace Attack on Woo-Lam and Yahalom-Lowe

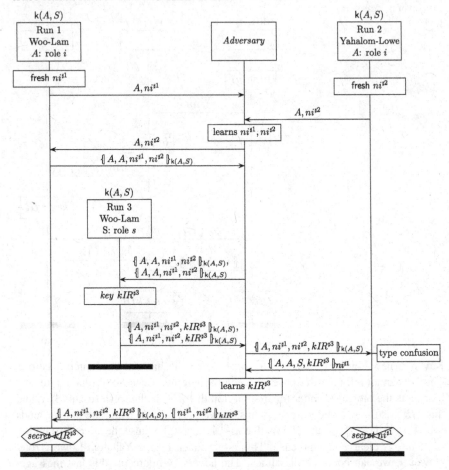

Fig. 6.3 A two-protocol attack

6.4.1 Protocol Updates

The experiments have shown that multi-protocol attacks are likely for protocols that use similar messages. We describe here a practical scenario where such similarities arise in practice.

It often occurs that security protocols are broken in some way, and that this is discovered after the protocol is deployed. The problem can be fixed by issuing a security update. This is effectively a second protocol that is very similar to the first one and shares the same key structure. Such a situation makes multi-protocol attacks very likely.

As an example, we show in Fig. 6.4 a broken authentication protocol. It is suscep-tible to a man-in-the-middle attack, similar to the one described in [106]. For our

Fig. 6.4
Needham-Schroeder: Broken

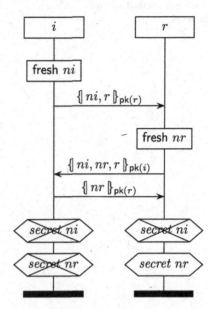

protocol Broken

purposes, we only assume this protocol has been distributed to and is being used by clients, and that we need to update it with a security fix. The easiest way to fix the protocol is to replace the name in the first message, resulting in the protocol in Fig. 6.5. This protocol is also known as the Needham-Schroeder-Lowe protocol as we have seen before, which can be proven to be correct when run in isolation.

If the broken protocol is updated in such a way that the old version of the protocol can still be run by some clients, then there is a multi-protocol attack possible on the new protocol, as shown in Fig. 6.6. In this attack, the adversary uses two instances of the old protocol (denoted by "Broken i" and "Broken r") to learn the value of a nonce $ni^{\#1}$. Then, an instance of the responder role of the new protocol ("NSL r") is completed using the initiator role of the old protocol. Thus, an agent completing the responder role of the new protocol claims that the nonces $ni^{\#1}$ and $nr^{\#3}$ are secret. The adversary can learn the nonce $ni^{\#1}$ by attacking the old protocol. He can then use messages from the old protocol to make a run of the new protocol accept this nonce. Hence the claim of the run of the new protocol that $ni^{\#1}$ is secret is false.

In this example, agent B executes one run of the old, broken protocol and one of the updated protocol. Because the protocol messages of these two runs are not interleaved it is not necessary for B to execute them at the same time. Therefore, the attack already applies during the transition from the old protocol to the new protocol.

The cause of the problems is that the messages of the updated protocol often closely resemble the messages of the original protocol. Because of this, many possibilities are available for an adversary to insert messages from one protocol at unforeseen places in the other protocol, which opens the door for multi-protocol attacks.

Fig. 6.5 The
Needham-Schroeder-Lowe
protocol

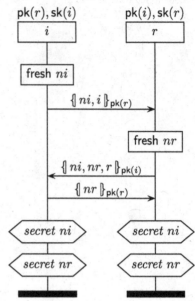

6.4.2 Ambiguous Authentication

We use the term "ambiguous authentication" to refer to two or more protocols that share a similar initial authentication phase. This can lead to ambiguity, where protocol mismatches occur between communicating partners.

In particular, authentication protocols are often used to set up session keys for other protocols. The resulting protocol then consists of the sequential execution of the authentication protocol and the protocol that uses the session key. Often the same protocols are used for authentication, which are then composed with different follow-up protocols. In such cases ambiguous authentication can occur: although the authentication protocol is correct in isolation, there can be a multi-protocol attack involving different follow-up protocols.

In the experiments, ambiguous authentication occurred frequently among similar protocols, as in protocol families, and among broken protocols and their fixed variants.

We give an example of this phenomenon. Consider the protocol pattern "Service 1", shown in Fig. 6.7. In this figure, there is a large rectangle denoted protocol P. For this rectangle, we can substitute any protocol that authenticates the partners and generates a fresh shared secret. (For example, we could insert here the Needham-Schroeder-Lowe protocol from Fig. 6.5, and take either of the nonces as the fresh secret ta.) This protocol P is then extended by a single message that sends the secret tb, encrypted with the fresh secret value from P, from the initiator i to the responder r. Assuming that P is correct, we can prove that the complete protocol for Service 1 as a single protocol is correct.

trace Protocol Update Attack

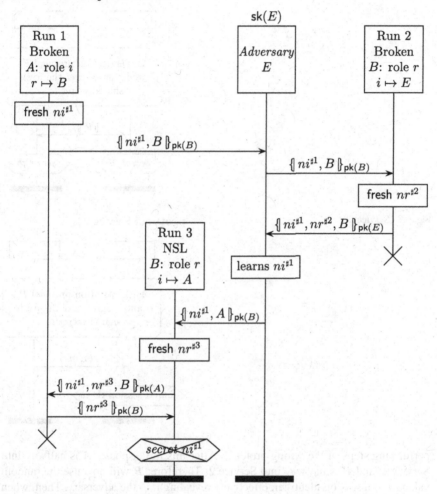

Fig. 6.6 NSL attack using the broken variant

Now we reuse the protocol P to implement another protocol referred to as the Service 2 protocol. See Fig. 6.8. Here we again use the same base protocol, but we extend it by sending a session identifier and some message m. For the session identifier, we use the fresh random value ta from the base protocol. (If we substitute Needham-Schroeder-Lowe for P, the protocol for Service 2 is correct in isolation.)

If we run Service 1 in parallel with Service 2, the combined protocols are broken. The attack is shown in Fig. 6.9. In this attack, the adversary simply reroutes the initial messages from Service 1 to Service 2. A executes its side of protocol steps of Service 1 as in the normal execution of the protocol. B on the other hand also executes its side correctly, but using the steps from Service 2. Because both services use the same initial sequence of messages, they cannot detect that the other agent is

Fig. 6.7 Service 1

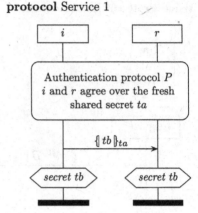

Fig. 6.8 Service 2

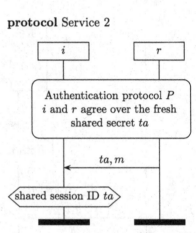

performing steps of the wrong protocol. After this initial phase, A is halfway into Service 1, and B is halfway into Service 2. Therefore, B will now use the random value ta as a session identifier, effectively revealing it to the adversary. Then, when A uses this value ta as a session key for the secret tb, the adversary can decrypt it. Thus the security claim of Service 1 is violated.

6.5 Preventing Multi-protocol Attacks

Analysis of the experiments has also indicated what is required to effectively prevent multi-protocol attacks.

Strict Type Detection   As noted in [92], it is possible to prevent type-flaw attacks by adding type information to the messages occurring in a protocol. This significantly reduces the number of possible attacks on a single security protocol, and is therefore advisable even when not considering a multi-protocol environment.

Fig. 6.9 Attack on combined   **trace** Ambiguous authentication attack
services 1 and 2

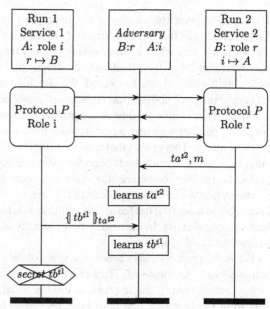

The experiments detailed here have shown that making sure no type-flaw attacks can occur prevents many multi-protocol attacks. In fact, 84 % of the attacks in the test set cannot occur in a setting without type-flaw errors. Ensuring that all messages are typed is therefore also a preventive measure for a large class of multi-protocol attacks. For details on preventing type-flaw attacks we refer the reader to [92, 103].

Tagging   Additionally, it is recommended to include unique constants (often called *tags*) in encryptions, signatures, and hashes occurring in each protocol. If these constants uniquely determine the protocol and the position of the crypto-graphic primitive within it, no confusion can occur among protocols that adhere to this convention. In this case, the resulting protocols also meet the disjoint encryption requirement from [90]. This approach is not only useful for preventing multi-protocol attacks, but also removes the risk of message confusion for protocols executed in isolation. This form of tagging was used to repair, e.g., the ISO/IEC 9798 standard for entity authentication [20].

Verification   In some cases it is undesirable to modify a set of protocols unless it can be proven that a vulnerability exists. In such cases verification of (multi-protocol) attacks is a realistic option. We have shown here that using suitable tools such as developed in this book it is possible to perform automated analyses of concurrent protocols.

6.6 Summary

The experiments in this chapter show that multi-protocol attacks on protocols from the literature exist in large numbers, and are realistic. The problem of multi-protocol attacks is not limited to a small subset of the protocols. Out of the 38 protocols, we found that 29 of them had security claims that are correct in isolation but for which multi-protocol attacks existed. We identified two common and realistic attack scenarios: protocol updates and ambiguous authentication.

Some of the security claims of the protocols are correct in isolation, and are even correct in parallel with any other protocol from the set, but are broken by a three-protocol attack. This proves that it is not sufficient to check for two-protocol attacks only. Here we have not investigated the existence of attacks involving four or more protocols, but we conjecture that there are many multi-protocol attacks on these protocols that we have not yet detected. Using formal models and tools has proven invaluable in assessing the feasibility of these attacks, and has allowed us to conduct such large-scale tests. In fact, many of the attacks are intricate and would be hard to find without tool support.

For multi-protocol environments, it is absolutely necessary to address the interaction between the protocols. This can only be done by looking at all the protocols in the environment: a single protocol can cause all others to break. Taking protocols from the literature that have been proven to be correct in isolation gives no guarantees at all for multi-protocol environments.

6.7 Problems

6.1 Construct a protocol P with two roles that uses long-term asymmetric keys. Design the protocol such that it achieves synchronisation for both of its roles, but at the same time causes at least one of the claims of the *NSL* protocol to be violated when *NSL* is executed in parallel with P.

Use the Scyther tool to verify that your protocol meets the above requirements.

6.2 Give reasons or sketch practical scenarios where it is beneficial for different protocols to use the same long-term keys.

6.3 Discuss why the use of password-based protocols can increase the possibility of multi-protocol attacks.

Chapter 7
Generalising NSL for Multi-party Authentication

Abstract We present a protocol for multi-party authentication for any number of parties, which generalises the Needham-Schroeder-Lowe protocol. We show that the protocol satisfies injective synchronisation of the communicating parties and secrecy of the generated nonces.

As a second application of the methods and tools developed in this book, we present a protocol for multi-party authentication for any number of parties, which generalises the Needham-Schroeder-Lowe protocol (*NSL*; see Sect. 4.5). We show that the protocol satisfies injective synchronisation of the communicating parties and secrecy of the generated nonces. For p parties, the protocol consists of $2p - 1$ messages, which we show to be the minimal number of messages required to achieve the desired security properties in the presence of a Dolev-Yao style adversary with compromised agents. The underlying communication structure of the generalised protocol can serve as the core of a range of authentication protocols.

The *NSL* protocol was designed for two parties that want to authenticate each other. This property is often referred to as bilateral authentication. In many settings, such as in modern e-commerce protocols, there are three or more parties that need to authenticate each other. In such settings we could naively instantiate multiple *NSL* protocols to mutually authenticate all partners. For p parties, such mutual authentication would require $\binom{p}{2} = (p \times (p-1))/2$ instantiations of the protocol, and three times as many messages. In practice, when multi-party authentication protocols are needed, protocol designers instead opt to design new protocols.

In this chapter we use our methodology to improve upon the approach that uses multiple instances of bilateral authentication, and to generalise the *NSL* protocol so as to obtain a multi-party authentication protocol with optimal message complexity (which turns out to be $2p - 1$ for p parties). We require that, in the setting of a Dolev-Yao adversary model with compromised agents, the generalised protocol satisfies at least the same security requirements as *NSL*. The situation where we have a family of protocols (one protocol for each p) is a bit different from that of a single protocol. Normally, a single protocol is proven correct in a context where we assume parallel sessions of it. For a protocol family, we assume that an agent may run sessions of different protocols of the family in parallel. This may increase the possibility of the

C. Cremers, S. Mauw, *Operational Semantics and Verification of Security Protocols*,
Information Security and Cryptography, DOI 10.1007/978-3-540-78636-8_7,
© Springer-Verlag Berlin Heidelberg 2012

protocol 4PNSL

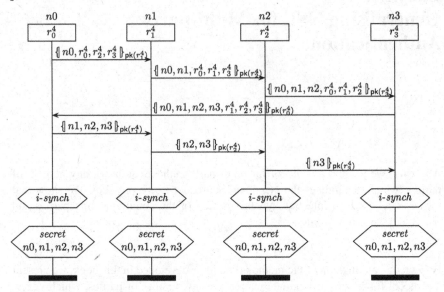

Fig. 7.1 Four-party generalised NSL

adversary attacking the protocol. Therefore, we require for each p that the protocol be correct, even if the agents run instances of it for different values of p in parallel.

We proceed as follows. In Sect. 7.1 we generalise the *NSL* protocol to any number of parties. In Sect. 7.2 we show the security properties that the protocol satisfies and sketch proofs of correctness and preconditions. Some variations of the pattern of the generalised protocol are presented in Sect. 7.3. In Sect. 7.4 we show that a previously generalised protocol for symmetric keys does not satisfy our authentication requirements.

7.1 A Multi-party Authentication Protocol

The basic idea behind the *NSL* protocol is that each agent has a challenge-response cycle to validate the other agent's identity, which is an instance of the loop principle from Sect. 5.6. These two challenge-response cycles are linked together by identifying the response of the second agent with its challenge.

Its generalisation follows the same line of thinking. Every agent conducts a challenge-response cycle with its neighbouring agent, while combining its own challenge with a response to another agent's challenge whenever possible. We first explain the four-party version of the protocol in some detail. Afterwards, we give the generalised specification for p parties.

The four-party protocol goes as follows (see Fig. 7.1). First, the initiating agent chooses which parties it wants to communicate with. It creates a new random value,

protocol MPNSL

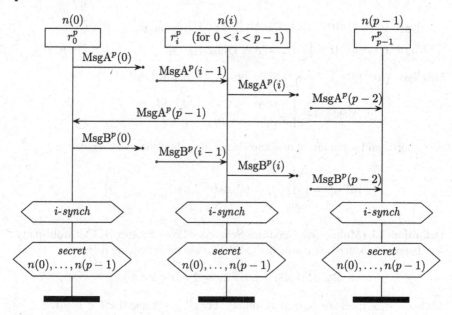

Fig. 7.2 Generalised NSL pattern

$n0$, and combines this with its name and the names of agents r_2^4 and r_3^4. The resulting message is encrypted with the public key of r_1^4, and sent to r_1^4. Upon receipt and decryption of this message, the second agent adds its own name and a fresh nonce, and removes the name of the next agent in the line from the message. This modified message is then encrypted with the public key of the next agent and sent along. This continues until each agent has added its nonce, upon which the message is sent back to the initiating agent. This agent checks whether the message contains the nonce it created earlier, and whether all agent names match. Then it can conclude that the other agents are authenticated. Next, in order to prove its own identity, it sends a message containing the other agents' nonces to r_1^4. The subsequent agents again check whether their own nonces are in the message, remove this nonce, and pass the resulting message on.

This four-party protocol can be generalised to any number of agents p. In Fig. 7.2 we schematically describe the communication structure of the protocol. The abstract messages are defined below. The function *next* determines the next role in the list of participants in a cyclic way. The ordered list $AL^p(x)$ contains all roles, except for role x. The protocol makes use of two types of messages. The first p messages are of type $MsgA^p$ and the final $p - 1$ messages are of type $MsgB^p$. The superscript denotes the parameter p of the protocol.

$$next^p(i) = r^p_{((i+1) \bmod p)},$$

$$\mathrm{AL}^p(x) = [r_0^p, r_1^p, \ldots, r_{p-1}^p] \setminus \{x\},$$

$$\mathrm{MsgA}^p(i) = \{\!| \, [n(0), \ldots, n(i)], \mathrm{AL}^p(next^p(i)) \,|\!\}_{\mathsf{pk}(next^p(i))} \quad 0 \leq i < p,$$

$$\mathrm{MsgB}^p(i) = \{\!| \, [n(i+1), \ldots, n(p-1)] \,|\!\}_{\mathsf{pk}(next^p(i))} \qquad\quad 0 \leq i < p-1.$$

Message i (for $0 \leq i < 2p-1$) of the protocol is defined by

$$\mathrm{Msg}^p(i) = \begin{cases} \mathrm{MsgA}^p(i) & \text{if } 0 \leq i < p, \\ \mathrm{MsgB}^p(i-p) & \text{if } p \leq i < 2p-1. \end{cases}$$

As a shorthand for the initial role knowledge of each of the roles, we define

$$\mathrm{MPK}_i^p = \bigcup_{j=0}^{p-1} r_j^p \cup \{ n(i), \mathsf{sk}(r_i^p), \mathsf{pk}(r_{(i+1) \bmod p}^p) \}.$$

Definition 7.1 (Multi-party Needham-Schroeder-Lowe Protocol) The Multi-party Needham-Schroeder-Lowe protocol (MPNSL) has the following roles:

$$dom(\mathrm{MPNSL}) = \{ r_i^p \mid p \geq 2 \wedge 0 \leq i < p \}.$$

The individual roles are defined as follows. For all $p \geq 2$ and $0 < i < p-1$,

$$
\begin{aligned}
\mathrm{MPNSL}(r_0^p) \; &= \bigl(\mathrm{MPK}_0^p, [&& \mathsf{send}_{(p,A,0)} && (r_0^p, & r_1^p, & \mathrm{MsgA}^p(0) & \;), \\
& && \mathsf{recv}_{(p,A,p-1)} && (r_{p-1}^p, & r_0^p, & \mathrm{MsgA}^p(p-1) & \;), \\
& && \mathsf{send}_{(p,B,0)} && (r_0^p, & r_1^p, & \mathrm{MsgB}^p(0) & \;)]\bigr), \\[4pt]
\mathrm{MPNSL}(r_i^p) \; &= \bigl(\mathrm{MPK}_i^p, [&& \mathsf{recv}_{(p,A,i-1)} && (r_{i-1}^p, & r_i^p, & \mathrm{MsgA}^p(i-1) & \;), \\
& && \mathsf{send}_{(p,A,i)} && (r_i^p, & r_{i+1}^p, & \mathrm{MsgA}^p(i) & \;), \\
& && \mathsf{recv}_{(p,B,i-1)} && (r_{i-1}^p, & r_i^p, & \mathrm{MsgB}^p(i-1) & \;), \\
& && \mathsf{send}_{(p,B,i)} && (r_i^p, & r_{i+1}^p, & \mathrm{MsgB}^p(i) & \;)]\bigr), \\[4pt]
\mathrm{MPNSL}(r_{p-1}^p) \; &= \bigl(\mathrm{MPK}_{p-1}^p, [&& \mathsf{recv}_{(p,A,p-2)} && (r_{p-2}^p, & r_{p-1}^p, & \mathrm{MsgA}^p(p-2) & \;), \\
& && \mathsf{send}_{(p,A,p-1)} && (r_{p-1}^p, & r_0^p, & \mathrm{MsgA}^p(p-1) & \;), \\
& && \mathsf{recv}_{(p,B,p-2)} && (r_{p-2}^p, & r_{p-1}^p, & \mathrm{MsgB}^p(p-2) & \;),]\bigr).
\end{aligned}
$$

We extend the above definition by adding secrecy claims for each nonce, as well as an injective-synchronisation claim, to the end of each role.

Note that in the above definition, the first (0) and last ($p-1$) roles are identical to the other roles ($0 < i < p-1$) except that respectively the first and last communication events are omitted.

The purpose of the protocol is to achieve authentication of all parties and secrecy of all nonces. We will make this precise in the next section, but first we make two observations. First, a run of role r_x^p receives messages $\mathrm{Msg}^p(x-1)$ (unless $x=0$) and $\mathrm{Msg}^p(x+p-1)$, and sends out messages $\mathrm{Msg}^p(x)$ and $\mathrm{Msg}^p(x+p)$ (unless $x=p$). Second, a nonce created by a run of role r_x^p occurs in p messages, viz. in the messages $\mathrm{Msg}^p(i)$, where $x \leq i < x+p$.

The protocol can be deployed in two main ways. First, it can be used in its most generic form, and have the initiating role choose the number of participants p. Agents receiving messages can deduce the chosen p at runtime from the number of agents in the first message, and their supposed role from the number of nonces in the message. Second, it can be restricted to a specific number of parties, e.g., to yield a four-party authentication protocol. For the analysis in the next section we use the generic form, where the number of parties p is not fixed. The properties that we prove will then automatically hold for specific instantiations as well, where only a certain number of parties are allowed.

7.2 Analysis

The multi-party authentication protocol described above satisfies secrecy of each of the nonces and authentication for all parties, in the form of injective synchronisation. Furthermore, it uses a minimal number of messages to achieve these properties.

7.2.1 Initial Observations

We start with some observations on how the generalised *NSL* protocol achieves authentication.

Our first observation is that the proposed multi-party authentication protocol performs an *all-or-none* authentication. This means that whenever an agent finishes its part of the protocol successfully, it will be sure that all other parties are authenticated to it. On the other hand, if any of the communication partners is not able to authenticate itself, the protocol does not terminate successfully. So, this protocol does not establish authentication of a subset of the selected agents.

A second observation concerning this protocol is the fact that authentication is only guaranteed if all agents indicated in the first message of the initiator are *honest*. This means that if any of the agents is compromised, the other agents in the list can be falsely authenticated. The reason is that, e.g., an agent performing role r_0^p only verifies the authenticity of the agent performing r_1^p. Verification of the identity of an agent performing role r_2^p is delegated to the agent performing role r_1^p, and so on. This chain of trust is essential to the design of an efficient multi-party authentication protocol. As is the case for the standard *NSL* protocol and most other authentication protocols, a session with a compromised partner does not have to satisfy authentication.

7.2.2 Proof of Correctness

We will show the proofs of the security claims of the generalised version of *NSL* in some detail. We start with a short proof outline.

Proof Outline   The proof exploits the fact that nonces generated by agents are initially secret, even if the adversary learns them later. Using the secrecy of the nonce up to the point where it is exposed, we establish a sequence of messages. If the nonce is exposed at the end of the sequence, we establish a contradiction, which is the basis of the secrecy proof. Once we know that the nonce of a role remains secret, we can use the same message sequence to establish synchronisation.

As a first step, we extend the notation AKN from Sect. 3.4 in Chap. 3. Given a trace $\alpha = [\alpha_1, \alpha_2, \ldots, \alpha_n]$, with $n = |\alpha|$, we define $AKN(\alpha, i)$ to denote the knowledge of the adversary after executing the first i events of α. Therefore, $AKN(\alpha, 0) = AKN_0$ is the initial adversary knowledge and, for $i \geq |\alpha|$, $AKN(\alpha, i) = AKN(\alpha)$ is the knowledge of the adversary after the execution of all events in the trace.

Recall that nonces created in runs are not known to the adversary initially. Even if the adversary learns them at some point, there is a point before which the nonce was not known.

Lemma 7.2 *Given a trace α, and a run term of the form $n^{\sharp\theta}$, we have that*

$$\exists j : AKN(\alpha, j) \vdash n^{\sharp\theta} \;\Rightarrow\; \exists i : AKN(\alpha, i) \nvdash n^{\sharp\theta} \;\wedge\; AKN(\alpha, i+1) \vdash n^{\sharp\theta}.$$

Proof We have that $AKN_0 \nvdash n^{\sharp\theta}$ by the definition of initial adversary knowledge. Furthermore, the adversary knowledge is nondecreasing according to the operational semantics rules from Table 3.4.   □

The previous result holds for all protocols in our model. In contrast, the following lemmas only hold for the MPNSL protocol, under the assumption of the *type matching* model from Definition 3.25. In this context, we can strengthen the previous lemma as follows. If a nonce created by some run is not known to the adversary, it cannot construct terms that have this nonce as a direct subterm himself. Thus, these messages must have been learned somewhere before.

Similarly to the *cont* function, we define a *message content* extraction function for send and receive run events.

Definition 7.3 (Message Contents of Event) The function

$$mcont: (RecvRunEv \cup SendRunEv) \to RunTerm$$

specifies the *message* contents of an event, i.e.,

$$mcont((inst, \mathsf{send}_\ell(R, R', m))) = \langle inst \rangle (m), \quad \text{and}$$

$$mcont((inst, \mathsf{recv}_\ell(R, R', m))) = \langle inst \rangle (m).$$

We use this definition here to establish the message contents of a received message before establishing the actual sender.

Lemma 7.4 *Let α be a trace of the MPNSL protocol, let $n^{\sharp\theta}$, m and k be run terms, such that $n^{\sharp\theta} \in unpair(m)$, and let i be an index $(1 \leq i \leq |\alpha|)$. Then we have*

$$\big(AKN(\alpha, i) \nvdash n^{\sharp\theta} \wedge \alpha_i \in RecvRunEv \wedge mcont(\alpha_i) = \{\!|\,m\,|\!\}_k\big) \Rightarrow$$

$$\big(\exists j : j < i \wedge \alpha_j \in SendRunEv \wedge mcont(\alpha_i) = mcont(\alpha_j)\big).$$

Proof First observe that the content of all messages of the MPNSL protocol are of the form $\{\!|\,m\,|\!\}_k$. Because α_i is a receive event, we conclude from the *recv* rule of the operational semantics that $AKN(\alpha, i) \vdash \{\!|\,m\,|\!\}_k$. Looking at the components of this term, we find that because $AKN(\alpha, i) \nvdash n^{\sharp\theta}$ and $n^{\sharp\theta} \in unpair(m)$, it must be the case that $AKN(\alpha, i) \nvdash m$. As the definition of the initial adversary knowledge (Definition 3.33) excludes run-local subterms, we conclude that $\{\!|\,m\,|\!\}_k$ cannot be in the initial adversary knowledge, because m contains $n^{\sharp\theta}$. Thus, for $\{\!|\,m\,|\!\}_k$ to be in the adversary knowledge, while $AKN(\alpha, i) \nvdash m$, it must be a subterm of a term that was previously sent. We identify this send event with α_j. We investigate the protocol send events, and observe that variables may not be instantiated with encryptions. This implies that $mcont(\alpha_j) = \{\!|\,m\,|\!\}_k$. □

Based on Lemma 7.4 one can establish the following property:

Lemma 7.5 *Let α be a trace of the MPNSL protocol, and let $n^{\sharp\theta}$ be an instantiated fresh value. If we have*

$$AKN(\alpha, i-1) \nvdash n^{\sharp\theta} \wedge \alpha_i \in SendRunEv \wedge n^{\sharp\theta} \sqsubseteq mcont(\alpha_i) \wedge runidof(\alpha_i) \neq \theta,$$

then we have

$$\exists i'', i' : i'' < i' < i \wedge runidof(\alpha_{i'}) = runidof(\alpha_i). \wedge$$

$$\alpha_{i''} \in SendRunEv \wedge n^{\sharp\theta} \sqsubseteq mcont(\alpha_{i''}) \wedge$$

$$\alpha_{i'} \in RecvRunEv \wedge mcont(\alpha_{i''}) = mcont(\alpha_{i'}).$$

Proof Given that $runidof(\alpha_i) \neq \theta$, the run to which α_i belongs is not the run that created the nonce. Thus, there must be a variable V of this run that is instantiated with the nonce. Variables are assigned only at receive events, and thus the run $runidof(\alpha_i)$ must have a preceding receive event $\alpha_{i'}$ of which the nonce is a subterm. By inspection of the protocol messages, it follows that this receive event is uniquely defined. Based on this event and the fact that the nonce is not known by the adversary, we find from Lemma 7.4 that there must be a previous send event with identical contents. □

Intuitively, the lemma states that if an agent sends out a nonce generated in a run (which can therefore not be part of AKN_0), then it is either its own nonce or it is one that it learned before from the send of some other agent.

The previous lemma gives us a preceding run for a message that is sent. If we repeatedly apply this lemma to a similar situation where a nonce is received, we can establish a sequence of events that must have occurred before a nonce is received. This is expressed by the next lemma.

Lemma 7.6 *Let α be a trace of the MPNSL protocol, and θ be the identifier of a run executing a role in which a nonce $n^{\sharp\theta}$ was created. If we have*

$$AKN(\alpha, i) \nvdash n^{\sharp\theta} \wedge \alpha_i \in RecvRunEv \wedge n^{\sharp\theta} \sqsubseteq mcont(\alpha_i) \wedge runidof(\alpha_i) \neq \theta,$$

then there exists a non-empty finite sequence of send events $\beta = [\beta_1, \beta_2, \ldots, \beta_m]$, such that the events in β are a subset of the events in α, and

$$runidof(\beta_1) = \theta \wedge mcont(\beta_m) = mcont(\alpha_i) \wedge$$

$$\left(\forall k : 1 \le k \le m : \beta_k \in SendRunEv \wedge \exists j, j' :' j < j < i \wedge \beta_k = \alpha'_j \wedge \right.$$

$$\alpha_j \in RecvRunEv \wedge n^{\sharp\theta} \sqsubseteq cont(\beta_k) \wedge cont(\beta_k) = cont(\alpha_j) \wedge$$

$$\left. \left(k < m \Rightarrow runidof(\alpha_j) = runidof(\beta_{k+1}) \right) \right).$$

Proof This lemma is the result of repeated application of the previous lemma. Note that the last conjunct expresses that if the nonce is received by a certain run, it is sent out later by that same run, unless it is the final receive event (expressed by $k = m$).   □

The resulting sequence of events is a chain of send events that include the nonce, where each sent message is received by the run of the next send. This lemma is used to trace the path of the nonce from its creator to a recipient of a message with it, as long as the nonce is not known to the adversary. In other words, β represents a subset of send events of α through which the nonce $n^{\sharp\theta}$ has passed before having reached α_i.

One can derive additional information from the sequence of events β as established by Lemma 7.6. Given a send event e, the type of message is either A or B, and is denoted as mtype(e). Type A contains agent names and nonces, whereas type B contains only nonces.

Lemma 7.7 *Assume the nonce $n^{\sharp\theta}$ was generated in the run θ that is executing role r_i^p, for some p and some i.*

Given a sequence of run events β established by application of Lemma 7.6 under the assumption the adversary does not know the nonce (yet), we have that there exists an index k, where $1 \le k \le |\beta|$, and a q such that

$$(k < |\beta| \Rightarrow role(\beta_{k+1}) = r_0^q) \wedge \forall 1 \le n \le |\beta| : mtype(\beta_n) = \begin{cases} A & if \ n \le k, \\ B & if \ n > k. \end{cases}$$

Proof This lemma follows from the protocol rules. When a run creates a nonce, it is sent out first as part of a message of type A. Messages of type A contain agent names, whereas messages of type B do not. The run that receives such a message sends it out again within a type A message (containing agent names), unless it is executing role r_0^q for some q, in which case it sends out the nonce within a type B message, without agent names. After receiving a message without agent names (type B), runs only send out type B messages. $\square$

In the lemma, the function of k is to point at the last message of type A, after which only messages of type B follow. Clearly, if $k = |\beta|$, there are only messages of type A. The first message of type B after k is executed by an agent in run r_0^p that sends out a type B message after receiving the type A message.

From the operational semantics it follows that if (θ, ρ, σ) occurs as an instantiation, then ρ is completely determined by θ. Given a context with instantiation (θ, ρ, σ), we define the function $\varrho()$ that maps a run identifier to its corresponding role-agent assignment, so $\varrho(\theta) = \rho$. Informally, this denotes the intended communication partners of the run.

This allows us to draw some further conclusions. Because the messages in the sequence β are received as they were sent, and because the messages up to k include a list of agents, we deduce:

- The runs executing the events $\beta_0, \ldots, \beta_k$ have the same role-number parameter q (the number of agents in the messages plus 1) and each run has the same role-agent assignment ρ.
- Given the role-number parameter q and the number of nonces in a message, we can uniquely determine the role in which a message occurs.

This leads to the following result.

Lemma 7.8 *Given a sequence β resulting from applying Lemma 7.6 for a nonce created in a run θ executing role r_x^q, and an index k resulting from Lemma 7.7, we have*

$$(k < |\beta| \Rightarrow role(\beta_{k+1}) = r_0^p) \wedge$$

$$\forall 1 \le n \le k : \varrho(runidof(\beta_n)) = \varrho(\theta) \wedge role(\beta_n) = r_{x+n-1}^q.$$

Proof All messages of type A explicitly contain the agent names, except for the name of the agent whom the message is for, which is encoded in the public key that is used. The number of agents defines the parameter q for both the send and receive events and, combined with the number of nonces, uniquely defines the role of which the send and receive events must be a part. $\square$

For all previous lemmas we required as a precondition that some nonce be secret. In order to identify the point up to which a given nonce is secret, we prove the following lemma:

Lemma 7.9 *Let α be a trace of the MPNSL protocol, let $n^{\sharp\theta}$ be a nonce that was created by a run θ, and let k be a trace index. Then we have*

$$AKN(\alpha, k) \vdash n^{\sharp\theta} \Rightarrow (\exists j : 1 \le j < k \wedge$$

$$AKN(\alpha, j-1) \nvdash n^{\sharp\theta} \wedge AKN(\alpha, j) \vdash n^{\sharp\theta} \wedge \alpha_j \in SendRunEv \wedge$$

$$ran(\varrho(runidof(\alpha_j))) \nsubseteq Agent_H \wedge n^{\sharp\theta} \sqsubseteq cont(\alpha_j)).$$

Proof Because the nonce is not known initially to the adversary, there must be a first point at which it is learned. This point is referred to by index j. From the semantics we have that α_j must be a send event.

Observe that for the MPNSL protocol, the initial adversary knowledge only contains the long-term private keys of the compromised agents. All messages that are sent by a run θ' are encrypted with public keys of agents from the set $ran(\varrho(\theta'))$, and the long-term private keys are not included in any sent messages. The adversary therefore has no means to learn any additional long-term private keys. Thus, from the inference rules we find that the adversary knowledge can only derive the contents of such a message if a run communicates with compromised agents. Because the protocol does not involve messages encrypted with keys other than long-term public keys, the nonce must be learned directly from the sent message and hence must occur as a subterm.   □

7.2.3 Secrecy of Nonces Created in Role r_0^p

Based on the previous lemmas we can prove that nonces generated in a run that performs role r_0^p (for some p), and tries to communicate with honest agents only, are kept secret.

Lemma 7.10 *Let α be a trace of the MPNSL protocol and let $n^{\sharp\theta}$ be a nonce created by a run θ in role r_0^p. Then we have that*

$$ran(\varrho(\theta)) \subseteq Agent_H \Rightarrow \forall i : AKN(\alpha, i) \nvdash n^{\sharp\theta}.$$

Proof We prove this by contradiction. We assume the generated nonce is learned by the adversary, and establish a contradiction, from which we conclude that the nonce cannot be learned by the adversary.

Let α be a trace in which a nonce $n^{\sharp\theta}$ was generated in a run θ executing role r_0^p. Assume that this run tries to communicate with honest agents only, so $ran(\varrho(\theta)) \subseteq Agent_H$. Further, assume that the nonce is learned by the adversary at some point. We apply Lemma 7.9 to find an event α_j of a run $\theta' = runidof(\alpha_j)$ where the nonce is first learned by the adversary. Thus we have $AKN(\alpha, j-1) \nvdash n^{\sharp\theta}$ and $AKN(\alpha, j) \vdash n^{\sharp\theta}$. Note that $\theta \neq \theta'$: The nonce could not have been created in run θ' because that would imply that θ' only communicates with honest agents, and hence only sends out messages encrypted with the public keys of honest agents, contradicting the assumption that the nonce is first learned after α_j. We apply Lemmas 7.6 and 7.7 to yield a sequence of events β and an index k, such that messages in β up to k are of type A, and all messages after k are of type B.

   We split cases based on the type of message of the send event at α_j. We distinguish two cases, and show that both lead to a contradiction.

- *The message sent at α_j is of type A.* Then we have that $j \leq k$, and from Lemma 7.8 we conclude $\varrho(\theta') = \varrho(\theta)$. Because θ communicates with honest agents only, and θ' does not, we arrive at a contradiction.
- *The message sent at α_j is of type B.* Then the message does not contain agent names and $j > k$, and therefore we cannot immediately draw conclusions regarding the honesty of the involved agents. Because we know $n^{\sharp\theta}$ was produced in the run θ, β_1 must be executed in this run. Connecting the type A messages in a backwards fashion, we find that all runs executing the events β_i for $i \leq k$ have the same choice of the role parameter p and agree on all agent names: therefore they are also all honest. Furthermore, because θ performs role r_0^p, we can conclude that the first message contains only the nonce of θ, and each subsequent run adds its own nonce as specified by the protocol, until it can only be accepted again by run θ, and hence $k = p - 1$, and we have that for all $1 \leq i \leq k$, $role(\beta_i) = r_{i-1}^p$. Revisiting the protocol description, it is clear that the final message sent in this sequence can only be received by θ, which does not include its nonce in the next message that it sends (which is of type B). This contradicts the assumption that the next message, β_{k+1}, is of type B and contains the nonce.   □

7.2.4   Non-injective Synchronisation of Role r0

Given that the secrecy of nonces generated by role r_0^p holds, the following is straightforward:

Lemma 7.11 *Non-injective synchronisation holds for role r_0^p.*

Proof We only give a sketch of the proof. Given a trace α with a run θ executing role r_0^p, we have that the nonce $n^{\sharp\theta}$ generated by this run is secret on the basis of Lemma 7.10. Thus, if the agent completes its run, there must have been two indices j and i ($j < i$) such that α_j is an instantiation of $\mathsf{send}_{(p,A,0)}(r_0^p, r_1^p, \mathrm{MsgA}^p(0))$ and α_i is an instantiation of $\mathsf{recv}_{(p,A,p-1)}(r_p^p - 1, r_0^p, \mathrm{MsgA}^p(p-1))$. If we use Lemmas 7.6 and 7.7 we find that the events in the sequence β are exactly the events that are required to exist for the synchronisation of the role r_0^p. The messages of these events are received exactly as they were sent, which is required for synchronisation. This leaves us with only one proof obligation. We have to show that the sequence β contains all the messages of type A, in the right order, after the start of run θ, and before the end of run θ. This follows directly from the role assignment in Lemma 7.8.   □

7.2.5 Secrecy of Nonces Created in Role r_x^p for $x > 0$

Lemma 7.12 *Given a trace α and a nonce $n^{\sharp\theta}$ created by a run θ executing role r_x^p with $x > 0$, we have that*

$$ran(\varrho(\theta)) \subseteq Agent_H \Rightarrow \forall i : AKN(\alpha, i) \nvdash n^{\sharp\theta}.$$

Proof Proof by contradiction, similar to that of Lemma 7.10.   □

Theorem 7.13 (Secrecy of Generated Nonces) *For the MPNSL protocol, we have that all nonces created in runs θ for which we have $ran(\varrho(\theta)) \subseteq Agent_H$ are secret.*

Proof A direct result of Lemmas 7.10 and 7.12.   □

7.2.6 Non-injective Synchronisation of Role r_x^p for $x > 0$

For non-injective synchronisation of role r_x^p for $x > 0$, we not only have to prove that all messages of type A have occurred as expected, but also have all messages of type B. Further, we have to prove that for each role r_y^p there must be a single run that sends and receives the actual messages.

Lemma 7.14 *Non-injective synchronisation holds for role r_x^p, where $x > 0$.*

Proof Based on the secrecy of the nonce generated in such a role, we determine an index k and a sequence β that precedes the last receive event of the role, with $role(\beta_0) = r_x^p$. Because the sequence must include an event of role r_0^p, for which non-injective synchronisation holds, we merge the sequences for both (as in the previous lemma). This gives us a complete sequence of send and receive events that exactly meet the requirements for non-injective synchronisation. The messages of these events are received exactly as they were sent. The requirement of the existence of all messages of type A follows from Lemma 7.8, which allows us to conclude that there is a run for each role in the protocol. Furthermore, the nonce of each of these runs is present in the message sent at α_k. If we examine the protocol rules, we see that the message of type B is only accepted by runs whose own nonce is contained in the message. Therefore we have that the run executing role r_1^p must be equal to $runidof(\alpha_{k+1})$, and that the receive event must be labelled with $(p, B, 0)$. Similarly, we establish that the correct messages have been consistently received and sent by the runs that created the nonces. Thus all conditions for non-injective synchronisation are met.   □

Theorem 7.15 (Non-injective Synchronisation) *For the MPNSL protocol, we have that for all runs θ with $ran(\varrho(\theta)) \subseteq Agent_H$, non-injective synchronisation holds.*

Proof A direct result of Lemmas 7.11 and 7.14. □

The synchronisation property implies that the received values are authenticated.

Theorem 7.16 (Secrecy of the Contents of Nonce Variables) *Let θ be a run in a trace of the MPNSL protocol, such that $ran(\varrho(\theta)) \subseteq Agent_H$. Then we have that all nonce variables in run θ are instantiated with nonces that are secret.*

Proof Based on Theorem 7.15, we obtain that the nonce variables of run θ must be instantiated with nonces that have been created in some run θ' with $\varrho(\theta) = \varrho(\theta')$. Hence we can use Theorem 7.13 to establish secrecy. □

7.2.7 Injective Synchronisation of All Roles

In Chap. 4 we formalised the notion of injectivity and proved that for synchronising protocols, inspecting them at a syntactic level suffices for concluding injectivity. This syntactic criterion, the *loop-property*, clearly holds for all roles of the MPNSL protocol. Therefore, the synchronisation proof presented above implies injective synchronisation as well.

Theorem 7.17 (Injective Synchronisation) *For the MPNSL protocol, we have that for all runs θ with $ran(\varrho(\theta)) \subseteq Agent_H$, injective synchronisation holds.*

Proof Follows from Theorem 5.31 and Theorem 7.15. □

7.2.8 Type-Flaw Attacks

We have assumed that type-flaw attacks are not possible, i.e., agents can verify whether an incoming message is correctly typed. There are several reasons for doing this.

Without this assumption, there are type-flaw attacks on the MPNSL protocol. This is not restricted to interactions between roles with the same role number parameter p. There are also multi-protocol type-flaw attacks that involve instances of roles with different choices of p, similar to the multi-protocol attacks described in Chap. 6. Thus, ensuring correct typing is crucial for the MPNSL protocol. Solutions for preventing type-flaw attacks using type information are examined in detail in [92]. Such type information can be easily added to each message, but a simple tagging scheme will also suffice. If we add a tuple (p, i) to each message $Msg^p(i)$ inside the encryption, where p is the number of participants for the protocol instance, and i is the message number, the protocol becomes robust against type-flaw attacks and multi-protocol attacks that include other instances of itself. In the correctness proofs above, we used the fact that the tag could be derived from the type. If we explicitly add such a tag, the proofs work in the same way for untyped models, except that the tag is now explicit instead of being derived from the type.

Note that the type-flaw attacks are not due to the specific ordering of the nonces and agent names within the messages. In particular, if one reverses the order of the agent or the nonce list, or interleaves the lists, there also exist type-flaw attacks on the resulting protocol family for some choice of p.

7.2.9 Message Minimality

As discussed in Sect. 5.6.1, the loop property is instrumental to achieving injectivity. Although other options exist, such as fine-grained time stamps or incremental counters from a large domain, the challenge-response pattern provides a clear guarantee of the injectivity of the authentication. Phrased in terms of such challenge-response behaviour, we can say that in order to achieve injective synchronisation, each role must send a challenge that is replied to by all other roles.

From this requirement we can easily derive the minimal number of messages to achieve injective synchronisation using challenge-response. Consider the first message sent by some role r_x^p, and call it m. In order to achieve a loop to all other roles after this first message, every role will have to send at least one message after m. Including message m, this will yield at least p messages. Next we observe that every role must take part in the protocol, and we consider the first message sent by each of the roles. If we take r_x^p to be the last of the p roles that becomes active in the protocol, it must be the case that before r_x^p sends its first message, at least $p - 1$ messages have been sent. Adding this to the p messages that must have been sent after that message yields a lower bound of $2p - 1$ messages.

7.3 Variations on the Pattern

The communication structure from Fig. 7.2 can be instantiated in several different ways to obtain authentication protocols satisfying different requirements. In this section we list some of the more interesting possibilities.

Generalised Bilateral Key Exchange First, we observe that the nonces generated in the protocol are random and unknown to the adversary, which makes them suitable keys for symmetric encryption. Furthermore, if we examine the proofs, the authentication of the messages is derived from the encryption of the messages only of type A, not of type B. As with the Bilateral Key Exchange protocol (BKE) described in [44], we can opt to replace the asymmetric encryption for the messages of type B by symmetric encryption with the nonce of the recipient. We can then omit

protocol 4PBKE

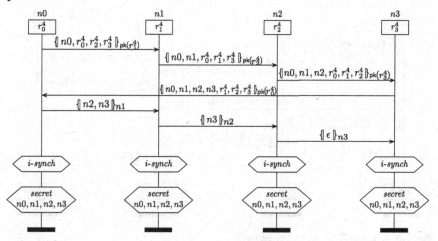

Fig. 7.3 Four-party BKE protocol

this nonce from the list. We use ϵ to denote a constant representing the empty list. This yields the following message definitions. Figure 7.3 illustrates the four-party BKE protocol.

$$\mathrm{MsgA}^P(i) = \{\!| \, [n(0), \ldots, n(i)], \mathrm{AL}^P(next^P(i)) \, |\!\}_{\mathsf{pk}(next^P(i))},$$

$$\mathrm{MsgB}^P(i) = \begin{cases} \{\!| \, [n(i+2), \ldots, n(p-1)] \, |\!\}_{n(i+1)} & \text{if } i < p-1, \\ \{\!| \, \epsilon \, |\!\}_{n(i+1)} & \text{if } i = p-1. \end{cases}$$

Using Secret Keys   If secrecy of the nonces is not required, we can use the secret key of the sender of a message for encryption, instead of the public key of the receiver. This gives the following protocol.

$$\mathrm{MsgA}^P(i) = \{\!| \, [n(0), \ldots, n(i)], \mathrm{AL}^P(ri) \, |\!\}_{\mathsf{sk}(r_i^P)},$$

$$\mathrm{MsgB}^P(i) = \{\!| \, [n(i+1), \ldots, n(p-1)], \mathrm{AL}^P(ri) \, |\!\}_{\mathsf{sk}(r_i^P)}.$$

Figure 7.4 illustrates the four-party version of this protocol. Although this protocol is minimal in the number of messages, it is not minimal in the complexity of the messages. For instance, in the first message of role r_0^4, we can take the role names outside the encryption operator.

Rearranging Message Contents   In the proofs of correctness, we have used some (but not all) information that distinguishes the messages in the protocol. In particular, we used:

protocol 4PNSLsk

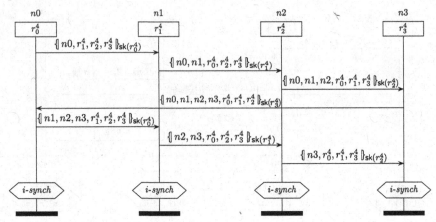

Fig. 7.4 Four-party NSL secret-key protocol

- *The ordered agent list* AL. We used this to derive the parameter p from an incoming message. Further, the order in the list is required to be able to determine that the agent list of the sender is identical to the agent list of the recipient.
- *The list of nonces.* We used the number of nonces to derive the role an agent is supposed to assume (given p).

A direct consequence of this is that the exact order of the agent list and nonce list is not relevant. We could redefine messages of type A so as to start with a reversed list of roles, followed by the list of nonces.

As a second observation, we note that besides depending on the distinct type of each message, the proof did not depend on the fact that there is no other content inside the encryption besides nonces and agent names. Thus, we can add any payload inside the encryption, as long as we ensure that it cannot be confused with an agent term or a nonce.

This opens up several possibilities for establishing keys between pairs of agents inside of the generalised *NSL* protocol. Next, we discuss one such option.

Key Agreement Protocols   In the field of cryptographic protocols many so-called group key agreement protocols have been developed. Although these have different goals from the protocol mentioned here, we see some possibility of using the underlying structure of the developed protocols for these purposes.

The generalised *NSL* protocol presented here can be turned into a naive group key agreement protocol by deriving a session key using a hash function over all the nonces, e.g., $h(n(0)\ldots n(p-1))$. This would constitute a fresh authenticated session key, which is shared by all the participants.

protocol 3PBNV1

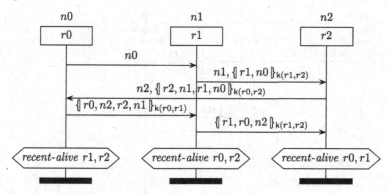

Fig. 7.5 BNV Protocol 1, three-party version

7.4 Weaker Multi-party Authentication Protocols

In this section we show one of the two multi-party authentication protocols designed by Buttyán, Nagy and Vajda [40] that use symmetric encryption. Their notion of authentication corresponds to our notion of *recent aliveness* as defined in Sect. 4.3.1. From Definition 1 in the paper [40]:

> We say that A authenticated B if there exists a bounded time interval I in the local time of A such that A is convinced that B was alive (i.e., sent some messages) in I.

The protocol is shown in Fig. 7.5. We write $k(r0, r1)$ to denote the key shared by the agent in role $r0$ and the agent in role $r1$. Recent aliveness is established by a challenge-response loop, and the authors make sure no reflection attack (which can arise from using symmetric keys) is possible.

However, the protocol does not satisfy agreement or synchronisation. In Fig. 7.6, we show that for three parties already the protocol does not satisfy agreement. The attack involves three runs. The first run is of agent A executing role $r0$. This agent wants to authenticate B and C, so in the first run B and C correspond to roles $r1$ and $r2$, respectively. In the second run, agent B executes role $r1$. In conflict with A's role assignment, B executes the protocol with some agent D for $r0$. The third run is an execution of role $r2$ by agent C, having the same role/agent correspondence as agent A.

The attack proceeds as follows. Agent A sends the first message to B, but the adversary modifies it in such a way that it seems to originate from D. In the figure, this is expressed by extending the contents of the first message with the identities of the intended or observed sender and receiver. B accepts this message and gives the expected reply to C. Because the first component of this message is not cryptographically protected, the adversary changes the nonce to the arbitrary value X. Next, agent C replies with a message to A. Again, the first component of the message is modified by the adversary to a random value Y. The resulting message corresponds to the message expected by A, so A decides that the protocol has successfully finished and, thus, that agreement with all communication partners is satisfied. Clearly,

trace 3PBNV1-attack

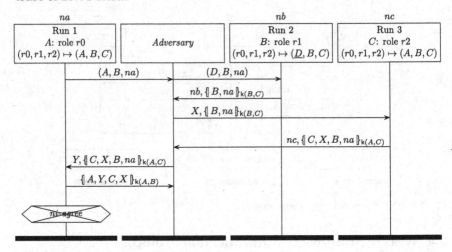

Fig. 7.6 Attack on BNV Protocol 1, three-party version

agreement does not hold because the agents do not agree on the nonces nb and nc and, moreover, the first message received by B seemed to come from D, while it originated from A.

7.5 Problems

7.1 Give a protocol specification (following Definition 3.13) of the four-party generalised *NSL* protocol from Fig. 7.1.

7.2 Find a type-flaw attack on the four-party generalised *NSL* protocol from Fig. 7.1.

7.3 Consider the following centralised multi-party authentication protocol. One agent acts as the authentication server. It starts by executing bilateral authentication protocols with each of the other agents. If all these authentication attempts succeed, it then sends a confirmation to all agents, to indicate that all agents have been successfully authenticated.

(i)   Draw an MSC and give a formal specification of the protocol.
(ii) Determine the number of messages required for this protocol as a function of the number of parties.
(iii) Specify the security requirement(s) that this protocol must satisfy. Formulate the assumptions (e.g., with respect to the honesty of the parties).
(iv) Consider an instantiation of this protocol with four parties. Prove, either manually or with computer tool support, that this instantiated protocol satisfies the security requirements.

protocol 3PBNV2

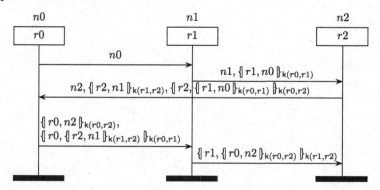

Fig. 7.7 BNV Protocol 2, three-party version

(v) Prove that for any number of parties the protocol satisfies the security requirements.

7.4 Consider the Generalised Bilateral Key Exchange protocol from Sect. 7.3.

(i) Consider an instantiation of this protocol with four parties. Prove, either manually or with computer tool support, that this instantiated protocol satisfies the security requirements.
(ii) Prove that for any number of parties the protocol satisfies the security requirements.

7.5 Consider the Multi-party *NSL* protocol with private keys from Sect. 7.3.

(i) Consider an instantiation of this protocol with four parties. Prove, either manually or with computer tool support, that this instantiated protocol satisfies the security requirements.
(ii) Prove that for any number of parties the protocol satisfies the security requirements.
(iii) Which parts of the messages of the four-party protocol can be taken outside the encryption operator without affecting correctness of the protocol?

7.6 Prove that protocol 3PBNV1 from Fig. 7.5 satisfies recent aliveness. Does it satisfy recent aliveness in the correct role? If so, give a proof; otherwise, give an attack.

7.7 Figure 7.7 contains the second authentication protocol from [40]. Show that this protocol does not satisfy agreement.

7.8 Design and verify a multi-party authentication protocol using symmetric encryption that satisfies injective synchronisation.

Chapter 8
Historical Background and Further Reading

Abstract We provide historical background on our approach, we give pointers for further reading and we describe alternative approaches. We only cover those approaches that are closely related to ours.

8.1 Historical Background

8.1.1 Models

The foundation for the symbolic analysis of security protocols was laid by Dolev and Yao in their 1981 and 1983 papers [75, 76]. They introduced a model in which the adversary (a) has full control over the network and (b) is limited to certain cryptographic primitives and operations. This second aspect later became known as the perfect cryptography assumption. Instead of modelling cryptographic algorithms and operations such as encryption in full detail, Dolev and Yao modelled abstract terms with limited operations. For example, given a term representing an encryption, the adversary cannot derive any information unless he knows the term representing the corresponding decryption key. If he knows the decryption key, he learns the term representing the encrypted message. This strong abstraction allowed them to define an algorithm for deciding security for a very restricted class of protocols.

8.1.2 Initial Tools

After Dolev and Yao's foundational work, the concept of symbolic analysis of security protocols was picked up by the formal methods community. Several research groups applied or developed their own techniques for analysing security protocols. Some early examples are Kemmerer's use of the FDM tool suite and the Ina Jo specification language to show how protocols can be analysed [98], in 1986. Kemmerer also pointed out that such methods are useful during the design phase of a system in order to explore alternatives or detect flaws early. In 1987, Millen et al. developed the Interrogator tool [117] for finding attacks on security protocols, using a

C. Cremers, S. Mauw, *Operational Semantics and Verification of Security Protocols*,
Information Security and Cryptography, DOI 10.1007/978-3-540-78636-8_8,
© Springer-Verlag Berlin Heidelberg 2012

backward search implemented in Prolog. Later, in 1992, the Longley-Rigby tool followed a similar approach [105]. A more extensive tool, the NRL Protocol Analyzer (NPA), was developed by Meadows [111]. NPA would later be used in many case studies of real-world protocols, such as [112], and would serve as the blueprint for the development of Maude-NPA [81], which we will discuss in Sect. 8.2.3. In 1996, Kemmerer, Meadows, and Millen compared their approaches [99].

8.1.3 Logics

In 1989 Burrows, Abadi, and Needham published their ground-breaking work on a logic for the verification of authentication properties [39]. In this logic, later known as BAN logic, predicates have the form "P believes X". Such predicates are derived from a set of assumptions, using derivation rules like "If P believes that P and Q share key K, and if P sees message $\{\!|X|\!\}_K$ then P believes that Q once said X". This rule implies an assumption on the agent model, which is not made in most other approaches, namely, that an agent can detect and ignore its own messages. An important property of the logic is that it does not distinguish between the different runs (or threads) of an agent. One implication of this design choice is that the logic uses a relatively weak notion of authentication. The authentication properties verified for most protocols have the form "A believes that A and B share key K" (or "...share secret X"), and "A believes that B believes that A and B share key K". This weak form of agreement is sometimes even further simplified to *recent aliveness*. Furthermore, BAN logic models an external adversary, i.e., it does not consider compromised agents. This allowed Burrows, Abadi, and Needham to provide a proof of the Needham-Schroeder protocol, on which Lowe would later find an attack.

One criticism made of BAN logic is that it did not have a semantics, and many authors pointed out that some of its axioms could not be sound. Subsequently, many researchers developed extensions to BAN logic or tried to provide a semantics, e.g., [5, 39, 87, 126, 151, 152]. One core problem was how to connect the high-level reasoning about the view of agents with a low-level semantics based on runs. Ultimately, these attempts led either to complex solutions or retained the original logic's problems. These issues, combined with advances in the development of automated tools, caused a decline in interest in the logic-based approaches, such as BAN and its successors, during the mid-1990s.

Interest in the logic approaches was reinvigorated from 2001 onwards with the Protocol Composition Logic [78]. Early versions of this logic closely resembled the setup of the BAN logic, in the sense that reasoning occurs at the agent level, without distinguishing between the different runs of a single agent. This setup inherits some of BAN's limitations, for example in terms of properties that can be proven. One of the main features of the Protocol Composition Logic is its intent to reason compositionally, i.e., to allow for reusing proofs of individual protocols when proving that their composition is correct. This approach can be seen as a specialised version of the Owicki-Gries approach [127] for proving concurrent programs correct. Later versions of PCL [65, 66] switched to a run-based model. However, the scope of the base logic was limited and soundness problems persisted [54]. Attempts to address these problems increased the complexity of the logic and corresponding protocol proofs significantly [67].

8.1.4 Tool Proliferation

Early approaches to symbolic verification tended to re-establish known results about protocols: they either verified protocols known to be correct or automatically detected known attacks. As Kemmerer had observed in 1996 [98], this area of research could obtain justification by, for example, finding *new* attacks. In 1996, Lowe used the FDR model checker as a backend in the Casper protocol analysis tool [107]. When applied to the Needham-Schroeder public-key protocol, which was previously proven correct in BAN logic, the tool automatically finds an attack. This is the now-classical man-in-the-middle attack. The reason that the Needham-Schroeder protocol could be proven correct in BAN logic was that the underlying assumptions on the adversary were different. In particular, in BAN logic, the man-in-the-middle attack was not captured. In Lowe's model, the long-term private keys of some agents may be known to the adversary. In such a model, like in ours, one aims to still achieve security for those communications that involve only honest agents.

Lowe's example showed that a protocol that had been assumed to be secure for two decades was vulnerable to an attack that could be detected automatically. This triggered an increased interest in the development of automatic protocol analysis tools. The first new approaches were based on explicit-state model-checking, in which a model-checking algorithm considers all possible messages that an agent may receive. This includes both the use of general-purpose model checkers, such as FDR [141] and Murφ [122] as well as the development of special-purpose model checkers, such as Brutus [45]. In order for these methods to work, the message space had to be finite and trace length had to be bounded, which allows these model checkers to generate all possible traces in a forward fashion.

In parallel, researchers developed constraint-based algorithms that tried to avoid branching on all possible messages an agent could receive, and instead handle this case symbolically: a received message must be derivable from a certain set (the adversary's knowledge), and the only requirement is that there exists such a message. This direction was first described by Huima in 1999 [93] and led to a long line of work in which these constraint-based techniques were extended and optimised [17, 22, 46, 118, 157]. These methods allow the adversary to derive an infinite set of messages, but still bound the length of the traces considered.

An alternative approach is to perform a backward search, starting from the negation of the property, as we have done in this book. In contrast to the tools mentioned previously, this allows for unbounded verification, i.e., without bounding the number of runs. The underlying ideas to this approach were first described by Song for her Athena tool [147, 148]. These ideas were later extended and led to Scyther [55] and ultimately the Tamarin prover [114, 143].

Until 1997, most tools were based on the model-checking approach. An alternative approach was proposed in 1997, when Paulson applied the interactive theorem prover Isabelle [125] to the protocol verification problem, resulting in the Inductive Method [130, 131]. In this approach, one formalises the system (i.e., the agents running the protocol along with the adversary) as a set of possible communication traces. First, the system is modelled as an inductively defined set of traces. Then, one states and inductively proves theorems expressing that the system in question has certain desirable properties, i.e., each system trace satisfies properties such as authentication or secrecy. The proofs are usually carried out under strong restrictions, e.g., that all variables are strictly typed and that all keys are atomic. The inductive approach requires significant user interaction, but has been applied to many protocols. These include simple authentication protocols like the Needham-Schroeder-Lowe public-key protocol and the Otway-Rees protocol [131], key distribution protocols like Yahalom [133], recursive authentication protocols [131], and non-repudiation protocols like Zhou-Gollmann [29]. Moreover, the method has been applied to a number of industrial-strength protocols. These include Kerberos Version 4 [27, 28], a version of SSL/TLS [132], and parts of SET [23–26, 134].

In 2001, Blanchet developed the ProVerif tool [33], which was subsequently used in many case studies. ProVerif uses over-abstraction to avoid reasoning about specific runs or unbounded number of nonces. ProVerif's abstraction has proven remarkably effective and its scope has been continuously expanding. We discuss ProVerif in more detail in Sect. 8.2.3.

An alternative approach, based on SAT-solving, was taken by Armando and Compagna for the SATMC [13] tool. This tool converts the protocol security problem for a bounded number of runs and a bounded message space into a satisfiability problem in propositional logic, using techniques from research on planning problems. This satisfiability problem is then given to a generic SAT-solver. Moreover, it has been extended with support for specifying properties in a fragment of the linear-time temporal logic LTL [135].

8.1.5 Multi-protocol Attacks

Multi-protocol attacks were first described in 1997 by Kelsey, Schneier and Wagner in [97]. They are also sometimes called cross-protocol attacks. Kelsey et al. showed that, for any given correct protocol, another correct protocol can be constructed, such that when these two protocols are executed in parallel, the adversary can exploit the second protocol to mount an attack against the first protocol.

In the following years, some multi-protocol attacks were manually found or constructed [7, 158]. From 2006 onwards, the Scyther tool was used to find several new multi-protocol attacks, e.g., [53, 110].

The existence of multi-protocol attacks implies that in order to preserve security properties when composing protocols, certain requirements must be met. There is a long line of research, both in the formal methods and the cryptographic communities, that attempts to establish minimal conditions under which protocols can be safely composed. In the symbolic setting, several (incomparable) sufficient conditions for compositionality have been established, e.g., [8, 48, 68, 90]. Alternative conditions and restricted application domains have also been studied, e.g., in [41, 42, 88].

The definition of multi-protocol attacks presented in this book does not put any constraints on the adversary's behaviour. A more restricted definition is given in [69], in which the adversary is only allowed to replay a message from one protocol into another.

8.1.6 Complexity Results

As tool development expanded, many researchers attempted to establish the complexity of the problems occurring in symbolic protocol analysis. Early on, in 1999, it was discovered that the secrecy problem, that is, determining if the adversary could learn a specific term during protocol execution, is undecidable [77]. In 2001, it was shown that if the number of runs is bounded, the secrecy problem is decidable [139, 140]. Later, several other sub-classes of the problem were isolated and their complexity analysed. See [156] for an overview and corrections to earlier results.

8.1.7 Divergence Between Symbolic and Computational Models

While the formal methods community made progress on establishing complexity results and developing tool support for their symbolic models, the cryptographic community developed their own security definitions, e.g., for defining the security of key exchange protocols. Such security definitions are known as computational models. They consider probability distributions on bit strings, instead of abstract terms. Furthermore, they model adversaries as arbitrary Turing Machines with polynomial runtime, instead of restricting them to a fixed set of operations. Protocols only meet such security definitions if it can be shown that an adversary that can successfully attack the protocol with non-negligible probability, can also efficiently solve a known hard problem (such as factoring). Thus, in many ways, these computational models are more detailed than the symbolic Dolev-Yao style models, and are assumed to provide a stronger security guarantee. However, their inherent complexity made them unlikely candidates for tool support at that time.[1]

---

[1] Several years later, researchers started to work on automated tool support for computational models, e.g., [35].

Nonetheless, this alternative style of defining security was also considered by researchers from the formal methods community. In 1998, Lincoln et al. presented a probabilistic framework for reasoning about protocols [104]. Its complexity however did not lead to uptake. In 2000, Gollmann wrote on the discrepancy between the research of the cryptographic community and that of the formal methods community [86], recommending reconciliation. Part of this discrepancy between the symbolic and computational approaches, which concerns the soundness of symbolic encryption with respect to a passive adversary, was addressed in 2000 by Abadi and Rogaway [4]. This lead to many follow-up works, see [50] for an overview.

However, there was another way to reduce the gap between the two approaches that does not require reasoning about bit-strings. In the Dolev-Yao model, and as we have assumed in this book, two terms are equivalent if and only if they are syntactically equivalent. This assumption makes it hard to faithfully model the algebraic properties assumed by some typical cryptographic primitives, such as Diffie-Hellman exponentiation. One way to model such algebraic properties more faithfully is to consider term equivalence with respect to an equational theory. For example, one could consider $exp(exp(g, a), b)$ to be equivalent to the term $exp(exp(g, b), a)$. It is straightforward to adapt the models with such an equational theory, but it is not trivial to provide the corresponding tool support. In 2003, Millen and Shmatikov presented early results with respect to bounded analysis of products and Diffie-Hellman exponentiation [119]. Later works extended these results, e.g., Basin et al. [21]. We list more extensions for specific tools in Sect. 8.2.3. For an overview of the algebraic properties used in cryptographic protocols, see Cortier et al. [49].

In the meantime, the cryptographic community made significant advances in establishing new primitives and developing protocols that are resilient against increasingly stronger adversaries. Early research on reconciling the two areas focused mostly on extending Abadi and Rogaway's results for more primitives and active adversaries, e.g., [16]. Later, Basin and Cremers revisited the discrepancies with respect to the adversary models and types of compromise used by the two communities [19, 57], and provided a formal framework and extension of the Scyther tool to support more adversary models.

8.1.8 Bridging the Gap Between Symbolic Analysis and Code

In symbolic analysis, protocol models often only consider the cryptographic functions and the send and receive steps, abstracting away from application-driven control flow and details of how the transmitted payloads are computed or interpreted. As a result, there is a significant gap between the results of a symbolic analysis and the security of a concrete implementation of such a protocol.

Researchers have also tried to reduce this gap between the symbolic models and the concrete implementations. One approach is to separate the implementation of the cryptographic primitives from the rest of the code. One then verifies that the part of the code that uses the cryptographic libraries meets its security properties. This code is then combined with a concrete implementation of low-level primitives, in a way that guarantees that the security properties are preserved. This approach is especially suitable for programming languages that allow for direct formal analysis, such as functional programming languages. Examples of this approach include Bhargavan et al.'s formally verified core of TLS [30], and works such as [31]. Another approach is to perform symbolic analysis on the concrete code, essentially extracting a symbolic model from the code in a sound way. An example of this approach is [6]. Yet another approach is to follow a formal development process based on refinement [32, 123, 150]. Starting from a set of functional and security requirements, one constructs a series of models with an increasing level of detail that gradually realise the requirements. Models are linked by refinement proofs, which imply property preservation. This process can be continued towards the code level.

8.2 Alternative Approaches

The framework and tool support presented in this book is not a silver bullet. There are presently many different approaches, each of which has its own strengths. In this section we give an overview of alternative approaches and their most important distinguishing features.

8.2.1 Modelling Frameworks

Applied-Pi Calculus

A prominent modelling formalism for security protocols is the applied-pi calculus [2]. It can be seen as a generalisation of the spi-calculus [3], which in turn is based on the Pi calculus [120, 121] by Milner, Parrow, and Walker. The applied-pi calculus is a process calculus that is a general formalism for specifying and reasoning about concurrent processes. It provides a rich term algebra that enables modelling of a variety of cryptographic operators. One of the reasons for the success of the applied-pi calculus is that the ProVerif tool accepts a substantial fragment of the applied-pi calculus as one of its two input languages. Unlike the role scripts defined here, it directly allows for the specification of branching and looping behaviour.

Strand Spaces

The Strand spaces approach [155] is closely related to our approach. It provides an elegant way to reason about protocol executions in the presence of a Dolev-Yao adversary. In Strand spaces, a protocol is implicitly modelled as a collection of (parameterised) strands, with additional constraints that imply which parameters denote freshly generated values (nonces), and which denote variables. The main difference with respect to our approach is that we provide a totally ordered formal semantics that makes the relation between a protocol and its behaviour explicit, whereas Strand spaces describe protocol execution using a partial order on the events. The notion of a strand is similar to our notion of run, and a strand space is the set of all possible combinations of strands, reflecting our semantical model of interleaved runs. The notion of a bundle closely corresponds to our notion of realisable trace pattern, and allows one to effectively reason about classes of traces. The Strand spaces approach also differs from our approach in the way in which some subtleties are handled, e.g., nonce generation, the handling of initial adversary knowledge and honest/compromised agents. In our model, such concepts are explicit and solved at a syntactical level where possible, whereas in the Strand spaces model these are often formalised as additional requirements on, e.g., nonce occurrence (that somehow exist outside the base model), or encoded as the parameters of a strand. Similarly, there is no strict distinction between fresh values and variables within a strand. These design choices allow for flexibility in modelling but it is less clear how to interpret some of the modelling possibilities in an operational semantics.

The Strand spaces approach has been used to prove many theoretical results [72, 90, 91, 153, 154] and is the basis of several tools [46, 118, 137, 148]. Additionally, there are many extensions to the Strand spaces formalism, e.g., Mixed Strand spaces for multi-protocol analysis [154], and a variant to capture state and progress [89].

8.2.2   Security Properties

Each security protocol framework has its own distinct means for defining security properties. Furthermore, specifying security properties is a research area in itself, and models and logics have been developed with the specific purpose of modelling security properties, such as [47, 82, 144].

Secrecy

With respect to specific security properties, we find that secrecy is handled in a similar way by the majority of models, as we did here. An alternative notion of secrecy is called *strong secrecy* [34] and is based on indistinguishability: the adversary should not be able to distinguish between two processes that are identical except for the term that is supposed to be secret. It was later shown that under certain restrictions the standard notion of secrecy (as used here) implies strong secrecy [51].

Authentication

For authentication properties, the situation is significantly more complicated. Historically, many different interpretations of authentication exist for communication

protocols. Early authentication concepts simply mention that one "end" of a communication channel can assure itself regarding the identity of the other end, as in,
e.g., [124, 136]. An identity is considered to be an "end". These concepts seem very
similar to Lowe's later definition of *aliveness* in [108]. For this form of authentication, it is only required that the party to be authenticated performs some action to
prove its identity (i.e., applying its secret key) regardless of the context or to whom
it is proving its identity. This is a rather weak form of authentication.

In 1996, Roscoe introduced the distinction between extensional and intensional
specifications of security properties [138]. This distinction stems from the observation that some security properties are specified independently from the protocol
structure, focusing on the intent of the protocol design, whereas other properties are
directly connected to the protocol structure. For example, the purpose of the protocol may be to authenticate a key (and nothing else). A definition of authentication
using such (protocol independent) knowledge is called an *extensional specification*.
In contrast, if one specifies the property directly on the protocol structure, it is called
an *intensional specification*. For example, synchronisation is an intensional security
property. We will use this distinction below to classify alternative definitions of authentication.

Extensional Specifications of Authentication   In extensional specifications, the
authentication goal is not derived from the protocol specification, but is instead specified independently. For example, the ISO/IEC 9798-1 [83] standard states that authentication requires verification of an entity's claimed identity. Commenting on this
definition, Gollmann pointed out in [85] that the concept of a sender of a message
should be treated with caution, and that replays should be prevented. Gollmann ar-
gued that authentication of an entire communication session is done by first setting
up a session key, and that further messages are authenticated on the basis of this
key. Based on this assumption, he identified four authentication goals. These goals
explicitly assume that the protocols are implemented using private keys and session
keys, which limits the application domain of the definitions.

In [108], Lowe introduced a hierarchy of authentication properties. Many of these
are formalised by extensional specifications, e.g., to express authentication of data.
This builds on the earlier work of Diffie et al. [71] and Gollmann [85], resulting in
four different forms of authentication, viz. aliveness, weak agreement, non-injective
agreement and injective agreement. On top of this, agreement on subsets of data
items and recentness are considered (two topics we do not address here). In the
course of time many subtly different extensional authentication properties have been
proposed. Most of these derive directly from the work by Lowe.

In [36], Boyd proposes an alternative hierarchy of extensional goals for authentication protocols. Boyd's goals focus on the establishment of keys and the expected
end results for the user of the protocol. Similar to Gollmann, Boyd assumes that
authentication is interpreted in the context of a key exchange protocol. In this view,
the authenticated objects are the communications that are secured by a session key,
which is the output of a key establishment protocol. Boyd's perspective leads to
definitions that differ from the ones considered here.

Some more advanced notions of authentication can be found in [100], where mechanisms are sketched to prevent *message stream modification*. This can be prevented by achieving three subgoals: determine message authenticity, integrity, and ordering. Although no formalisation is provided, this concept is akin to our notion of non-injective synchronisation.

Intensional Specifications of Authentication   In 1996, Roscoe introduced in [138] intensional specifications. At a high level, these can be viewed as authentication of communications. The definitions we have given in Chap. 4 are all intensional specifications. Roscoe's work did not identify subclasses and did not consider the notion of injectivity. Instead, Roscoe informally sketched the notion of "canonical intensional specification", which seems similar to non-injective synchronisation.

An early informal intensional formulation of authentication was given in 1992 by Diffie et al. in [71]. Here, participants are required to have matching message histories. The message history is allowed to be partial, if the last message sent is never received, which corresponds to our notion of messages that *causally precede* a claim. Because their definition includes recording the time at which each message is sent and received, it corresponds closely to non-injective synchronisation.

Multi-party Authentication

Regarding the definition of multi-party authentication, we find that much research has been performed in the computational setting, e.g., [14, 15, 38]. As a result, these definitions usually only consider a static adversary, and do not consider the dynamic behaviour of the protocol and the adversary. These protocols are typically assumed to employ a multicast primitive, and based on this primitive their complexity can be analysed, as in, e.g., [96, 115]. The protocols in this category are designed to meet different goals than the protocols presented here.

In the symbolic analysis of security protocols, protocols usually consist of two or three roles only. Most of the frameworks, except for Paulson's Inductive Method, assume that the protocols have a fixed number of participants, and are therefore not suited for analysis of parameterised protocol specifications. Hence, they cannot be used to analyse multi-party protocols in general, but they can be used to analyse specific instances of such protocols. For example, ProVerif [33] has been used to analyse instances of the GDH protocols from [15]. In spite of the success of the symbolic analysis methods, few multi-party protocols have been constructed in this setting. A notable exception is [40], in which the authors construct two challenge-response protocols for any number of parties. However, the protocols described there satisfy neither synchronisation nor agreement, as was shown in Sect. 7.4.

Beyond Trace Properties

The properties we have mentioned in this chapter until now, except for strong secrecy, are all trace properties: they can be defined as predicates over traces. A protocol is said to satisfy a (trace) property if it is satisfied by all of its traces. In contrast, there are many interesting security properties that cannot be expressed as trace properties. Such properties are often defined using indistinguishability: the adversary should not be able to distinguish between two systems. Examples include strong secrecy as well as several privacy and anonymity notions. There exists tool support for some of these properties, such as strong secrecy, whereas other interesting properties are still the subject of active research.

8.2.3 Tools

There are several tools we would like to mention as alternatives to the Scyther tool. Although it is possible to perform efficiency analysis on commonly supported protocol models [59], the tools mainly differ in the type of protocol- and property specification that they can effectively analyse.

Tamarin Prover

Along the lines of the work already discussed here, the Tamarin prover [114, 143] offers support for a strict generalisation of the Scyther modelling framework. It also supports both automatic and interactive verification: the user can inspect the search tree and locally override the choices made by the heuristics, and the user can provide additional axioms, either for more precise modelling or in case the tool is not able to verify the property directly. It furthermore provides support for equational theories, including Diffie-Hellman, bilinear pairings, and arbitrary subterm-convergent rewrite systems specifying equational theories. Tamarin supports trace properties specified using a guarded fragment of first-order logic with quantification over timepoints. Its features make it especially suitable for analysis of stateful systems, such as cryptographic APIs, as well as the analysis of key exchange protocols with respect to their intended security properties.

Tamarin has been successfully applied in the analysis of the TESLA protocol, the YubiKey protocol, and many authenticated key exchange protocols, both for establishing unbounded verification and finding attacks [114, 143].

ProVerif

As we already mentioned before, a widely used tool for security protocol analysis is ProVerif [33]. Protocols are either directly specified as Horn clauses, or in a fragment of the applied-pi calculus, which is then translated into a corresponding set of Horn clauses. ProVerif can analyse protocols with respect to an unbounded number of runs, based on two abstractions. First, protocol steps are encoded using Horn clauses, which means that the number of repetitions of the corresponding protocol rule is ignored. Second, fresh values such as nonces are replaced by representatives of equivalence classes. A basic example of such an equivalence class is the set of nonces used by A for communication with B, represented by $n(A, B)$. The abstractions used in ProVerif have proven to be very effective for verifying security protocols. In the case that the abstraction-based algorithm discovers a counterexample, the tool attempts to construct a concrete trace. If this succeeds, a concrete attack is reported. If this construction fails, the tool reports that the result is unknown. Moreover, the algorithm may not terminate.

ProVerif allows the user to specify secrecy properties, as well as (forms of) observational equivalences for processes, which allows expressing strong secrecy [34] and certain privacy properties. Additionally, one can specify authentication properties, which are known as *correspondence properties* in the applied-pi calculus. Because of its support of non-trace properties such as observational equivalence, it was also instrumental in the first attempts at automated analysis of e-voting protocols [146].

Stateful protocols such as cryptographic APIs have turned out to be harder to deal with in ProVerif, because of its abstraction methods and focus on the adversary's knowledge [9]. There exist preprocessing tools that allow ProVerif, under some restrictions, to deal with exclusive-or [102], Diffie-Hellman [101] and bilinear pairing [128]. ProVerif has been used in a large number of case studies, such as JFK [1] and other protocols [9, 101, 102, 146].

Maude-NPA

The Maude-NPA tool [79, 81] is a descendant of the NRL Protocol Analyser. Of all protocol analysis tools, it provides the most extensive support for equational reasoning. In particular, it directly supports exclusive-or [142] and homomorphic encryption [80]. In Maude-NPA, protocols are specified using a Strand-spaces-like language. It uses a backward search strategy, which is implemented in rewriting logic. Starting from some specified insecure state the tool verifies if it can be reached from the initial state.

Its predecessor, the NRL protocol analyser, was used to verify, for example, the Internet Key Exchange protocol [112].

CPSA

The Strand spaces formalism [155] has tool support in the form of the CPSA tool [137], whose algorithm is based on the authentication tests method [91] in combination with the concept of skeletons [74]. Essentially, the CPSA algorithm computes the complete characterisation of a protocol role and possibly additional events, using an extended version of the Strand spaces model.

As noted before, the term *complete characterisation* was introduced in [72, 73] in the context of the strand space framework. CPSA relies on an algebraic theory of skeletons and shapes: skeletons are comparable to trace patterns without adversary events, and shapes are similar to realisable trace patterns without adversary events. A characterisation is defined as the set of shapes of a skeleton.

Given a skeleton, CPSA determines the set of shapes, by exploiting the idea of authentication tests [91]. For characterisation of the Needham-Schroeder responder role, CPSA determines exactly one shape, which captures the correct execution and the attack at the same time, while in our approach we find two realisable trace patterns. This is a result of their choice to exclude adversary events: in terms of shapes, the normal behaviour is a special case of the attack. In terms of realisable trace patterns, the attack and the normal behaviour are not instances of each other, as one strictly requires decrypt and encrypt events, and the other does not.

AVANTSSAR Tool Suite

The AVANTSSAR tool suite [10] is an extension of the AVISPA tool suite [11] for the analysis of security protocols. Similar to the AVISPA tool suite, it supports bounded protocol verification. It additionally provides support for the modelling of business processes and policies. In AVANTSSAR, the specifications are translated into a set-rewriting based formalism. This specification is then passed through to one of its three backends, Cl-Atse [157], OFMC [22], or SATMC [13], to attempt falsification or bounded verification.

The AVISPA tool suite, the predecessor to AVANTSSAR, has been applied to many industrial case studies, including several IEEE standards and the SAML 2.0 single sign-on standard [12].

Scyther-Proof

The Scyther-proof tool [113] uses a variant of the algorithm presented in this book. The main additional feature is that it generates proof scripts for use with the Isabelle-HOL theorem prover [129]. The generated proof scripts include an embedding of the operational semantics and a proof that the desired security property is correct, closely resembling the search tree explored by Scyther. These proof scripts can be machine-checked by Isabelle/HOL. The correctness of these proofs is thus independent of potential flaws in the Scyther-proof tool.

After Scyther was used to detect flaws in the ISO/IEC 9798 standard for entity authentication protocols, the Scyther-proof tool was applied to provide machine-checked correctness proofs of the repaired protocols [20].

References

1. M. Abadi, B. Blanchet, C. Fournet, Just fast keying in the pi calculus. ACM Trans. Inf. Syst. Secur. **10**(3), 9 (2007)
2. M. Abadi, C. Fournet, Mobile values, new names, and secure communication, in *28th ACM SIGPLAN-SIGACT Symposium on Principles of Programming Languages (POPL'01)*, ed. by C. Hankin, D. Schmidt, London, UK (ACM, New York, 2001), pp. 104–115
3. M. Abadi, A.D. Gordon, A calculus for cryptographic protocols: the Spi calculus. Inf. Comput. **148**, 1–70 (1999)
4. M. Abadi, P. Rogaway, Reconciling two views of cryptography (the computational soundness of formal encryption), in *IFIP International Conference on Theoretical Computer Science (IFIP TCS'00)*, ed. by J. van Leeuwen, O. Watanabe, M. Hagiya, P.D. Mosses, T. Ito, Sendai, Japan (2000), pp. 3–22
5. M. Abadi, M. Tuttle, A semantics for a logic of authentication, in *10th ACM Symposium on Principles of Distributed Computing (PODC'91)*, Montreal, Canada (ACM, New York, 1991), pp. 201–216
6. M. Aizatulin, A.D. Gordon, J. Jürjens, Extracting and verifying cryptographic models from C protocol code by symbolic execution, in *18th ACM Conference on Computer and Communications Security (ACM CCS'11)*, ed. by Y. Chen, G. Danezis, V. Shmatikov, Chicago, USA (ACM, New York, 2011), pp. 331–340
7. J. Alves-Foss, Multiprotocol attacks and the public key infrastructure, in *21st National Information Systems Security Conference (NISSC'98)*, Arlington, USA (NIST, Gaithersburg, 1998), pp. 566–576
8. S. Andova, C.J.F. Cremers, K. Gjøsteen, S. Mauw, S.F. Mjølsnes, S. Radomirović, A framework for compositional verification of security protocols. Inf. Comput. **206**(2–4), 425–459 (2008)
9. M. Arapinis, E. Ritter, M.D. Ryan, StatVerif: verification of stateful processes, in *24th IEEE Computer Security Foundations Symposium (CSF'11)* (IEEE Computer Society, Los Alamitos, 2011), pp. 33–47
10. A. Armando, W. Arsac, T. Avanesov, M. Barletta, A. Calvi, A. Cappai, R. Carbone, Y. Chevalier, L. Compagna, J. Cuéllar, G. Erzse, S. Frau, M. Minea, S. Mödersheim, D. von Oheimb, G. Pellegrino, S.E. Ponta, M. Rocchetto, M. Rusinowitch, M. Torabi Dashti, M. Turuani, L. Viganò, The AVANTSSAR platform for the automated validation of trust and security of service-oriented architectures, in *18th International Conference on Tools and Algorithms for the Construction and Analysis of Systems (TACAS'12)*, ed. by C. Flanagan, B. König, Tallinn, Estonia. Lecture Notes in Computer Science, vol. 7214 (Springer, Berlin, 2012)
11. A. Armando, D.A. Basin, Y. Boichut, Y. Chevalier, L. Compagna, L. Cuellar, P.H. Drielsma, P. Heám, O. Kouchnarenko, J. Mantovani, S. Mödersheim, D. von Oheimb, M. Rusinowitch, J. Santiago, M. Turuani, L. Viganò, L. Vigneron, The AVISPA tool for the automated val-

C. Cremers, S. Mauw, *Operational Semantics and Verification of Security Protocols*,
Information Security and Cryptography, DOI 10.1007/978-3-540-78636-8,
© Springer-Verlag Berlin Heidelberg 2012

idation of internet security protocols and applications, in *17th International Conference on Computer Aided Verification (CAV'05)*, Edinburgh, UK. Lecture Notes in Computer Science, vol. 3576 (Springer, Berlin, 2005), pp. 281–285

12. A. Armando, R. Carbone, L. Compagna, J. Cuéllar, M.L. Tobarra, Formal analysis of SAML 2.0 web browser single sign-on: breaking the SAML-based single sign-on for Google apps, in *6th ACM Workshop on Formal Methods in Security Engineering (FMSE'08)*, ed. by V. Shmatikov, Alexandria, USA (ACM, New York, 2008), pp. 1–10

13. A. Armando, L. Compagna, SAT-based model checking for security protocols analysis. Int. J. Inf. Secur. **7**(1), 3–32 (2008)

14. G. Ateniese, M. Steiner, G. Tsudik, Authenticated group key agreement and friends, in *5th ACM Conference on Computer and Communications Security (ACM CCS'98)*, San Francisco, USA (ACM, New York, 1998), pp. 17–26

15. G. Ateniese, M. Steiner, G. Tsudik, New multiparty authentication services and key agreement protocols. IEEE J. Sel. Areas Commun. **18**(4), 628–639 (2000)

16. M. Backes, B. Pfitzmann, M. Waidner, A composable cryptographic library with nested operations, in *10th ACM Conference on Computer and Communications Security (ACM CCS'03)*, ed. by S. Jajodia, V. Atluri, T. Jaeger (ACM, New York, 2003), pp. 220–230

17. D.A. Basin, Lazy infinite-state analysis of security protocols, in *Secure Networking (CQRE'99)*, ed. by R. Baumgart, Düsseldorf, Germany. Lecture Notes in Computer Science, vol. 1740 (Springer, Berlin, 1999), pp. 30–42

18. D.A. Basin, C.J.F. Cremers, Degrees of security: protocol guarantees in the face of compromising adversaries, in *Computer Science Logic, 24th International Workshop (CSL'10)*, Brno, Czech Republic. Lecture Notes in Computer Science, vol. 6247 (Springer, Berlin, 2010), pp. 1–18

19. D.A. Basin, C.J.F. Cremers, Modeling and analyzing security in the presence of compromising adversaries, in *15th European Symposium on Research in Computer Security (ESORICS'10)*, Athens, Greece. Lecture Notes in Computer Science, vol. 6345 (Springer, Berlin, 2010), pp. 340–356

20. D.A. Basin, C.J.F. Cremers, S. Meier, Provably repairing the ISO/IEC 9798 standard for entity authentication, in *1st International Conference on Principles of Security and Trust (POST'12)*, ed. by P. Degano, J.D. Guttman, Tallinn, Estonia. Lecture Notes in Computer Science, vol. 7215 (Springer, Berlin, 2012), pp. 129–148

21. D.A. Basin, S. Mödersheim, L. Viganò, Algebraic intruder deductions, in *12th International Conference on Logic for Programming, Artificial Intelligence and Reasoning (LPAR'05)*, Montego Bay, Jamaica. Lecture Notes in Artificial Intelligence, vol. 3835 (Springer, Berlin, 2005), pp. 549–564

22. D.A. Basin, S. Mödersheim, L. Viganò, OFMC: a symbolic model checker for security protocols. Int. J. Inf. Secur. **4**(3), 181–208 (2005)

23. G. Bella, F. Massacci, L.C. Paulson, The verification of an industrial payment protocol: the SET purchase phase, in *9th ACM Conference on Computer and Communications Security (ACM CCS'02)*, ed. by V. Atluri, Washington, USA (ACM, New York, 2002), pp. 12–20

24. G. Bella, F. Massacci, L.C. Paulson, Verifying the SET registration protocols. IEEE J. Sel. Areas Commun. **21**(1), 77–87 (2003)

25. G. Bella, F. Massacci, L.C. Paulson, An overview of the verification of SET. Int. J. Inf. Secur. **4**(1–2), 17–28 (2005)

26. G. Bella, F. Massacci, L.C. Paulson, P. Tramontano, Formal verification of cardholder registration in SET, in *6th European Symposium on Research in Computer Security (ESORICS'00)*, ed. by F. Cuppens, Y. Deswarte, D. Gollmann, M. Waidner, Toulouse, France. Lecture Notes in Computer Science, vol. 1895 (Springer, Berlin, 2000), pp. 159–174

27. G. Bella, L.C. Paulson, Using Isabelle to prove properties of the Kerberos authentication system, in *Workshop on Design and Formal Verification of Security Protocols*, ed. by H. Orman, C. Meadows, Piscataway, USA (DIMACS, Rutgers, 1997)

28. G. Bella, L.C. Paulson, Kerberos version IV: inductive analysis of the secrecy goals, in *5th European Symposium on Research in Computer Security (ESORICS'98)*,

ed. by J.-J. Quisquater, Y. Deswarte, C. Meadows, D. Gollmann, Louvain-la-Neuve, Belgium. Lecture Notes in Computer Science, vol. 1485 (Springer, Berlin, 1998), pp. 361–375

29. G. Bella, L.C. Paulson, Mechanical proofs about a non-repudiation protocol, in *14th International Conference on Theorem Proving in Higher Order Logics (TPHOLs'01)*, ed. by R.J. Boulton, P.B. Jackson, Edinburgh, UK. Lecture Notes in Computer Science, vol. 2152 (Springer, Berlin, 2001), pp. 91–104

30. K. Bhargavan, C. Fournet, R.J. Corin, E. Zalinescu, Cryptographically verified implementations for TLS, in *15th ACM Conference on Computer and Communications Security (ACM CCS'08)*, ed. by P. Ning, P.F. Syverson, S. Jha, Alexandria, USA (ACM, New York, 2008), pp. 459–468

31. K. Bhargavan, C. Fournet, A.D. Gordon, Modular verification of security protocol code by typing, in *37th ACM SIGPLAN-SIGACT Symposium on Principles of Programming Languages (POPL'10)*, ed. by M.V. Hermenegildo, J. Palsberg, Madrid, Spain (ACM, New York, 2010), pp. 445–456

32. P. Bieber, N. Boulahia-Cuppens, Formal development of authentication protocols, in *6th BCS-FACS Refinement Workshop*, London, UK (1994)

33. B. Blanchet, An efficient cryptographic protocol verifier based on Prolog rules, in *14th IEEE Computer Security Foundations Workshop (CSFW'01)*, Cape Breton, Canada (IEEE Computer Society, Los Alamitos, 2001), pp. 82–96

34. B. Blanchet, Automatic proof of strong secrecy for security protocols, in *25th IEEE Symposium on Security & Privacy (S&P'04)*, Oakland, USA (IEEE Computer Society, Los Alamitos, 2004), pp. 86–100

35. B. Blanchet, A computationally sound mechanized prover for security protocols. IEEE Trans. Dependable Secure Comput. **5**(4), 193–207 (2008)

36. C. Boyd, Towards extensional goals in authentication protocols, in *Workshop on Design and Formal Verification of Security Protocols*, ed. by H. Orman, C. Meadows, Piscataway, USA (DIMACS, Rutgers, 1997)

37. C. Boyd, A. Mathuria, *Protocols for Authentication and Key Establishment. Information Security and Cryptography* (Springer, Berlin, 2003)

38. E. Bresson, O. Chevassut, D. Pointcheval, J.J. Quisquater, Provably authenticated group Diffie-Hellman key exchange, in *8th ACM Conference on Computer and Communications Security (ACM CCS'01)*, ed. by M.K. Reiter, P. Samarati, Philadelphia, USA (ACM, New York, 2001), pp. 255–264

39. M. Burrows, M. Abadi, R.M. Needham, A logic of authentication. ACM Trans. Comput. Syst. **8**(1), 18–36 (1990)

40. L. Buttyán, A. Nagy, I. Vajda, Efficient multi-party challenge-response protocols for entity authentication. Period. Polytech. **45**(1), 43–64 (2001)

41. R. Canetti, Universally composable security: a new paradigm for cryptographic protocols. IACR Cryptology ePrint Archive, Report 2000/067 (2000)

42. R. Canetti, C. Meadows, P. Syverson, Environmental requirements for authentication protocols, in *Software Security—Theories and Systems, Mext-NSF-JSPS International Symposium (ISSS'02)*, ed. by M. Okada, B.C. Pierce, A. Scedrov, H. Tokuda, A. Yonezawa, Tokyo, Japan. Lecture Notes in Computer Science, vol. 2609 (Springer, Berlin, 2002), pp. 339–355

43. N. Chomsky, Three models for the description of language. IRE Trans. Inf. Theory **2**(3), 113–124 (1956)

44. J.A. Clark, J.L. Jacob, A survey of authentication protocol literature: Version 1.0. Unpublished article (1997)

45. E.M. Clarke, S. Jha, W. Marrero, Verifying security protocols with Brutus. ACM Trans. Softw. Eng. Methodol. **9**(4), 443–487 (2000)

46. R.J. Corin, S. Etalle, An improved constraint-based system for the verification of security protocols, in *9th International Static Analysis Symposium (SAS'02)*, ed. by M.V. Hermenegildo, G. Puebla, Madrid, Spain. Lecture Notes in Computer Science, vol. 2477 (Springer, Berlin, 2002), pp. 326–341

47. R.J. Corin, A. Saptawijaya, S. Etalle, A logic for constraint-based security protocol analysis, in *27th IEEE Symposium on Security & Privacy (S&P'06)*, Berkeley, USA (IEEE Computer Society, Los Alamitos, 2006), pp. 155–168

48. V. Cortier, S. Delaune, Safely composing security protocols. Form. Methods Syst. Des. **34**(1), 1–36 (2009)

49. V. Cortier, S. Delaune, P. Lafourcade, A survey of algebraic properties used in cryptographic protocols. J. Comput. Secur. **14**(1), 1–43 (2006)

50. V. Cortier, S. Kremer, B. Warinschi, A survey of symbolic methods in computational analysis of cryptographic systems. J. Autom. Reason. **46**(3–4), 225–259 (2011)

51. V. Cortier, M. Rusinowitch, E. Zalinescu, Relating two standard notions of secrecy. Log. Methods Comput. Sci. **3**(3), 1–29 (2007)

52. C.J.F. Cremers, The Scyther tool: automatic verification of security protocols. http://people. inf.ethz.ch/cremersc/scyther/index.html (accessed 18 Sept 2012)

53. C.J.F. Cremers, Feasibility of multi-protocol attacks, in *1st International Conference on Availability, Reliability and Security (ARES'06)*, Vienna, Austria (IEEE Computer Society, Los Alamitos, 2006), pp. 287–294

54. C.J.F. Cremers, On the protocol composition logic PCL, in *ACM Symposium on Information, Computer & Communication Security (ASIACCS'08)*, ed. by M. Abe, V. Gligor, Tokyo, Japan (ACM, New York, 2008), pp. 66–76

55. C.J.F. Cremers, The Scyther tool: verification, falsification, and analysis of security protocols, in *20th International Conference on Computer Aided Verification (CAV'08)*, ed. by A. Gupta, S. Malik, Princeton, USA. Lecture Notes in Computer Science, vol. 5123 (Springer, Berlin, 2008), pp. 414–418

56. C.J.F. Cremers, Unbounded verification, falsification, and characterization of security protocols by pattern refinement, in *15th ACM Conference on Computer and Communications Security (ACM CCS'08)*, ed. by P. Ning, P.F. Syverson, S. Jha, Alexandria, USA (ACM, New York, 2008), pp. 119–128

57. C.J.F. Cremers, Session-state reveal is stronger than eCK's ephemeral key reveal: using automatic analysis to attack the NAXOS protocol. Int. J. Appl. Cryptogr. **2**(2), 83–99 (2010)

58. C.J.F. Cremers, Key exchange in IPsec revisited: formal analysis of IKEv1 and IKEv2, in *16th European Symposium on Research in Computer Security (ESORICS'11)*, ed. by V. Atluri, C. Díaz, Leuven, Belgium. Lecture Notes in Computer Science, vol. 6879 (Springer, Berlin, 2011), pp. 315–334

59. C.J.F. Cremers, P. Lafourcade, P. Nadeau, Comparing state spaces in automatic protocol analysis, in *Formal to Practical Security*, ed. by V. Cortier, C. Kirchner, M. Okada, H. Sakurada. Lecture Notes in Computer Science, vol. 5458 (Springer, Berlin, 2009), pp. 70–94

60. C.J.F. Cremers, S. Mauw, Operational semantics of security protocols, in *Scenarios: Models, Transformations and Tools, International Workshop, 2003, Revised Selected Papers*, ed. by S. Leue, T. Systä, Dagstuhl, Germany. Lecture Notes in Computer Science, vol. 3466 (Springer, Berlin, 2005)

61. C.J.F. Cremers, S. Mauw, Generalizing Needham-Schroeder-Lowe for multi-party authentication. Computer Science Report CSR 06-04, Eindhoven University of Technology (2006)

62. C.J.F. Cremers, S. Mauw, E.P. de Vink, Defining authentication in a trace model, in *1st International Workshop on Formal Aspects in Security and Trust (FAST'03)*, ed. by T. Dimitrakos, F. Martinelli, Pisa, Italy (2003), pp. 131–145. IITT-CNR technical report

63. C.J.F. Cremers, S. Mauw, E.P. de Vink, A syntactic criterion for injectivity of authentication protocols, in *2nd Workshop on Automated Reasoning for Security Protocol Analysis (ARSPA'05)*, ed. by P. Degano, L. Viganò, Lisbon, Portugal. Electronic Notes in Theoretical Computer Science, vol. 135 (Elsevier, Amsterdam, 2005), pp. 23–38

64. C.J.F. Cremers, S. Mauw, E.P. de Vink, Injective synchronisation: an extension of the authentication hierarchy. Theor. Comput. Sci. **367**(1–2), 139–161 (2006)

65. A. Datta, A. Derek, J.C. Mitchell, D. Pavlovic, Secure protocol composition, in *1st ACM Workshop on Formal Methods in Security Engineering (FMSE'03)*, ed. by M. Backes, D.A. Basin, Washington, USA (ACM, New York, 2003), pp. 11–23

66. A. Datta, A. Derek, J.C. Mitchell, A. Roy, Protocol Composition Logic (PCL), in *Computation, Meaning, and Logic: Articles dedicated to Gordon Plotkin*, ed. by L. Cardelli, M. Fiore, G. Winskel. Electronic Notes in Theoretical Computer Science, vol. 172, (2007), pp. 311–358

67. A. Datta, J.C. Mitchell, A. Roy, S. Stiller, Protocol composition logic, in *Formal Models and Techniques for Analyzing Security Protocols*, ed. by V. Cortier, S. Kremer (IOS Press, Lansdale, 2011)

68. S. Delaune, S. Kremer, M.D. Ryan, Composition of password-based protocols, in *21st IEEE Computer Security Foundations Symposium (CSF'08)*, Pittsburgh, USA (IEEE Computer Society, Los Alamitos, 2008), pp. 239–251

69. X. Didelot, COSP-J: a compiler for security protocols. Master's thesis, University of Oxford, Computing Laboratory (2003)

70. W. Diffie, M.E. Hellman, New directions in cryptography. IEEE Trans. Inf. Theory **22**(6), 644–654 (1976)

71. W. Diffie, P.C. van Oorschot, M.J. Wiener, Authentication and authenticated key-exchanges. Des. Codes Cryptogr. **2**(2), 107–125 (1992)

72. S. Doghmi, J.D. Guttman, F.J. Thayer, Skeletons and the shapes of bundles, in *7th International Workshop on Issues in the Theory of Security (WITS'07)*, Braga, Portugal (2007)

73. S.F. Doghmi, J.D. Guttman, F.J. Thayer, Searching for shapes in cryptographic protocols, in *13th International Conference on Tools and Algorithms for the Construction and Analysis of Systems (TACAS'07)*, ed. by O. Grumberg, M. Huth, Braga, Portugal. Lecture Notes in Computer Science, vol. 4424 (Springer, Berlin, 2007), pp. 523–537

74. S.F. Doghmi, J.D. Guttman, F.J. Thayer, Skeletons, homomorphisms, and shapes: characterizing protocol executions, in *23rd Conference on the Mathematical Foundations of Programming Semantics (MFPS XXIII)*, New Orleans, USA. Electronic Notes in Theoretical Computer Science, vol. 173 (Elsevier, Amsterdam, 2007), pp. 85–102

75. D. Dolev, A.C. Yao, On the security of public key protocols (extended abstract), in *22nd IEEE Symposium on Foundations of Computer Science (FOCS'81)*, Nashville, USA (IEEE Computer Society, Los Alamitos, 1981), pp. 350–357

76. D. Dolev, A.C. Yao, On the security of public key protocols. IEEE Trans. Inf. Theory **29**(2), 198–207 (1983)

77. N.A. Durgin, P.D. Lincoln, J.C. Mitchell, A. Scedrov, Undecidability of bounded security protocols, in *Formal Methods and Security Protocols (FMSP'99)*, Trento, Italy (1999)

78. N.A. Durgin, J.C. Mitchell, D. Pavlovic, A compositional logic for protocol correctness, in *14th IEEE Computer Security Foundations Workshop (CSFW'01)*, Cape Breton, Canada (IEEE Computer Society, Los Alamitos, 2001), pp. 241–272

79. S. Erbatur, S. Escobar, D. Kapur, Z. Liu, C. Lynch, C. Meadows, J. Meseguer, P. Narendran, S. Santiago, R. Sasse, Effective symbolic protocol analysis via equational irreducibility conditions, in *17th European Symposium on Research in Computer Security (ESORICS'12)*, ed. by S. Foresti, M. Yung, F. Martinelli, Pisa, Italy. Lecture Notes in Computer Science, vol. 7459 (Springer, Berlin, 2012), pp. 73–90

80. S. Escobar, D. Kapur, C. Lynch, C. Meadows, J. Meseguer, P. Narendran, R. Sasse, Protocol analysis in Maude-NPA using unification modulo homomorphic encryption, in *13th International ACM SIGPLAN Conference on Principles and Practice of Declarative Programming (PPDP'11)*, ed. by P. Schneider-Kamp, M. Hanus, Odense, Denmark (ACM, New York, 2011), pp. 65–76

81. S. Escobar, C. Meadows, J. Meseguer, Maude-NPA: cryptographic protocol analysis modulo equational properties, in *Foundations of Security Analysis and Design V, FOSAD 2007/2008/2009 Tutorial Lectures*, ed. by A. Aldini, G. Barthe, R. Gorrieri. Lecture Notes in Computer Science, vol. 5705 (Springer, Berlin, 2009), pp. 1–50

82. R. Focardi, F. Martinelli, A uniform approach for the definition of security properties, in *World Congress on Formal Methods in the Development of Computing Systems (FM'99)*, ed. by J.M. Wing, J. Woodcock, J. Davies, Toulouse, France. Lecture Notes in Computer Science, vol. 1708 (Springer, Berlin, 1999), pp. 794–813

83. International Organization for Standardization. Information technology—security techniques—entity authentication, part 1: general model. ISO/IEC 9798-1 (1991)

84. T. Genet, F. Klay, Rewriting for cryptographic protocol verification, in *17th International Conference on Automated Deduction (CADE'00)*, ed. by D.A. McAllester, Pittsburgh, USA. Lecture Notes in Artificial Intelligence, vol. 1831 (Springer, Berlin, 2000), pp. 271–290

85. D. Gollmann, What do we mean by entity authentication, in *17th IEEE Symposium on Security & Privacy (S&P'96)*, Oakland, USA (IEEE Computer Society, Los Alamitos, 1996), pp. 46–54

86. D. Gollmann, On the verification of cryptographic protocols—a tale of two committees, in *Workshop on Secure Architectures and Information Flow 1999*, London, UK. Electronic Notes in Theoretical Computer Science, vol. 32 (Elsevier, Amsterdam, 2000), pp. 42–58

87. L. Gong, R.M. Needham, R. Yahalom, Reasoning about belief in cryptographic protocol analysis, in *11th IEEE Symposium on Security & Privacy (S&P'90)*, Oakland, USA (IEEE Computer Society, Los Alamitos, 1990), pp. 234–248

88. L. Gong, P. Syverson, Fail-stop protocols: an approach to designing secure protocols, in *5th International Working Conference on Dependable Computing for Critical Applications (DCCA'95)*, Urbana-Champaign, USA (1995), pp. 44–55

89. J.D. Guttman, State and progress in Strand Spaces: proving fair exchange. J. Autom. Reason. **48**(2), 159–195 (2012)

90. J.D. Guttman, F.J. Thayer, Protocol independence through disjoint encryption, in *13th IEEE Computer Security Foundations Workshop (CSFW'00)*, Cambridge, UK (IEEE Computer Society, Los Alamitos, 2000), pp. 24–34

91. J.D. Guttman, F.J. Thayer, Authentication tests and the structure of bundles. Theor. Comput. Sci. **283**(2), 333–380 (2002)

92. J. Heather, G. Lowe, S. Schneider, How to prevent type flaw attacks on security protocols. J. Comput. Secur. **11**(2), 217–244 (2003)

93. A. Huima, Efficient infinite-state analysis of security protocols, in *FLOC Workshop on Formal Methods and Security Protocols (FMSP'99)*, ed. by N. Heintze, E. Clarke, Trento, Italy (1999)

94. FET Open Project IST-2001-39252. AVISPA: automated validation of internet security protocols and applications. http://www.avispa-project.org/ (accessed 18 Sept 2012)

95. ITU-TS, Recommendation Z.120: Message Sequence Chart (MSC) ITU-TS, Geneva (1999)

96. J. Katz, M. Yung, Scalable protocols for authenticated group key exchange, in *23rd Annual International Cryptology Conference (CRYPTO'03)*, ed. by D. Boneh, Santa Barbara, USA. Lecture Notes in Computer Science, vol. 2729 (Springer, Berlin, 2003), pp. 110–125

97. J. Kelsey, B. Schneier, D. Wagner, Protocol interactions and the chosen protocol attack, in *5th International Workshop on Security Protocols*, ed. by B. Christianson, B. Crispo, T.M.A. Lomas, M. Roe, Paris, France. Lecture Notes in Computer Science, vol. 1361 (Springer, Berlin, 1997), pp. 91–104

98. R.A. Kemmerer, Analyzing encryption protocols using formal verification techniques, in *Workshop on the Theory and Application of Cryptographic Techniques (EUROCRYPT'86)*, ed. by I. Ingemarsson, Linköping, Sweden (1986), p. 48

99. R.A. Kemmerer, C. Meadows, J.K. Millen, Three systems for cryptographic protocol analysis. J. Cryptol. **7**, 79–130 (1994)

100. S.T. Kent, Encryption-based protection for interactive user/computer communication, in *5th Symposium on Data Communications (SIGCOMM'77)*, Snowbird, USA (ACM, New York, 1977), pp. 5.7–5.13

101. R. Küsters, T. Truderung, Using ProVerif to analyze protocols with Diffie-Hellman exponentiation, in *22nd IEEE Computer Security Foundations Symposium (CSF'09)*, Port Jefferson, USA (IEEE Computer Society, Los Alamitos, 2009), pp. 157–171

102. R. Küsters, T. Truderung, Reducing protocol analysis with XOR to the XOR-free case in the Horn Theory based approach. J. Autom. Reason. **46**(3–4), 325–352 (2011)

103. Y. Li, W. Yang, C. Huang, On preventing type flaw attacks on security protocols with a simplified tagging scheme. J. Inf. Sci. Eng. **21**(1), 59–84 (2005)

104. P. Lincoln, J.C. Mitchell, M. Mitchell, A. Scedrov, A probabilistic poly-time framework for protocol analysis, in *5th ACM Conference on Computer and Communications Security (ACM CCS'98)*, ed. by L. Gong, M.K. Reiter, San Francisco, USA (ACM, New York, 1998), pp. 112–121

105. D. Longley, S. Rigby, An automatic search for security flaws in key management schemes. Comput. Secur. **11**(1), 75–89 (1992)

106. G. Lowe, Breaking and fixing the Needham-Schroeder public-key protocol using FDR, in *2nd International Conference on Tools and Algorithms for the Construction and Analysis of Systems (TACAS'96)*, ed. by T. Margaria, B. Steffen, Passau, Germany. Lecture Notes in Computer Science, vol. 1055 (Springer, Berlin, 1996), pp. 147–166

107. G.L. Lowe, Casper: a compiler for the analysis of security protocols, in *10th IEEE Computer Security Foundations Workshop (CSFW'97)*, Rockport, USA (IEEE Computer Society, Los Alamitos, 1997), pp. 18–30

108. G. Lowe, A hierarchy of authentication specifications, in *10th IEEE Computer Security Foundations Workshop (CSFW'97)*, Rockport, USA (IEEE Computer Society, Los Alamitos, 1997), pp. 31–44

109. G. Lowe, Towards a completeness result for model checking of security protocols, in *11th IEEE Computer Security Foundations Workshop (CSFW'98)*, Rockport, USA (IEEE Computer Society, Los Alamitos, 1998), pp. 96–105

110. A. Mathuria, A.R. Singh, P.V. Sharavan, R. Kirtankar, Some new multi-protocol attacks, in *15th International Conference on Advanced Computing and Communications (ADCOM'07)*, Guwahati, India (IEEE Computer Society, Los Alamitos, 2007), pp. 465–471

111. C. Meadows, The NRL protocol analyzer: an overview. J. Log. Program. **26**(2), 113–131 (1996)

112. C. Meadows, Analysis of the Internet Key Exchange Protocol using the NRL protocol analyzer, in *20th IEEE Symposium on Security & Privacy (S&P'99)*, Oakland, USA (IEEE Computer Society, Los Alamitos, 1999), pp. 216–231

113. S. Meier, C.J.F. Cremers, D.A. Basin, Strong invariants for the efficient construction of machine-checked protocol security proofs, in *23rd IEEE Computer Security Foundations Symposium (CSF'10)*, Edinburgh, UK (IEEE Computer Society, Los Alamitos, 2010), pp. 231–245

114. S. Meier, B. Schmidt, The Tamarin prover: source code and case studies. http://hackage.haskell.org/package/tamarin-prover (accessed 18 Sept 2012)

115. D. Micciancio, S. Panjwani, Optimal communication complexity of generic multicast key distribution, in *Advances in Cryptology—International Conference on the Theory and Application of Cryptographic Techniques (EUROCRYPT'04)*, ed. by J. Camenisch, C. Cachin, Interlaken, Switzerland. Lecture Notes in Computer Science, vol. 3027 (Springer, Berlin, 2004), pp. 153–170

116. J.K. Millen, A necessarily parallel attack, in *FLOC Workshop on Formal Methods and Security Protocols (FMSP'99)*, ed. by N. Heintze, E. Clarke, Trento, Italy (1999)

117. J.K. Millen, S.C. Clark, S.B. Freedman, The Interrogator: protocol security analysis. IEEE Trans. Softw. Eng. **13**(2), 274–288 (1987)

118. J.K. Millen, V. Shmatikov, Constraint solving for bounded-process cryptographic protocol analysis, in *8th ACM Conference on Computer and Communications Security (ACM CCS'01)*, ed. by M.K. Reiter, P. Samarati, Philadelphia, USA (ACM, New York, 2001), pp. 166–175

119. J.K. Millen, V. Shmatikov, Symbolic protocol analysis with products and Diffie-Hellman exponentiation, in *16th IEEE Computer Security Foundations Workshop (CSFW'03)*, Pacific Grove, USA (IEEE Computer Society, Los Alamitos, 2003), pp. 47–61

120. R. Milner, J. Parrow, D. Walker, A calculus of mobile processes, I. Inf. Comput. **100**(1), 1–40 (1992)

121. R. Milner, J. Parrow, D. Walker, A calculus of mobile processes, II. Inf. Comput. **100**(1), 41–77 (1992)

122. J.C. Mitchell, M. Mitchell, U. Stern, Automated analysis of cryptographic protocols using Murφ, in *18th IEEE Symposium on Security & Privacy (S&P'97)*, Oakland, USA (IEEE Computer Society, Los Alamitos, 1997), pp. 141–151

123. C. Morgan, The shadow knows: refinement and security in sequential programs. Sci. Comput. Program. **74**(8), 629–653 (2009)

124. R.M. Needham, M. Schroeder, Using encryption for authentication in large networks of computers. Commun. ACM **21**(12), 993–999 (1978)

125. T. Nipkow, L.C. Paulson, M. Wenzel, *Isabelle/HOL—A Proof Assistant for Higher-Order Logic*. Lecture Notes in Computer Science, vol. 2283 (Springer, Berlin, 2002)

126. P.C. van Oorschot, Extending cryptographic logics of belief to key agreement protocols, in *1st ACM Conference on Computer and Communications Security (ACM CCS'93)*, ed. by D.E. Denning, R. Pyle, R. Ganesan, R.S. Sandhu, V. Ashby, Fairfax, USA (ACM, New York, 1993), pp. 232–243

127. S. Owicki, D. Gries, An axiomatic proof technique for parallel programs I. Acta Inform. **6**(4), 319–340 (1976)

128. A. Pankova, P. Laud, Symbolic analysis of cryptographic protocols containing bilinear pairings, in *25th IEEE Computer Security Foundations Symposium (CSF'12)*, ed. by S. Chong, Cambridge, USA (IEEE Computer Society, Los Alamitos, 2012), pp. 63–77

129. L.C. Paulson, *Isabelle: A Generic Theorem Prover*. Lecture Notes in Computer Science, vol. 828 (Springer, Berlin, 1994)

130. L.C. Paulson, Proving properties of security protocols by induction, in *10th IEEE Computer Security Foundations Workshop (CSFW'97)*, Rockport, Massachusetts (IEEE Computer Society, Los Alamitos, 1997), pp. 70–83

131. L.C. Paulson, The inductive approach to verifying cryptographic protocols. J. Comput. Secur. **6**(1–2), 85–128 (1998)

132. L.C. Paulson, Inductive analysis of the Internet protocol TLS. ACM Trans. Inf. Syst. Secur. **2**(3), 332–351 (1999)

133. L.C. Paulson, Relations between secrets: two formal analyses of the Yahalom protocol. J. Comput. Secur. **9**(3), 197–216 (2001)

134. L.C. Paulson, SET cardholder registration: the secrecy proofs, in *1st International Joint Conference on Automated Reasoning (IJCAR'01)*, ed. by R. Goré, A. Leitsch, T. Nipkow. Lecture Notes in Artificial Intelligence, vol. 2083 (Springer, Berlin, 2001), pp. 5–12

135. A. Pnueli, The temporal logic of programs, in *18th IEEE Symposium on Foundations of Computer Science (FOCS'77)*, Providence, USA (IEEE Computer Society, Los Alamitos, 1977), pp. 46–57

136. G.J. Popek, C.S. Kline, Encryption and secure computer networks. ACM Comput. Surv. **11**(4), 331–356 (1979)

137. J.D. Ramsdell, The cryptographic protocol shapes analyzer (CPSA). http://hackage.haskell.org/package/cpsa (accessed 18 Sept 2012)

138. A.W. Roscoe, Intensional specifications of security protocols, in *9th IEEE Computer Security Foundations Workshop (CSFW'96)*, Dromquinna Manor, Kenmare, Ireland (IEEE Computer Society, Los Alamitos, 1996), pp. 28–38

139. M. Rusinowitch, M. Turuani, Protocol insecurity with finite number of sessions is NP-complete, in *14th IEEE Computer Security Foundations Workshop (CSFW'01)*, Cape Breton, Canada (IEEE Computer Society, Los Alamitos, 2001), pp. 174–187

140. M. Rusinowitch, M. Turuani, Protocol insecurity with a finite number of sessions and composed keys is NP-complete. Theor. Comput. Sci. **299**(1–3), 451–475 (2003)

141. P.Y.A. Ryan, S. Schneider, *Modelling and Analysis of Security Protocols: The CSP Approach* (Addison-Wesley, Reading, 2001)

142. R. Sasse, S. Escobar, C. Meadows, J. Meseguer, Protocol analysis modulo combination of theories: a case study in Maude-NPA, in *6th International Workshop on Security and Trust Management (STM'10)*, ed. by J. Cuéllar, J. Lopez, G. Barthe, A. Pretschner, Athens, Greece. Lecture Notes in Computer Science, vol. 6710 (Springer, Berlin, 2010), pp. 163–178

143. B. Schmidt, S. Meier, C.J.F. Cremers, D.A. Basin, Automated analysis of Diffie-Hellman protocols and advanced security properties, in *25th IEEE Computer Security Foundations Symposium (CSF'12)*, ed. by S. Chong, Cambridge, USA (IEEE Computer Society, Los Alamitos, 2012), pp. 78–94

144. S. Schneider, Security properties and CSP, in *17th IEEE Symposium on Security & Privacy (S&P'96)*, Oakland, USA (IEEE Computer Society, Los Alamitos, 1996), pp. 174–187

145. C.E. Shannon, A mathematical theory of communication. Bell Syst. Tech. J. **27**(3–4), 379–423, 623–656 (1948)

146. B. Smyth, M.D. Ryan, S. Kremer, M. Kourjieh, Towards automatic analysis of election verifiability properties, in *Joint Workshop on Automated Reasoning for Security Protocol Analysis and Issues in the Theory of Security (ARSPA-WITS'10)*, ed. by A. Armando, G. Lowe, Paphos, Cyprus. Lecture Notes in Computer Science, vol. 6186 (Springer, Berlin, 2011), pp. 146–163

147. D. Song, Athena: a new efficient automatic checker for security protocol analysis, in *12th IEEE Computer Security Foundations Workshop (CSFW'99)*, Mordano, Italy (IEEE Computer Society, Los Alamitos, 1999), pp. 192–202

148. D. Song, S. Berezin, A. Perrig, Athena: a novel approach to efficient automatic security protocol analysis. J. Comput. Secur. **9**(1–2), 47–74 (2001)

149. Security Protocols Open Repository (SPORE). http://www.lsv.ens-cachan.fr/spore (accessed 18 Sept 2012)

150. C. Sprenger, D.A. Basin, Refining key establishment, in *25th IEEE Computer Security Foundations Symposium (CSF'12)*, ed. by S. Chong, Cambridge, USA (2012), pp. 230–246

151. S.G. Stubblebine, R.N. Wright, An authentication logic with formal semantics supporting synchronization, revocation, and recency. IEEE Trans. Softw. Eng. **28**(3), 256–285 (2002)

152. P.F. Syverson, P.C. van Oorschot, A unified cryptographic protocol logic. CHACS Report 5540-227 NRL (1996)

153. F.J. Thayer, J.C. Herzog, J.D. Guttman, Honest ideals on Strand Spaces, in *11th IEEE Computer Security Foundations Workshop (CSFW'98)*, Rockport, USA (IEEE Computer Society, Los Alamitos, 1998), pp. 66–77

154. F.J. Thayer, J.C. Herzog, J.D. Guttman, Mixed Strand Spaces, in *12th IEEE Computer Security Foundations Workshop (CSFW'99)*, Mordano, Italy (IEEE Computer Society, Los Alamitos, 1999), pp. 72–82

155. F.J. Thayer, J.C. Herzog, J.D. Guttman, Strand Spaces: proving security protocols correct. J. Comput. Secur. **7**(2–3), 191–230 (1999)

156. F.L. Tiplea, C. Enea, C.V. Birjoveneanu, Decidability and complexity results for security protocols, in *Verification of Infinite-State Systems with Applications to Security (VISSAS'05)*, ed. by E.M. Clarke, M. Minea, F.L. Tiplea, Timisoara, Romania. NATO Security Through Science Series D: Information and Communication Security, vol. 1 (IOS Press, Lansdale, 2006), pp. 185–211

157. M. Turuani, The CL-Atse protocol analyser, in *17th International Conference on Rewriting Techniques and Applications (RTA'06)*, ed. by F. Pfenning, Seattle, USA. Lecture Notes in Computer Science, vol. 4098 (Springer, Berlin, 2006), pp. 227–286

158. W.G. Tzeng, C.M. Hu, Inter-protocol interleaving attacks on some authentication and key distribution protocols. Inf. Process. Lett. **69**(6), 297–302 (1999)

159. T. Woo, S. Lam, A lesson on authentication protocol design. Oper. Syst. Rev. **28**(3), 24–37 (1994)

Index